Assessment Live!

Assessment Live!

10 Real-Time Ways for Kids to Show What They Know— and Meet the Standards

Nancy Steineke

Heinemann
Portsmouth, NH

Heinemann
361 Hanover Street
Portsmouth, NH 03801–3912
www.heinemann.com

Offices and agents throughout the world

The author and publisher wish to thank those who have generously given permission to reprint borrowed material:

Lyrics from "Build Me Up Buttercup," words and music by Tony McCauley and Michael D'Abo. Copyright © 1968, 1969 (Copyrights Renewed) by EMI Unart Catalog Inc., Unichappell Music, Inc. and State Music Ltd. All rights on behalf of itself and State Music Ltd. Reprinted by permission from Alfred Publishing Co., Inc. and Hal Leonard Corporation.

Excerpt from "Shereen's Jeans" from *Stick Figure: A Diary of My Former Self* by Lori Gottlieb. Copyright © 2000 by Lori Gottlieb. Published by Simon & Schuster, Inc. Reprinted by permission of the publisher, the author, and the author's agents, Scovil Galen Ghosh Literary Agency, Inc.

"The Termite" from *Candy is Dandy: The Best of Ogden Nash* by Ogden Nash with an Introduction by Anthony Burgess. Copyright © 1942 by Ogden Nash. Published by Curtis Brown, Ltd. and André Deutsch. Reprinted by permission from the publishers.

Library of Congress Cataloging-in-Publication Data
Steineke, Nancy.
    Assessment live! : 10 real-time ways for kids to show what they know—and meet the standards / Nancy Steineke.
       p. cm.
    Includes bibliographical references.
    ISBN-13: 978-0-325-02177-5
    ISBN-10: 0-325-02177-5
    1. Educational evaluation—United States.   2. Educational tests and measurements—United States. 3. Education—Standards—United States.   4. Academic achievement—United States—Testing. I. Title.
    LB2822.75.S74 2009
    379.1'58—dc22
                                                      2009018707

Editor: Smokey Daniels
Production: Abigail M. Heim
Typesetter: Gina Poirier Graphic Design
Cover design: Lisa Anne Fowler
Cover photographs: Nancy Steineke (front top and bottom right), Diane Titche (front bottom left), William Steineke (back)
Manufacturing: Valerie Cooper

Printed in the United States of America on acid-free paper
13   12   11   10   09   VP   1   2   3   4   5

Contents

Foreword

If I had a dime for every time I've been asked to share some ideas for more descriptive, engaging comprehension assessment, I'd be digging my toes into fine, white sand somewhere right now! Teachers throughout the country have been waiting for this book. In *Assessment Live!*, you'll find a lively, practical guide to not only assessing students' thinking, but engaging them in compelling, relevant learning *as a part of* the assessment process. Nancy Steineke has actually found a way (*many* ways) to make literacy assessment a vital part of the learning experience, a concept that researchers have written about for years. As I was absorbing every assessment approach she proposes, however, I was actually thinking of an audience she may never have considered—an audience I desperately wish would read *Assessment Live!* The audience? Businesspeople in this country.

I vividly recall a particular Board of Directors meeting for the Public Education & Business Coalition (PEBC is a Denver-based nonprofit in which I worked for sixteen years) in the late 1990s. We were seated in a lovely, wood-paneled bank conference room drinking rich coffee and eating very flaky croissants and everyone was dressed in "board meeting" suits—lots of navy and black, lots of pin stripes. One of the agenda items was an opportunity for the members of the board to discuss their hopes, needs, and priorities for incoming workers in the coming twenty years. They talked about the needs they saw in their businesses and, because Denver-area school superintendents and other educators were in the room, the board expressed their hopes with respect to how the PEBC might work with local school districts to improve the odds that entry-level workers (students straight from high school and college graduates alike) come to the workplace with appropriate skills. I was stunned silent by their priorities.

They said that they needed young workers who could think clearly and critically, articulate their thoughts cogently, orally and in writing; they wanted workers to collaborate, think flexibly, and solve problems in an agile, inventive way. They wanted creative thinkers rather than dogmatic rule-followers and they wanted them to be able to "flex" into a number of different roles, quickly changing perspectives to tackle new problems. They wanted, they said, thinkers and doers, but of the two they valued thinkers the most. They went on to say that they thought that these were the kinds of "skills" that should be taught K–12 and that students should be held accountable for agile thinking and collaborative actions. You'll get no argument from me on any of that, I thought.

I was stunned because this was the very same group I had listened to numerous times as they encouraged me to work with PEBC educators to raise test scores as measured by traditional high-stakes assessments. I thought briefly about the very real possibility that I might be shown the door if I expressed what I was thinking, but my frustration was at a peak and I feared that I might experience some kind of or implosion if I didn't speak up. I gathered my thoughts, tried to slow my pulse, and entered the conversation. I pointed out that, if this society indeed hopes for critical, collaborative, agile thinkers, then we educators, with their help, needed to think very differently about the ways we are "holding kids accountable." How on earth did we expect students to value the critical thinking skills they had just enumerated when their feedback from teachers, grades, tests, and entrance to college were all based on a hundred-year-old model of standardized, multiple-choice, dumbed down (I was really getting myself on a tear here) tests that didn't assess anything they had just said they valued most!

I recall hearing the thundering quiet following my diatribe and wondering how unemployment works and how long it lasts, and then the bank president whose conference room we were occupying leaned forward on his shiny table and said, "Well I never thought of it that way."

I suspect he speaks for many others (including some educators) in our society who may not have considered the disconnection between the proficiencies we seek among young entry-level workers and our teaching and assessment practices in the 13 to 17 years leading to their working life. Nancy Steineke has most certainly considered this anomaly—and she has a serious proposal for a solution.

In *Assessment Live!*, Nancy views assessment as an integral part of the learning process itself. She acknowledges that, in traditional assessment models, it is the adults who are doing the "heavy lifting." We design the assessments, prepare kids to take them, then score them later and lament that they reveal very little about students' thinking. Arguing convincingly that we need another paradigm for assessment, Nancy describes how activities that engage students in complex, multi-faceted demonstrations of learning can transfer the responsibility to students to reveal the quality of their thinking while seamlessly helping them learn the content more deeply and lastingly.

Teachers will devour the ten structures Nancy proposes in *Assessment Live!*, which represent a diverse set of tools teachers can use and adapt for a wide variety of learners across the range of content areas. Teachers will also love the detail Nancy offers to help students develop the skills required for these assessments. She writes clearly about the necessity of preparing kids in the early part of the semester to take full advantage of each type of demonstration. She emphasizes the need for team-building and work on students' oral language—the central tool they use to develop and express learning.

Nancy seems to have anticipated every conceivable glitch in the processes (having, no doubt, *experienced* every conceivable glitch in the processes) and has worked out just how to avoid them. As I was reading each live assessment, I would just start to think, "Yeah, but what would happen if . . . ," when Nancy would answer my question with a clever, precise response that can actually prevent the problems before they manifest. I began to wonder if she was reading my mind. I think the truth is that her experience has enabled her to write a book that is not only a practical guide to very engaging assessment and learning activities, but an important paradigm shift in assessment practice for American teachers.

Part of that shift relates to how teachers participate in the assessment process. Rather than standing as ultimate judge, Nancy sees us as coaches and observers, preparing kids before they begin the process and observing with a trained eye as students reveal their thinking as active, engaged learners. She helps us know what to look for in our role as observers and provides dozens of tools, including rubrics, to help teachers and students make informed judgments about the quality of the product. She also shows how numerous standards are met through performance assessments, calming any fears that students whose understanding is assessed in this way won't meet standards or score well on traditional assessments.

Nancy also asks us to reconsider our old ideas about the grade levels in which students can be asked to show what they know through performance assessments. The structures presented in *Assessment Live!* apply all the way across the 6–12 range, giving the lie to the notion that older students are too peer-focused to "perform" in this way and that younger kids aren't developmentally ready to synthesize their learning in a visible way. I can only imagine the power of these strategies if adapted and applied all along the K–12 grade continuum, and what critical thinkers and doers this Board of Directors would begin to find in their entry-level workforce!

I wish Nancy Steineke had been with me that day in the boardroom. I wish she had been able to describe as vividly as she does on these pages how students can bring their thinking to life by collaborating, thinking flexibly, and solving real-world problems in an agile, inventive way. I suspect that that group of business people and educators might have said, "Let's make this happen in all schools. Let's find a way to make our assessment practices match the skills we want students to bring with them into the higher-education and working worlds. Let's get behind schools that see the need to change the way they think about assessment. Let's stand back and watch kids really engage in learning again." I suspect that you'll feel that way after reading this book and I sincerely hope that you share it with colleagues with whom you can create your own movement for change in your school and district. Nancy leaves no doubt that it can be done.

—Ellin Oliver Keene

Acknowledgments

The students of Victor J. Andrew High School: My students supply the fun and energy that keep me going, and they willingly take the risks that enable all of us to become better learners.

Bill Steineke, my husband: He offers unwavering support and always manages to find a fresh supply of patience in the face of my authorial panics.

Smokey Daniels, friend and editor: There is no better person to help me talk through an idea. And when the prose is rough, he sure knows how to polish it up.

Abby Heim, production editor: Her willingness to make the book its best included two rounds of copyedits and page proofs as well as repeated fiddling with the cover and interior design. Oh, and then there's my 300 emails she had to respond to!

Charles McQuillen, marketing director: Even the best book will languish unread unless someone is working hard to find its audience.

Ellin Oliver Keene, foreword author: I am deeply honored by Ellin's enthusiasm for this book and truly appreciate her recognition that assessment should reinforce not only content but also the skills students will need for higher education and the working world.

Diane Titche, contributor: Thank you for sharing your students' Tableaux scripts and photos.

Jim Gaither, contributor: Thank you for sharing your students' Alternative-Perspective Journals and Found Poetry.

Jim Vopat, friend and fellow author: Jim's timely feedback was always spot-on.

James Bond, personal assistant cat: Though he wasn't much help with revision, Mister Bond did a great job keeping me company as he slept atop my computer monitor.

Getting Started

The Lively Art
of Assessment

Let's face it. Most of the assessment our students encounter—and that we teachers design—is pretty lifeless. It's dry, it's drudgery, it often feels empty and anticlimactic. We have kids sit in silent rows, blackening circles on machine-readable forms—or they stay up all night snagging paragraphs off the Internet and pasting them into their "research papers." These kinds of traditional assessments often entail huge amounts of paperwork for teachers but provide very little timely and formative feedback for our kids.

But what if assessment could be lively, not lifeless? What if it could be informative, powerful, and (dare I say it) *fun*? That's what this book is about. My students and I are here to show you how to "go live" with demonstrations of learning. I have been teaching for thirty years in a Chicago-area high school full of regular American kids. And I can tell you, assessing their growth the lively way is much more accurate and energizing than the run-of-the-mill paper-and-pencil measures.

What's the difference between lifeless assessment and live assessment? Here's an illustration. Remember reading *The Great Gatsby*? It's a staple of most U.S. high school American literature classes. Take a look at the excerpts from this objective test and see how well you do.

Directions: Mark T = True or F = False for each of the numbered answers (An answer key is included at the end of the chapter.)

The following describe Tom:

1. adulterer
2. abusive
3. racist
4. business tycoon
5. gambler

The following describe Daisy:

6. ambitious, driven to succeed
7. bitter, unhappy
8. flirtatious
9. spoiled, childlike
10. generous

The following are contrasts in the novel:

11. the splendor of Gatsby's weekend parties; the destruction repaired on Monday morning
12. the good manners of the West Eggers at Gatsby's parties; the crudeness of Myrtle and Tom's gathering at the apartment
13. the wild festivity of Gatsby's parties; the sober isolation of Jay Gatsby at those parties
14. Myrtle Wilson entertaining in her Central Park West apartment; Myrtle pumping gas at her husband's garage

The following details were used to characterize Jordan:

15. she once killed a man with her car
16. she cheats to win a golf tournament
17. she knew Daisy before Tom met her
18. she never leaves a convertible top down in the rain
19. she shamelessly eavesdrops on her hosts when Tom receives a call from his mistress

The real reasons that Tom does not divorce Daisy to marry Myrtle are:

20. Daisy is Catholic
21. he has no serious interest in Myrtle; she is just another "fling"
22. Myrtle is beneath him socially, unlike Daisy
23. the present circumstance offers him greater control over both women
24. Daisy's beauty and family background make her a social trophy

Tom broke Myrtle's nose when Myrtle chanted Daisy's name. This act shows Tom's:

25. brutality, since he became violent and out of control
26. nobility, since he was defending his wife's honor
27. good judgment, since Myrtle deserved to be punished
28. quick thinking, since he reacts spontaneously
29. controlling nature, since he knows this violent act will silence Myrtle

I have more questions; these are just a taste. Unless you are currently teaching American literature, you might have had some trouble recalling all the details. More important, how effective was this assessment in getting you to think more deeply about F. Scott Fitzgerald's most famous work? Did it spur a resolution to put *The Great Gatsby* on your books-to-reread list and maybe get a friend to read it with you as well? Did remembering those characters—Tom, Myrtle, Jordan, and Daisy—get you "worked up" when you started thinking about what jerks they were? As you read through these questions, did you feel any palpable emotions at all?

Now here's another assessment, created by a class of juniors that had just finished reading *Gatsby*. It's a song written to the tune of "Maxwell's Silver Hammer" from the Beatles' *Abbey Road* album. They wrote the song together and then sang it together several times.

Wilson's Silver Pistol
Daisy is depressed; Myrtle's joy is not suppressed
Both want Tom alone
Jordan hears a clandestine phone call
Oh, oh, oh, oh

Tom B's cheating ways led Daisy to go astray
Has some tea at Nick's
Finds that Gatsby watches her green light
Patiently

But as their love is just heating up
A man will ruin it all

CHORUS
Bang, bang, Wilson's silver pistol
Shot out at Gatsby's head
Bang, bang, Wilson's silver pistol
Made sure that Jay was dead

Nineteen-seventeen, Daisy Fay was just eighteen
Dating many boys
But her favorite was soldier Gatsby
Oh, oh, oh, oh

Gatsby left the states, Daisy missed her soul mate
Married Tom next June
Threw away the letter from Gatsby
Oh, no, no, no

But even as Jay dreams of return
A man will ruin it all

CHORUS

George he finds the leash, then he starts to really freak
Locks his wife right up
Plans a move out West and he tells Tom
So, oh, oh, oh

In the hotel room, Jay and Tom begin to fume
Daisy can't decide
Then she speeds and hits Myrtle Wilson
Oh, no, no, no

And hunting for the yellow death car
A man will ruin it all

CHORUS

Searching East-West Egg, George thinks justice should be paid
Pistol in his hand
He will find the car that killed Myrtle
Oh, no, no, no

Last day for the pool, why was Gatsby such a fool?
Sunning all alone
Jay's an easy target for Wilson
Oh, no, no, no

And as Jay's soaking up those fall rays
A man will ruin it all

CHORUS

Now did THIS make you want to read the book? If you said yes, then you are responding as my students do. Though none immediately announce they are going to reread *Gatsby* (probably because I've already passed out *The Crucible*), I know they might because that song is going to stay in their heads far longer than those test questions. Thanks to the song they have a personal investment, a hook.

Though both "tests" capture understanding of plot and character, I would argue that the second assessment is better than the first. The answer becomes clearer when we think about why we assess. Is it only to measure content retention at the moment the test is administered or do we hope for deeper, more durable outcomes? Might assessment also help in developing a positive attitude toward learning, extending and refining knowledge, using knowledge to create something original, practicing productive habits of mind (Marzano, Pickering, and McTighe 1993), and storing one's learning in long-term memory? I'd argue that the song does an equal job in the content retention department but is vastly superior when we consider those other assessment components.

Why Live Assessments?

First, I'm not suggesting you throw away all your multiple-choice tests, nor am I saying that the kids will no longer be writing papers. But I do believe that we need to move toward a more balanced use of assessments, a balance that enables all of our kids to learn, do their very best, and effectively show what they know.

As you probably noticed, most of the thinking for the *Gatsby* test was done by the teacher, not the kids. To design this objective assessment, a teacher had to carefully review the text as well as all the class notes and then hone a collection of questions that best represented what was studied. If you've ever created one of these objective tests from scratch, you know they take hours! And who's doing all the reviewing of the material? You! Then, after you've slaved away creating the perfect test, it only takes the kids fifteen minutes to finish—and once done they run to hand it in as if they can't wait to get the darn thing off their desk. That's not surprising. From their perspective, taking tests is often frustrating, boring, and pointless. Have you ever memorized information for a test only to forget it as soon as the test is finished? Your students have too. In their article, "What Can Student Drawings Tell Us About High-Stakes Testing in Massachusetts?" (Wheelock, Bebell, and Haney 2000) reveal some disturbing news about student attitudes toward testing. When asked to draw pictures of themselves taking the MCAS, Massachusetts' high-stakes exam, most of the drawings depicted anger, helplessness, boredom, anxiety, or withdrawal.

This book is about assessments that don't make kids angry, withdrawn, or anesthetized—but rather, engaged. If you saw the value in song parodies as a way for students to show what they know, there are nine similar, highly structured and productive assessment activities coming in the pages ahead. Live assessment puts the students in control and gives them full responsibility: they take the content they have studied and use it to create something new. The final product, their creation, is then performed before a real audience in real time. While an objective test is primarily a product of the teacher's efforts, live assessment is a product of the students' efforts. They're the ones who must return to their notes and text in order to create an informed performance. But that's not all. Aside from this who's-really-doing-the-work issue, there are several more very compelling reasons for choosing a more balanced diet of assessment.

If you'd like to jump ahead and look at some of the book's ten practical, live assessments, this might be a good time flip forward to Chapters 3–12. If you want to hear more of the research and rationale behind this kind of assessment, read on.

Brain Research

A key function of our brains is forgetting. Did you know that the brain discards 99 percent of the information it receives? The primary purpose of our brain is to perpetuate our survival, and most information received by the brain is immediately tagged as unimportant to survival. That's why it's so hard to get the kids to remember all the information we try to cram into their heads. We think it's important, the district curriculum guide may label it as vital, but students' brains do not. However, everyone's brains do sit up and take notice when information has a strong emotion attached to it, which makes perfect sense when survival is at stake. If the emotion coming through the circuits is screaming, "Danger Will Robinson!" the brain has to notice immediately and take the appropriate evasive action to ensure safety.

That doesn't mean we want to scare the heck out of kids so they'll remember something, but it does mean that they'll remember more information when it is connected to some sort of emotional investment. Positive yet powerful feelings connected with learning trigger chemicals that help us better retrieve information (Jensen 1998). Emotions connect memory networks to other memory networks (Sylwester 1995, Wolfe 2001a). That's why live assessment is so brain-friendly. All of the projects described in later chapters get students emotionally involved. In addition, working with others to create a product and then performing it live before an audience produces strong emotions, emotions that create stronger neural pathways so that information can be later retrieved. These performances are a celebration of learning, and also an emotionally charged experience that can forge memory connections and lead to better knowledge retention.

Here's another thing about memory: Information is not stored all in one place. When students learn through a variety of sensations (visual, aural, spatial, etc.), that information gets stored in more places, resulting in better memory retrieval (Sylwester 1995). Furthermore, our brain is wired in a way that responds to rhyme and rhythm. So a song or poem enables students to remember far more than if they tried to memorize the same information in prose form (Wolfe 2001b). We also will remember information presented in a novel context (Wolfe 2001b). All ten of the live assessments described in this book offer this novelty, that "something different" from what students typically encounter hour to hour, day to day. And since the brain's main goal is to forget what it doesn't need, it takes multiple rehearsals to get new information into long-term memory. Effective rehearsal requires the learner to manipulate and synthesize information. When students embark on a performance project, they must review the content and informally reteach it to one another, thus initiating multiple rehearsals. Creating a performance and then practicing repeatedly before taking it before an audience is exactly the kind of rehearsal the brain requires for consolidation, the condition that renders new memories more stable (Wolfe 2001b).

Boys' Life

If the chairs in your classroom are separate from the desks, you will have noticed that it's the boys who tip them back, balancing precariously as they rock back and forth. I always thought they did this to annoy me. Turns out it has nothing to do with me. Something the brain craves, particularly for boys, is movement. Believe it or not, that chair tipping is stimulating their brains (Jensen 1998). In their research on boy readers, Jeff Wilhelm and Michael Smith (2002) discovered that boys want to do something physically while they're reading: draw something, act it out, respond kinesthetically. All the assessments in this book are kinesthetic in nature. Boys also respond to gentle competition (Goff 2005). Academic controversy, described in Chapter 3, capitalizes on both boys' need for movement and their enjoyment of competition.

Bottom line: The way boys are hardwired makes them seem antsy, particularly when we want them to stay seated hour after hour. Live assessments offer boys the chance to get up and move around to create a product or rehearse a performance. The bonus is that attaching physical movement to content increases the likelihood that the information will be remembered—not just by the boys, but by all of your students (Jensen 1998): Yes, girls thrive on motion, too.

Multiple Intelligences

Ninety-five percent of the material presented in school favors two kinds of thinking: verbal/linguistic and logical/mathematical (Lazear 1991). This does a disservice to all students because, as Howard Gardner has shown, there are at least five other ways of knowing (1993). Those students who do not excel in linguistic or mathematical intelligences suffer because they never get to show what they know in a way that suits their learning style and reveals their strengths. Here's a little-known fact: When Dr. Martin Luther King, Jr. took the Graduate Record Exam, he scored in the bottom 10 percent for both the math and verbal sections (Bond 2006). Imagine if Dr. King had been able to express himself only through his Graduate Record Exam score! Though a splendidly gifted writer, it was his words combined with his intrapersonal and kinesthetic intelligences that inspired a movement.

On the flip side, when a variety of intelligences remain unaddressed, all students ultimately suffer because they are not challenged sufficiently. Kids need to learn how to use all their intelligences in order to stretch their thinking. Even though all of us have intelligences we favor, we can all become better at the others. Just because I'm not a good artist doesn't mean I couldn't become a better one if I practiced. And becoming better at drawing would offer me yet another way to express my thoughts and communicate my ideas. All of the live assessments described require the use of several different intelligences, enabling students to shine in various ways while building up their weaker areas.

Future Employment

The U.S. Department of Labor estimates that by the time our students turn forty, they will have held ten or more jobs. On top of that, many jobs of the future haven't even been created yet! This means that our students are going to have to be lifelong learners. They are going to have to be flexible and versatile in their thinking. They are going to have to be creative. Live assessments encourage the kind of thinking students will need in their future, multiple careers.

Performance assessment cultivates both interpersonal and presentation skills that are called upon in almost any job. The collaborative nature of live assessments helps kids learn how to work productively with others. Students must develop a game plan, offer leadership, honor and respect ideas, negotiate, assign tasks, and remain accountable to the group. In business lingo, these are referred to as *interpersonal skills*, qualities that employers consistently list in the top five competencies they look for in workers.

Public speaking skills are also vital in many jobs. The Toastmasters organization helps adults hone their public speaking ability. A community college in my neighborhood offers a course on "schmoozing" in which participants learn to how to make eye contact, introduce themselves, look friendly, and have something interesting to say. If you doubt the importance of such skills, just log on to any job-finding website and see how highly such simple interpersonal abilities are ranked in "help wanted" ads. Granted, once students leave school, they may not be performing memorized poems or scenes from plays as part of their employment. However, they will still need those presentation skills for networking at a job fair, interviewing, persuading their supervisor that a raise is in order, or making a PowerPoint presentation to possible clients.

Authentic Audience

For 99 percent of the work kids do in school, the teacher is the only audience. Try as we may, the publication possibilities for traditional papers remain limited. In addition, written assessments, whether assigned by the teacher or mandated by the state, typically have a single audience of the teacher or an anonymous disembodied reader, sitting somewhere far away. Having an authentic audience is what makes student work feel real and worth the effort. Performing for the class ups the ante and necessitates repeated rehearsals (an essential component of memory) because the kids want to look good in front of their classmates. A real audience also provides a strong emotional hook, which further enhances memory. When students perform live, their audience is present to respond immediately to the work. And if you videotape the performances and show them to next year's classes, the audience expands exponentially.

Learning and Assessment

A performance requires students to use higher-order thinking skills. They'll need to revisit, rethink, and re-create the text. Creating a script or visualization requires students to imagine, infer, extend, connect, compare, and imagine. The final product is the result of synthesis, the act of manipulating and transforming knowledge in order to create something new and different.

Though many of the performances described in later chapters work well as summative assessments, students also receive feedback and formative assessment throughout the process as you and classmates observe the performances taking shape and offer suggestions. Have you ever conferred with a student, recommended a mentor text, pointed out an aspect of craft, encouraged him to "give it a try," and then read a final draft that looked exactly like the previous one? There is little motivation to revise for an audience of one, but when preparing for a public performance, feedback is taken more seriously. Even in the best environment, it is often hard to get kids to act on feedback. However, when students will be performing before their peers, their desire to do their best skyrockets and feedback is heeded.

Performances offer the opportunity for collaborative assessment as well. Students can be held accountable for creating high-quality projects when they have collaborated on the creation of the grading rubrics from the beginning. Afterward, students reflect on their own performances using the rubric and constructive audience feedback.

Standardized Test Preparation

A recent study by the Consortium on Chicago School Research (2008) made some important discoveries. For tests such as the ACT, devoting substantial time to test preparation caused scores to decline. Yes, I said *decline*. What *did* work for increasing the reading and English subtest scores? A rich learning environment in which students talked about their reading with others, debated, examined craft, revised writing with peers, and explored an author's influences. Live assessments consistently offer students these opportunities.

Performance Assessments

Local school boards and state education departments are beginning to acknowledge the limitations of standardized testing for revealing our students' accomplishments. Rhode Island is the first state to require high school students to pass a performance assessment in addition to the standardized tests already in place. This is how Lewis Cohen, executive director of the Coalition of Essential Schools, describes performance assessment:

> Students today need a rich palette of skills, but close-ended multiple-choice questions measure student ability to recall discrete facts rather than their ability to engage in complex thinking and problem solving. Thus most of today's state assessments are widening the gap between the skills students are acquiring in school and those they need for the globalized and technology infused society they must live in. By contrast performance assessments allow students to demonstrate 21st Century skills including Critical Thinking and Problem Solving, Communication, Creativity and Innovation, Collaboration, Information and Media Literacy, and Contextual Learning. More powerful teaching and learning performance assessments require students to demonstrate what they know and can do. They engage the student in real world multi-disciplinary tasks and provide a richer, more sophisticated and more honest view of student learning. (Cohen, Pecheone, and Littlefield 2008)

Performance assessment is gaining momentum as dissatisfaction grows with the limited information conventional standardized tests provide. In order to get students ready for their ultimate senior year performance, they have to start practicing well ahead of time. And that practice must include engaging the students in discussion, using project-based assignments, offering them multiple ways to show what they know, and affording them opportunities to apply information in creative ways (Davidson 2008). These are all skills readily demonstrated in live assessments.

But What About State Standards?

Though deep down many of us know that live assessments are valuable, we may initially find them hard to defend in this era of standards. For a while, in the face of my own administration's demand for numerous district assessments, I eliminated the performances that earlier had given my students real opportunity to show what they knew in multiple ways. I administered the mandated assessments with the sinking feeling that they were unsatisfactory and inaccurate, giving me only a snapshot of student achievement versus a complete photo album. I wasn't happy and neither were the kids. I found my predicament ironic: My strict focus on the official assessments was very likely decreasing my students' chances of doing their best! That was when I reinserted performance assessments into my syllabus and built my case for them, a strong rationale that clearly demonstrated how these performance assessments taught and reinforced the very skills needed for the pen-and-paper assessments required of my students at every turn.

First, I made a list of the typical skills these projects required (see Figure 1.1).

The newsflash was that these were *the same skills* students typically used on high-stakes tests, even the ACT, the official test taken by all juniors in Illinois whether or not they intend to go to a four-year institution. My list seemed impressive until I realized that some Assessment and Standards aficionados might scoff at my exercise. After all, any

FIGURE 1.1 Typical Skills Required by Live Assessments

Reading	Writing	Speaking and Listening
■ Interpret facts	■ Convey information using a variety of genres	■ Listen and respond respectfully
■ Pick out important details	■ Utilize a writing process	■ Speak clearly
■ Summarize and draw conclusions	■ Organize for structural clarity	■ Share ideas, collaborate successfully to complete a project
■ Determine the author's purpose	■ Revise	■ Rehearse effectively
■ Make connections between texts	■ Research information	■ Organize a PowerPoint presentation
■ Make inferences	■ Support ideas with specific details	■ Interpret text orally
■ Visualize	■ Argue a position that acknowledges multiple viewpoints	■ Use effective movement and body language to convey a message
■ Extend text logically	■ Satirize or parody existing literary works	■ Speak extemporaneously
■ Determine character traits		■ Speak informally
■ Recognize an author's tone by style and word choice		■ Prepare and present an original speech

skills, strategies, or classroom activities worth pursuing *must* be traced back to those all-important state standards, not some personal list of standards I dreamed up.

So I perused the official state standards of Illinois, New York, and California and found them remarkably similar. If these government documents were student papers, I'd definitely smell a whiff of plagiarism. Where did these standards originate? WikiHowtoCheat? The next thing I discovered was an absolute delight: These state standards are like the bible. You can quote them chapter and verse to support just about *anything* you are doing in your classroom. I once caught a presentation given by Samantha Bennett. In her conclusion, she boldly stated, "Your state standards are your friend. Embrace them. Use them." That statement stunned me; I was speechless, being in the camp that would rather excise than embrace the state standards. But Sam Bennett was right.

Figure 1.2 is a condensed compilation of various standards I found for the three states I investigated. Notice any similarities between my skills list in Figure 1.1 and this state standards list? Yep, overlap galore. Those standards *are* my new best friends!

FIGURE 1.2 Selected Standards in Illinois, New York, and California

Reading	Writing	Speaking and Listening
■ Interpret and evaluate the impact of ambiguities, subtleties, contradictions, ironies, and incongruities in a text	■ Use precise language	■ Use elements of classical speech in formulating rational arguments and applying the art of persuasion and debate
■ Analyze interactions between main and subordinate characters in a literary text	■ Develop the main ideas through supporting evidence	■ Analyze historically significant speeches
■ Evaluate the qualities of style	■ Synthesize information from multiple sources	■ Assess how language and delivery affect the mood and tone
■ Analyze characteristics of subgenres (e.g., satire, parody) that are used in poetry, prose, plays, novels, short stories, essays, and other basic genres	■ Revise writing to improve the logic and coherence	■ Apply appropriate interviewing techniques
	■ Draw comparisons between specific incidents and broader themes	■ Use appropriate rehearsal to achieve command of the text and skillful artistic staging
	■ Write historical investigative reports	

continues

Reading	Writing	Speaking and Listening
■ Read, view, and interpret texts and performances in every medium	■ Use tone and language appropriate to the audience and purpose	■ Recite poems, selections from speeches, or dramatic soliloquies with attention to performance details
■ Recognize unstated assumptions	■ Use prewriting activities	
■ Recognize and analyze the relevance of literature to contemporary and/or personal events and situations	■ Use the writing process	■ Listen respectfully and responsively
	■ Take notes from written and oral texts	
	■ Maintain a writing portfolio	■ Apply delivery techniques such as voice projection and demonstrate physical poise
■ Share reading experiences with a peer or adult; engage in a variety of collaborative conversations	■ Evaluate written work for its effectiveness and make recommendations for its improvement	■ Use nonverbal communication techniques to help disclose message
■ Read with fluency	■ Write for real situations	■ Recognize the use and impact of effective language
■ Explain and justify interpretation	■ Use electronic formats	
	■ Evaluate research information in a logical manner	■ Respond to constructive criticism
		■ Determine points of view, clarify positions, make judgments, and form opinions
		■ Use social communication in workplace settings
		■ Deliver impromptu and planned oral presentations
		■ Orally present original work supported by research

Now I had one pretty good argument for any administrator who happened to walk in on a performance assessment versus a timed essay. And you know what? The kids were doing just as well on their mandated assessments without me teaching to the test because I was still teaching the skills that would be tested.

Clearing the Path for Live Assessments

People have lots of reasons for not using performance assessments: they take up too much class time, they're hard to grade, the kids are shy, the groups don't get along, performances are disappointing. All these things *could* go wrong. But I am going to show you how each potential problem can be easily prevented or solved. If the conditions are right, your kids will be dying to perform. And about that shyness . . . have you ever seen couples passionately kissing in the hallway right outside your door while several hundred students stream by between bells? Your kids are not shy—but they *are* afraid of ridicule, a different problem specifically addressed in Chapter 2.

The number one problem that deters teachers from exploring live assessment is this: How do you grade a live performance objectively? In previous eras, writing assignments received a letter grade and a teacher comment. Today, essays are more commonly graded against a rubric, resulting in a precise numerical score. Totally objective, right? Not really. Unless *all* teachers are trained to grade *each* mandated paper in exactly the same way (interrater reliability), teachers will subjectively interpret a rubric based on their own preconceived notions. In *Rethinking Rubrics in Writing Assessment* (2006), Maja Wilson asks, "What happens when a student misses the mark on a rubric attribute yet displays 'non-rubric' craft that isn't worth any points according to the scoring guide? What if it's the most brilliant paper you've ever read, but it just doesn't fit the rubric constraints? Does the student fail? Does the teacher say, 'Wow, this is the best paper I've read in the last thirty years, but it just doesn't fit our district's rubric definition in regards to organization. Would you rewrite this as a traditional five paragraph essay?'"

In our desire for objective assessment, the quest for rubrics has reached a fevered pitch bordering on religion. Don't buy into it. Though we can make our rubrics look highly scientific, they are not. Rubrics are just tools, like hammers and saws, and that's the status we should give them. Rubrics are handy tools that help us define performance criteria for our kids, with our kids. I use rubrics consistently in my classroom (and in this book), but I don't think they represent Truth. If a student wants to stray from the rubric in the name of creativity or a better idea, that's a conversation worth having.

Sometimes teachers avoid assessments other than traditional essays and tests because they are uncertain how to grade them and assign a point value. The great thing about rubrics is that one can be created for any performance or product. Check this out:

BACON RUBRIC

	5	4	3	1
Appearance	Flat	Curled	Folded	Shrunken
Color	Medium brown	Golden brown	Dark brown	Burnt/ undercooked
Texture	Crisp	Hard	Limp	Greasy feel
Temperature	Hot	Warm	Cool	Cold

This rubric is for real. Twenty-five years ago, I used to teach home economics (now rechristened family and consumer life science). Recently, when I finally decided to pitch all my old "quick breads" handouts, I ran across this rubric. I am passing it on to you with the hope it will free you from the anxiety-producing uncertainty that arises when frying bacon. Now you know exactly what will earn you some fives. "But what if I like my bacon a little curly and a bit limp?" You've got two choices: realign your personal preferences with the rubric or (better) modify the rubric. Now is the time for the class to have a discussion of what makes a great piece of bacon. Rubrics are living documents, awaiting revision as the need arises!

The task of assessing a performance using a rubric is no more/less difficult than assessing an essay or a slice of bacon. Good rubrics offer a concrete way to define quality. I use rubric scoring sheets in my classroom and alongside every assessment activity in this book because I know that in most school districts we must assign a point value to everything the kids do. But never forget that you and your students are the ones in charge. The best rubrics are the ones co-created by you and your students. And in Chapter 2 I will offer you a way to show your students how to think about quality and develop rubric descriptors that help them monitor their work and produce high-caliber performances. You'll find students enjoy collaborating on rubrics for live assessments because everyone has a stake. Unlike a bad paper, which only the teacher gets to suffer through, every student has to suffer through a boring, poorly executed performance. There is a real incentive for kids to take the creation of these rubrics seriously.

The Live Assessment Workshop Model

Unlike traditional assessments, all of the models in this book are collaborative and require that groups of students work together in order to create a final performance. Very often the collaboration begins with reviewing content and possible further research. Next, students work together and use the material to create a piece of writing from which their live performance will emerge. Finally, students take their original work and rehearse its interpretation, its staging, its physical drama. For students the work can be intense yet very engaging. Now, you're probably wondering: where do I fit in? I'm not lecturing or leading a large group discussion or grading piles of essays.

The teacher's role now is that of the ultimate coach. In the beginning you'll present the game plan and help students imagine the assessment. You'll also determine what live assessment skills students might be lacking and then lead them in minilessons to strengthen any weaknesses and in turn ensure their success as they engage in one of the live assessment models. Then as students begin to workshop their performances, you will be monitoring, listening in, offering advice, asking questions, giving feedback, and redirecting students based on the quality criteria set forth in the rubric. This live assessment workshop is just like writing workshop except that the products have expanded beyond the printed page.

How to Read This Book

Some people think that professional books for teachers should never be called "cookbooks." I beg to differ. Cookbooks are wonderful creative tools that allow you to meld your own taste and personality with someone else's basic ideas to create an experience that people enjoy. This initial chapter should have convinced you that "cooking" is something worth doing. Chapter 2 gives you the basics you need to know so that whatever "recipes" you try will be successful. For example, a cake is guaranteed to flop if you put the batter into an ice-cold oven. The activities in Chapter 2 will "preheat the oven" so the live assessment strategies come out golden brown! Of course, new recipes tried for the first time are seldom perfect. There are always some minor adjustments between the initial experiment and the version you serve to company. Therefore, when picking a live assessment strategy to try, choose one you think you can reuse a few times with the same class so that the performance can be refined and perfected.

Chapters 3 through 12 are the recipes: live assessment activities. Each chapter begins with an introduction offering a description and rationale for the activity followed by a list of applicable standards and skills typical of most state assessments in the categories of reading, writing, and speaking and listening. Also, as in a recipe, the amount of class time needed is indicated. While some activities take only a class period and others several, all are easily doable. The steps are outlined, and I've tried hard not to leave out any key ingredients! Finally, at the end of each chapter, there's a quick outline of all the assessment's steps for easy reference.

A Story

For ten years, my classroom was next door to that of one of our speech teachers. Bob taught freshman speech five periods a day, semester after semester, year after year. Although I did not envy his opportunity to hear nine thousand demonstration speeches over the course of his career, I did notice that Bob never left school carrying more than his jacket, while I left day after day dragging home bags of papers to grade. Bob seemed to have plenty of time to coach diving, sponsor the junior class, coordinate all student activities, and go fishing on his boat every weekend. After several years of silent envy, I came up with two solutions. One, I could take over Bob's all-speech-all-the-time classes since he was nearing retirement. Or two, I could figure out how to expand my assessment repertoire so that every single unit assessment didn't end with a "Final Paper" that became the focus of my own weekend, while the kids cruised the local mall, texted each other, and otherwise enjoyed their free time. As my exploration progressed, my students didn't stop writing, but they did begin to use writing for assessment outcomes that moved beyond the limiting genre of the traditional essay. In fact, I watched them work much harder on researching, writing, and practicing their talk shows (one of the assessments later described) than I ever saw when they were taking essay tests.

There's an old saying that school is a place where young people go to watch old people work. Ain't it the truth?! But live assessments offer us a way to turn this backwards arrangement around. Live assessments reinforce vital subject matter while expanding kids' preparation and performance skills. They honor the learning goals you've set for your students while also reflecting the standards your state has mandated. They are rigorous yet offer students the opportunity for flexibility, creativity, and innovation. By now you should only have one question left: How do I get started?

Gatsby Test Answers

1.	T	6.	F	11.	T	16.	T	21.	T	26.	F
2.	T	7.	T	12.	F	17.	T	22.	T	27.	F
3.	T	8.	T	13.	T	18.	F	23.	T	28.	F
4.	F	9.	T	14.	T	19.	T	24.	T	29.	T
5.	F	10.	F	15.	F	20.	F	25.	T		

Getting Kids Ready to Go Live: Strategies for Building Confidence and Performance Skills

Last week my students completed a character study of Mayella Ewell from *To Kill A Mockingbird* exploring this question: How could Mayella tell a lie that ultimately sent Tom Robinson to his death? After reviewing key text pages and jotting notes, groups made a list of the reasons why Mayella's life was so hard, why she had the blues:

- Her father was an alcoholic and spent the entire welfare check on booze

- She had to take care of all seven of her siblings with no help from her father

- Her father had a vicious temper and beat her

- She was lonely and had no friends

- She lived next to the dump in an abandoned shack

- She was so poor that she had to depend on combing through the dump for what she needed

- Her shoes were made out of tires found in the dump

The following day, we sang a traditional blues song together and then each group began writing a blues verse from Mayella's perspective. As each team finished, they tested the "singability" of the song with me. Though I accompanied them on guitar, it would have been just as easy to sing along with a recording. Then they wrote down their lyrics on a transparency. The last part of the class featured the songs. In turn, each group came up to the front and sang their original verse. But they weren't alone; with the transparency, everyone got to sing along—and they did! As the performances progressed, there was much laughter and applause and by the time class ended, everyone had a much better understanding of Mayella Ewell. (To see some of my students writing and performing Shakespearean blues tunes, see the video DVD *Inquiry Circles in Middle and High School*

Classrooms: New Strategies for Comprehension and Collaboration [Stephanie Harvey and Harvey "Smokey" Daniels, Heinemann, 2009].)

Do you have trouble visualizing your own class jumping up to perform as their peers offer encouragement and support? Earlier I pointed out that kids are not as shy as we think they are. But kids are also seriously worried about getting up in front of an unsupportive audience. So, our job as teachers is not to give up on energizing performances but to train students how to work together based on the wealth of knowledge we can gain from the field of group dynamics.

Group dynamics, the study of how groups interact under various circumstances, was first pioneered by German Psychologist Kurt Lewin (1948, reissued 1997), whose research was later applied to school settings by Richard and Patricia Schmuck (2000) and David and Roger Johnson and Edythe Holubec (1993). Their combined research revealed something we teachers often overlook: Group behavior is predictable, not random. And when people are taught efficient, productive, and positive behaviors that are modeled, practiced, and reflected on, they collaborate consistently well.

The most important variable a teacher must shape from day one is the classroom climate. A positive climate where classmates are supportive and friendly opens the door to the risk taking necessary for any kind of academic gain. Conversely, a classroom steeped in competitiveness and hostility is a place where little learning can happen. We know that "Emotions stamp the brain with extra vividness" (Wolfe 2001a). If the emotional trigger is a putdown, the brain will perceive it as a threat and make a quick choice: fight or flight. Embarrassment and humiliation create long-lasting vibrant memories because the brain directly connects them with vulnerability. In a classroom, students can't literally take flight, but they can withdraw, become "invisible," and refuse to take any risks.

Students tend to treat people with whom they have friendly relationships better than those they don't, so at the beginning of the school year teachers need to provide ways for students to get to know one another. Yes, I am saying that we teachers must instruct our kids in the ways of friendship if we want them to collaborate in our classrooms. I have written about this in two previous books. *Reading and Writing Together: Collaborative Literacy in Action* (2002) is a yearlong guide to building an interdependent, cohesive, and productive classroom community. In *Mini-lessons for Literature Circles*, Harvey Daniels and I take a social-skills approach to the development of lively, autonomous student discussion groups—which depends upon building friendliness and support (2004).

We all have our favorite icebreaking activities that we do on the first few days of school. As a matter of fact, for most kids, the first few days of school amount to icebreaking overload. It's probably one of the few times in the year when students actually wish we'd crack open the textbook just to give them a break from all that icebreaking. So here's the new icebreaking rule: never spend more than ten minutes on any icebreaking activity, but (and here's the important part) KEEP DOING THEM THROUGHOUT THE YEAR! Did you hear that? Was I screaming too loudly? Typically we hit the "get-to-know-you" stuff hard in the beginning of the semester and then check it off the list. Now, instead of intense ice-breaking those first few days, spend five or ten minutes on it two or three times a week throughout the entire year. Also, according to Spencer Kagan (1994), one of the cooperative learning gurus, there are two types of icebreaking: teambuilding and classbuilding. While teambuilding focuses on small groups of students getting to know each other, class-building focuses on out-of-your-seat mingling activities that encourage students to get to know *everyone* in the room. Classbuilding activities create wider contacts and enable students to learn names and know each other beyond labels. For your classroom community to support live assessment, you need to consistently use both kinds of icebreaking.

Creating a Supportive Classroom Audience

Almost all of the live assessment warm-ups and performances in this book make use of small groups. As I already noted, the behavior of groups is predictable based on the interaction skills that students bring into your room. Therefore, a large group combined with socially unskilled members is a recipe for disaster, and there's a specific predictable reason for this that can be described in a formula:

$$N = \text{the number of students in a group}$$

$$(N - 1) = \text{the number of students in a group minus one}$$

$$N(N - 1) = \text{I: the number of potential interactions that can take place in a group}$$

For example, let's say your students are working in pairs. Here's the formula with 2 plugged in for the N.

$$2(2 - 1) = 2$$

See, that's why kids get so much work done in pairs; they can only talk to each other—only two interactions are possible. So if your students haven't had much successful practice working in groups, it's best to start them in pairs. Now, for comparison's sake, let's see how many interactions are possible in a group of six.

$$6(6 - 1) = 30$$

Whoa, did you see that number explode? In a group of six, there are thirty possible interactions that can take place. For example,

- One person talks and everyone else listens.

- Everyone talks and no one listens.

- Two people talk together while everyone else does their homework and ignores the group.

- The group splinters off into a trio, a pair, and one odd person out.

Etc., etc., etc.—you get the picture!

As evidenced, larger groups can be unwieldy. At the beginning of the year, it makes the most sense to start the small-group work in pairs, at least for the first couple of weeks. After monitoring how skilled students are with those they don't know well, you can decide whether to keep moving the students into new pairs or increase the size of the groups. No performance in this book requires a group larger than four people. If you do decide to expand beyond four, monitor those groups closely so that the quieter members are not ignored. And when you do see unequal distributions of air-time or workload, don't be afraid to coach the group—or turn the issue into a whole-class minilesson that could benefit everyone.

Teambuilding: Interviews

I've found that the most reliable, consistent teambuilding strategy is interviewing. In pairs or small groups, offer students a low-risk topic (favorite television show, movie, store, pizza place) and then give the groups a few minutes to interview each other on the topic; one minute a person is a good place to start. Also, before letting the groups loose on the topic, have the kids interview you and send one student to the board or overhead to record the questions. Encourage students to ask you open-ended versus yes/no or single-answer questions. Don't be afraid to coach and direct students to revise their questions so that they'll get a more complete answer out of you. But don't be too forth-coming. We teachers can talk about anything, including ourselves, for hours. Try to be more like the kids. Make them work to get the details out of you! Also, explain to the kids that their questions should build on your answers. In other words, they should ask follow-up questions rather than just a bunch of questions on the topic that aren't really related. For example:

Q: What kind of pizza do you like?

A: Thin crust cheese and sausage.

Q: Where's the best place to get that kind of pizza?

A: Enzo's; it's near my house.

Q: What is Enzo's like?

A: We mostly get carryout. It's a block from our house, just down the alley from us and they have the thinnest thin crust ever. In the summer, they'll even put on fresh tomatoes and basil from our garden as long as we bring extra for them.

Really listening to a partner's answers and then coming up with good follow-up questions takes practice. However, the ability to ask and answer will come in handy for many of the live assessment activities that follow.

How often should groups conduct these quick interviews? Probably for three or four days in a row when a new group has formed and, after that, at least twice a week in order to keep the connection and friendliness flowing. Groups should always conduct interviews in order to warm up the conversation before beginning any academic work together. This five minutes of small talk may seem like a throwaway, but it is critical to the work that follows because no one in a group is going to share their thoughts freely unless they already feel they can trust their members to be supportive. Getting to know each other just a little better before the work begins fuels this supportiveness. It's that opening conversation about pizza or pets that gets them invested in one another. And if you think about it, this is exactly how we grown-ups behave when we gather in small work groups—the meetings always begin with some socializing, chatting, sharing photos, and other kinds of warming-up behavior.

Once groups become familiar with the interview structure, have them brainstorm new topics and then as you use them, credit each group in turn. They like the recognition; they'd rather talk about their topics than your topics, and the next time you challenge them to come up with new topics they will attempt to be more creative. Also, the nice thing about interviews is that whenever you switch groups, the interview process stays the same but the conversations change with the new people.

Variation: Two Truths and a Lie

As groups get to know each other and are willing to take a bit more risk, assign your students to individually think of two or three facts about themselves that others do not know. Of course, tell them this is not to be a "tell all" exposé and they should definitely keep their intimate secrets just that! Next, the students need to think up one more personal fact, but this fact has to be false. (Totally plausible, but false.) Because these "facts" can be a little hard to think of on the spot, it's best to give the assignment and then complete the activity a day or two later. Here are some examples my students came up with. See if you can guess which one is the lie.

- I cut off my sister's hair while she was sleeping.

- A deer attacked me in my backyard.

- I was electrocuted by my dog and paralyzed for a year.

Give up? The girl did not cut off her sister's hair, but the other stories were true. The kids do a great job of scouring their past for experiences that really did happen but most people wouldn't believe.

On the designated day, students get together in their interview groups and decide who will go first. The volunteer presents their three facts and it is the group's job to conduct an interview that will ultimately determine which of the three is the lie. Now the skills of listening carefully and asking good follow-up questions really come in handy. At the end of two minutes, the group decides which truth is really the lie and then the interviewee reveals the ultimate truth. Then it's on to the next person. Unless the questions are deep and probing and the kids are begging you for more, allowing less time helps keep the groups more focused and the energy high.

Classbuilding: Trading Riddles

While teambuilding can be boisterous, students also generally remain in their seats, which enables a teacher to maintain a great degree of control. On the other hand, all classbuilding activities require mingling and moving around. This is good for burning off some energy but it is also an opportunity for some behavioral surprises. Therefore, start the teambuilding activities right away but hold off on the classbuilding activities until you know everyone's names or at least the names of the kids you might have to rein in.

Trading Riddles is a fun, low-risk classbuilding activity that follows some basic steps. Prepare riddle strips beforehand (some starter riddles are provided in Figure 2.1); you'll need one for each student. Pass out the strips and tell students they will be reused so they should be careful with them. Strips in hand, here are the steps for Trading Riddles. If these look familiar, they probably are, since they were adapted from the Spencer Kagan structure called Mix and Match (1994).

1. Wave your strip above your head to indicate you need a partner.

2. Once you've paired up, introduce yourself and find out your partner's name if you don't know it. Partner A then says, "_____ (insert name), I've got a really funny riddle; let me read it to you and see if you can guess the punch line."

3. Partner A reads the riddle and sees if Partner B can guess the answer. If not, tell him/her.

4. Partner B says, "_____ (insert name), that was a really funny riddle; now I'm going to read you mine."

FIGURE 2.1 **Sample Riddles**

Why did the lady hold her ears when she passed the chickens?
Because she didn't want to hear their fowl (foul) language.

If you put three ducks in a carton, what do you get?
A box of quackers.

What has four wheels and flies?
A garbage truck.

What is the first thing ghosts do when they get into a car?
They fasten their sheet (seat) belts.

What tree is hairy?
A fur (fir) tree.

What part of a car is the laziest?
The wheels. They are always tired.

A man had two sons and named them both Ed. How come?
Because two Eds (heads) are better than one.

When is a green book not a green book?
When it is red (read).

Why do people feel stronger on Saturdays and Sundays?
Because all the other days are weak (week) days.

Spell electricity with three letters.
NRG (energy).

What is an ant dictator called?
A tyrant.

What is the difference between a bus driver and a cold?
One knows the stops, the other stops the nose.

Which eye gets hit the most?
A bull's-eye.

When a girl slips on the ice, why can't her brother help her up?
He can't be a brother and assist her (a sister) too.

5. Partner B reads the riddle and sees if Partner A can guess the answer. If not, tell him/her.

6. After both partners have read their riddles, trade strips. Now you have a new riddle.

7. End by thanking your partner by name and looking for a new partner.

Five or six minutes is enough time for the kids to interact with eight or ten classmates. Be sure to repeat the activity a few times until the kids start to know the punch lines to most of the riddles. Then challenge them to pester their other friends and teachers with those corny riddles and encourage them to enjoy some wordplay and create a few riddles of their own. They'll come back in the following days filled with funny riddle reports and possibly new riddles.

Variation: Trading Questions

Follow the previous steps, but instead of using riddles use interview questions that students have thought up ahead of time. Have each student neatly print their class period and full name on the red line of an index card and then write an interesting (but not embarrassing, invasive, or school-inappropriate) question on the lined side below their name.

- What's your favorite subject in school?

- Where do you like to shop for clothes?

- Who cuts your hair?

- What's your favorite middle school memory?

Collect the cards the day before the activity so that you can weed out the ones that could be inappropriate or even evoke a sexual harassment suit. Catch the "comedians" at the door the following day, clean cards in hand. Wave the rejected card in one hand while simultaneously handing the culprit a clean card and saying, "I think you need a different question. Would you like some suggestions or can you revise on your own?" Most kids will understand exactly what you are talking about without any further discussion. Be sure to get the new question on the spot, before the student even walks in the door.

Before starting the activity, pass the cards back to the owners and then follow the same format as for the Riddle Trade, except instruct the students to interview their partners on the questions, asking some follow-up questions rather than just settling for a short answer. Also, remind them to trade the cards at the end of the interview so that they get to see and use the questions their classmates made up.

Making Positive, Supportive Behavior the Norm

Once you've had a chance to observe your students in these teambuilding and classbuilding situations, you may begin to find that their interaction skills need a bit of tweaking. You'll notice some students who only talk to their friends, ignore their partners, or don't take the time to really interview thoroughly. If you notice these behaviors, you need to be more explicit in teaching what it means to be a positive member of the classroom community. Though once in a while you're going to inherit a truly antisocial student, most kids really do want a positive classroom climate; they just need some training and practice to make it happen.

Start this training by defining *exactly* what friendliness and support looks and sounds like. Have the students fold a piece of paper in half lengthwise. Head the paper *Friendliness and Support.* Label the left-hand column *Looks Like* and the right-hand column *Sounds Like.* Then, ask students this question: If someone were being friendly and supportive to someone, what would it look like as you walked by—not hearing a word but just seeing the group work? What would the body language look like? Give students a minute to brainstorm and then record the answers on the board or overhead. Tell everyone to check off their own ideas on their sheets, but also to write down everything else that gets get put up on the board so that they each have a complete master list. Once that side looks complete, go to the *Sounds Like* column on the right. This time ask: What would group members say to each other that showed they were being friendly and supportive of one another? The items that go on this side are written in quotes to show that these are things people would actually say. It's good to give an example first: "Hi _____ (insert name), how's it going?" After pairs brainstorm for a minute or two, record all the ideas while the students write them down as well. A finished chart would look something like Figure 2.2.

Once the chart is finished, have the kids keep it handy for easy reference. Whenever students are working together, review the chart beforehand. Afterward, take time to add further examples to either column.

This handy device is what David Johnson, Roger Johnson, and Edythe Holubec, the trio of cooperative learning heavyweights, call a T-chart. When students are struggling with an interaction skill that is impeding performance, it's time to create a new T-chart. Let's say you've noticed that the kids are just hanging with their friends during Riddle Trade. The T-chart in Figure 2.3 will help solve the problem.

Remember that great story about blues songs at the beginning of the chapter? Before the kids get up in front of the class to perform, you'll want to define in concrete terms what it means to be a good audience member. This is a T-chart I have students return to

FIGURE 2.2

FRIENDLINESS AND SUPPORT

Looks Like	Sounds Like
Smiling	"Hi _____ (insert name), how's it going?"
Eye contact	
Nodding	"Pull up closer so we can hear you."
Leaning in	"_____ (insert name), glad you're here."
Sitting close together	"Wow, that was a good idea."
Looking interested	"What do you think; we want to hear your idea."
Ignoring other groups	
Laughing together	"Thanks for your help."

FIGURE 2.3 T-Chart

RIDDLE TRADE

Looks Like	Sounds Like
Smiling	"Hey, come over; I haven't worked with you yet."
Moving around the room	
Working with different partner each time	"What's your name? You forgot to tell me."
Laughing	"_____ (insert name), that was a pretty funny riddle."
Looking interested	
Eye contact on partner	"Come on, _____ (insert name), take a guess!"
Working in pairs	"_____ (insert name), read your riddle to me."
Waving riddle above head	

Figure 2.4

BEING A GOOD AUDIENCE MEMBER	
Looks Like	**Sounds Like**
Focused on performance	Respectful quiet during performance
Sitting up straight	Appropriate reaction to material
Looking interested	Applause when performance concludes
Desk cleared	Only performers are talking
	Audience uses transparency and sings along with performers (blues day)

every time there is a performance. Also, depending on the performance, different behaviors are expected from the audience. On "blues day," the audience is expected to support the performers by singing along. In contrast, when students are performing their scenes from *Othello*, the audience must remain respectfully quiet yet engaged.

The last T-chart example I've included (Figure 2.4) looks a little bit different than the other two since on the Sounds Like side there is nothing in quotes because the audience's job is to engage appropriately, not talk.

Focus and Listening

Part of being a performer or an audience member is paying attention to the action, whether it's the action you are creating or the action you are watching. As we set the stage for successful live assessments, students need to improve their focus as well as become comfortable taking risks and interacting positively with others in performance situations. The next three activities all require that the entire class stand in a circle facing each other. In these activities, students will be practicing self-control and maturity. These quick activities will help them learn to focus on their classmates without starting to laugh, make faces, or get distracted.

Applause Pass

Have students stand in a circle (or more of a square depending on your desk situation) facing each other. You do not need to move all the desks out of the way for this. It is just important that the kids are standing in close proximity and can see each other.

1. Model the action. Turn to the student next to you and tell them to face you and watch carefully. Tell your partner that when you clap, they should clap at exactly the same moment so that it sounds like one clap, not two. Try it a couple of times until you are clapping in unison.

2. Now ask for a volunteer to start. That person will turn to the person on their left. As partners, they will clap in unison. Then that person will turn to the partner on their left and continue the applause pass. This synchronized clapping continues until it has returned to the person who started the sequence.

3. While waiting for the applause to reach them, all students should practice good posture (a key element in all performance), remain quiet, and focus on the synchronized rhythm moving around the circle.

It will probably take a few rounds of practice for everyone to find the focus and timing to make the claps sound like one. Then you can try a couple of different variations. First, move the applause in the opposite direction. Everyone will have a new partner and a new challenge. Now, clap high (clapping above the head) or low (bending at the waist toward the floor). It's up to each student whether the clap will be high or low, so the receiver has to really pay attention. Next, ask for a volunteer to think up a simple rhythm. Now instead of a single clap in unison, partners will need to increase their concentration in order to make the entire series sound like one. Finally, combine the rhythm with the option of passing high or low.

Rainstorm

Like Applause Pass, Rainstorm requires the same circle or box configuration. Once again students are asked to respond physically and not talk. This sound-and-rhythm activity is intended to mimic a rainstorm. Though either activity can stand on its own, doing Rainstorm after students have mastered Applause Pass improves the Rainstorm because students will already be familiar with passing a sound as well as the importance of silence and concentration. One difference between Rainstorm and Applause Pass is that the sounds in this activity do not need to be created in unison. Actually, the more nonsynchronized, the better. For the first time through, it is better for the teacher to initiate the stages. However, once the kids understand, rehearse with different volunteers.

1. You will initiate an audible gesture that is then passed around the circle. Unlike Applause Pass each person will continue to make the sound until it returns to the originator who will then begin a different sound. Then the new sound will be passed. Tell students that they need to be absolutely quiet so that they can really get into the sound effects.

2. Start by rubbing your palms together (it's drizzling). Palm rubbing is picked up by each member in turn until the entire class is engaged.

3. Next, snap fingers right hand then left hand in a 1, 2–1, 2 pattern (rain is picking up). One by one students will move from palm rubbing to finger snapping until the new sound travels around the circle. If anyone shouts out, "I can't snap my fingers!" tell them to pretend they can and just make the gesture.

4. Now start clapping (it's raining hard!). If necessary, remind students that the clapping should not be in unison since all raindrops do not fall at the same time in the same rhythm. One by one students will move from finger snapping to clapping until the new sound travels around the circle.

5. Finally, start slapping your thighs (now the thunder has started). One by one students will move from clapping to thigh slapping until the new sound travels around the circle.

6. Return to clapping (the storm is starting to let up). One by one students will move from thigh slapping to clapping until the new sound travels around the circle.

7. Return to finger snapping. One by one students will move from clapping to finger snapping until the new sound travels around the circle.

8. Return to palm rubbing (the storm is about over). One by one students will move from finger snapping to palm rubbing until the new sound travels around the circle.

9. Finally, starting with you, going around the circle, one person at a time will stop the palm rubbing until there is only one person left making any sound. Then silence.

Like Applause Pass this activity takes some practice and refinement. Once the kids understand the pattern, ask for a volunteer to initiate the sounds and run through it again. When the class is comfortable with the steps, see if everyone can complete the activity with their eyes shut, relying only on their listening skills. Also, with their eyes shut, tell them to use their imaginations and really picture the rainstorm. Of course, I recommend that the teacher keep her eyes open!

Hand Jive

Simple group and line dances are a great way to energize the kids, increase coordination, and continue to work on focus and performance. The ultimate goal of these introductory activities is to get the kids to have fun and learn how to be supportive of each other while stepping just a little bit outside their comfort zone.

Remember that old movie *Grease?* You know, when John Travolta was young and everyone knew him as Vinnie Barbarino from *Welcome Back, Kotter?* Though most of the dances in that movie are way too complicated for most classrooms, there is one dance that isn't: The Hand Jive! Actually, this dance is barely a dance since all you move is your arms; your feet don't have to move at all. If you can't quite picture this dance and you don't have a copy of *Grease* at your fingertips, just take a moment to hop on YouTube. While Paramount has managed to keep original movie clips off this site, you will have no problem whatsoever finding plenty of people doing The Hand Jive on YouTube. Who knew it was so popular?

To do this dance, you'll need to get the tune first. If you type "Hand Jive" into iTunes, you'll find 123 different versions, but the one you want is called "Willie and the Hand Jive" performed by Johnny Otis. That version has a great Bo Didley sort of beat and is much slower than the version used in the film. The following moves are pretty easy, but I still recommend that you practice a few times in front of the mirror with the song before you spring this on your class. Like most line dances, the choreography has sixteen counts and then it repeats.

1. Pat hands on your knees twice. (counts 1, 2)

2. Clap your hands twice. (counts 3, 4)

3. Cross your hands (palms facing down) in front of your body, twice with right hand above and twice with right hand below. (counts 5, 6, 7, 8)

4. Make fists and pound hands together twice with the right hand on top and twice with left hand on top. (counts 9, 10, 11, 12)

5. Make a thumbs-up with your right hand and point backward over your right shoulder twice, as if you were hitchhiking. (counts 13, 14)

6. Make a thumbs-up with your left hand and point backward your over left shoulder twice, as if you were hitchhiking. (counts 15, 16)

7. Repeat sequence until you get to the chorus. Then just clap twice after the words "hand jive."

Now you're ready to teach it to your class. Rather than moving to the circle, have the kids just stand at their desks so that their focus is on you. First, teach the choreography without any music. Next, practice the entire routine a few times with everyone counting out loud one through sixteen. Now go ahead and put the music on and see how everyone does. Once the kids know the song, this is an activity you can throw in the last few minutes of class for some fun. If they're good, you can have sides of the room face each other and perform in turn, trying to outdo each other. Also, once the kids have the song down pat, try performing in a circle. See if they can still "hand jive" while looking at their friends. Remember, part of the whole point of all these activities is for them to learn self-discipline and focus and ignore distractions, so go ahead and remind them of that.

Too embarrassed, shy, nervous, uncoordinated to lead a Hand Jive session? Don't worry. You've got some options. Farm Hand Jive leadership out to some willing students. Believe me, they love to watch just about ANYTHING that's on YouTube. Of course, give them some extra credit for mastering the moves and teaching them to the rest of the class. Another solution is to invent your own rhythmic movements to a song. They wouldn't even have to be choreographed. Think "Simon Says." The whole point is for students to get more comfortable with movement and be able to focus and follow along.

Why Dancing?

You may find it hard to believe that your students will enjoy dancing, but if you've trained them in consistently being friendly and respectful then you might be surprised. I've seen a few energetic dance parties break out in my room once the kids have mastered the moves. But I bet this is your big question: How does dance fit into the classroom? I have plenty of answers. First, dance heightens kinetic awareness and improves coordination, both of which make a huge difference in any kind of performance whether it's a speech, job interview, or scene from Shakespeare. We already know that the brain responds positively to rhythm as well as physical movement, and dance combines both of these! Second, when a class can perform a dance together with some degree of precision, it is a bonding moment. This class this period has accomplished something together that, most likely, none of them will for the rest of the day. A group dance enhances community. Third, once the kids know a dance, you can work it into the curriculum. When you are studying *Romeo and Juliet* and the kids are acting out the scene where Romeo and his friends crash the Capulet's party, throw in a dance scene. Now everyone has a part! When you are studying the Declaration of Independence, don't you think Thomas Jefferson wanted to hit the floor once that job was done? After all, he was the one that got stuck writing most of it. Use dance to add some fun and spice things up!

Dance Variations

What works? There's always that good old standby the Hokey Pokey. The dance is silly and should bring forth some laughs, but dancers of the Hokey Pokey also have to listen and follow the instructions on the recording.

A line dance that also calls out its own moves is the Cha-Cha Slide. According to Wikipedia, the only site that offers historical background on this dance, the Cha-Cha Slide started out as an exercise routine, developed by DJ Casper for Bally's Total Fitness in 1996. By 2000, this aerobics choreography had broken out of the gym and hit the streets. Recognizing a dance with potential, Mr. C, not to be confused with DJ Casper, recorded the Cha-Cha Slide anthem, but refusing to be left in the dust, DJ Casper recorded his own version and then went on to record the Cha-Cha Slide Part 2. Go to iTunes and you'll find 63 different versions of this song. The version I have is the radio edit by Mr. C. It is short (3:46 minutes) and simple. On the longer versions, the moves go well beyond turn it out, take it left, take it back, stomp, hop, and cha-cha. And if you've never done the Cha-Cha Slide but now feel intrigued, you can find plenty of instructional video between YouTube and Wikipedia.

Finally, another line dance standby is the Electric Slide, father of the Cha-Cha Slide and like its son, still very popular at weddings. The Electric Slide is a four-corners dance comprising of a sixteen-count choreography pattern that repeats. Any moderately paced disco song works for this dance, but my favorites are "Le Freak" by Chic, "Get Down Tonight" by K.C. and The Sunshine Band, and "Play That Funky Music White Boy" by Wild Cherry. The downside to this dance is that you've got to know it since no one will be calling out the moves. The upside is it's pretty simple:

1. Right grapevine. (4 counts)

2. Left grapevine. (4 counts)

3. Take three steps backward and tap front foot. (4 counts)

4. Lean forward tap back foot, lean back tap front foot, lean forward tap front foot. (3 counts)

5. Put weight down on front foot and while doing so, turn to face the left and clap. (1 count)

6. Repeat all steps.

For further clarification and instruction, Google this dance or go straight to YouTube.

Teaching Performance Skills

What we've been working on with the class is a new group of skills that will help kids succeed when we open up performance. We started with basic citizenship: getting to know each other, being interested and friendly to each other, being supportive of one another. Once confident of the class' trustworthiness not to embarrass or ridicule a classmate, we moved on to more physical activities designed to improve focus and concentration as well as push the comfort zone ever so slightly. Now the ultimate goal is to turn your classes into a bunch of canned hams. The ones that can take a risk and really throw themselves into a role will be the most entertaining—and also the ones that later in life will be best able to throw themselves into the role of winning job interviewee. The rest of the activities in this chapter focus on specific skills that students will call upon in the various Assessment Live! projects outlined later in this book.

Learning How to Memorize as a Class

How many times has a student said to you, "I can't memorize"? As a matter of fact, for decades students had me completely convinced that they couldn't do this. It was far too demanding, challenging, impossible. Then I signed up for a weeklong residency program offered by Poetry Alive! I thought I'd learn strategies for helping my kids enjoy the reading and writing of poetry. I completely missed this paragraph in the brochure:

> Our week begins on Sunday night with a Poetry Alive! performance, and it ends Thursday night with you and your workshop partners performing your own Poetry Alive! show for the public. The daily sessions are designed to ease you toward your performance, so that by show time on Thursday night, your presentation will be safe, comfortable and polished.

Did you just read that? The fine print said we had to put on a show that Thursday night! To top it off, once I got there, our instructors told us that all the poetry had to be memorized! I was in shock. I hadn't memorized anything since the play I was in back in high school. But you know what? I shouldered through and did fine. That's when I learned two important things about memorization. First, anyone can memorize; it just takes consistent practice over an extended period of time. The key is to get the words into your long-term memory. Second, when it comes to performing from memorization, as long as you say something that makes sense, the audience will never know you didn't say quite what was on the original page. Remember that old saying "On with the show!"? Bottom line: If I could memorize and perform three poems given only four days, my kids could totally memorize pieces as long as I taught them how to do it and gave them ample time to work at it.

Since memorization takes serious concentration, work on this at the start of the period when the kids are fresh. The best way to introduce students to memorization is through call and response using a poem that rhymes. Before you begin, have the kids stand up, push their chairs in, and practice good posture: the confidence stance. You repeat a line of the poem; they repeat a line of the poem. You repeat the next line of the poem; they repeat the next line of the poem. You repeat the first two lines of the poem together; they repeat the first two lines of the poem together. And so on. I never actually hand out the piece they're memorizing until they've almost got it. That's when they're most interested in seeing the words on paper. Plus, if they have no handout, they can't cheat during the practice by peeking. For starting out, pick short, four-line poems that rhyme since it's much easier to memorize a rhythmical rhyming poem than a free verse one. My favorite for this first memorization outing is "The Termite" by Ogden Nash.

> Some primal termite knocked on wood
> And tasted it, and found it good!
> And that is why your Cousin May
> Fell through the parlor floor today.

Interestingly enough, when I first learned this poem at Poetry Alive!, a few of the words were changed:

> A **hungry** termite **spied** some wood
> **Tasted** it, and found it good!
> And that is why your **Auntie** May
> Fell through the parlor floor today.

Personally, I like the revised version better when working with kids because it seems just slightly easier to remember. Plus, it lends itself to a slew of gestures. Once the kids have the poem memorized, we add the gestures:

A hungry *(rub your tummy)* termite spied *(hand to forehead, on the look out)* some wood

Tasted it *(pretend to be eating wood like it was corn on the cob)* and found it good *(smack lips)*

And that is why your Auntie May

Fell through *(sweeping, dramatic gesture pointing to the floor)* the parlor floor today.

Once the kids have "The Termite" mastered (it won't take long), try "Fog" by Carl Sandburg. This famous poem only has twenty-one words in it, but it will take more practice because it doesn't rhyme. This is an important lesson for your students to understand if you plan to have them memorize lines from a script later on.

Now that students know the process of memorization, the next step is to teach them a longer piece. For this I like to use the "Witches Chant" from *Macbeth*, but not the whole thing. I cut out a whole two verses of recipe ingredients. This poem gives me the chance to introduce them to Shakespeare since we'll be reading *Othello* later on in the semester. Plus, *Macbeth* is the kind of gory story you can dramatically tell so that the kids get into it. Just like "The Termite," we memorize the lines call-and-response style, but this time I try to add some gestures as we go along: throw some entrails in, stir the pot, wriggling snake arms, bat wing arms, and so on. The gestures help with the memorization. You'll notice that this piece is substantially longer, but isn't as difficult as it looks because it rhymes—and it has this great Goth hook!

> Round about the caldron go:
> In the poisoned entrails throw.
> Toad, that under cold stone,
> Days and nights has thirty-one.
> Sweltered venom sleeping got,
> Boil thou first in the charmed pot!
>
> Double, double, toil and trouble;
> Fire, burn; and caldron, bubble

Fillet of a fenny snake,
In the caldron boil and bake;
Eye of newt, and toe of frog,
Wool of bat, and tongue of dog,
Adder's fork, and blind-worm's sting,
Lizard's leg, and owlet's wing,
For a charm of powerful trouble,
Like a hell-broth boil and bubble.

Double, double, toil and trouble;
Fire, burn; and caldron, bubble.

Cool it with a baboon's blood,
Then the charm is firm and good.

We work on this poem at the beginning of the period for a few minutes just about every day for about four weeks. As we work, the kids notice that they think they have it nailed one day and then they blank on certain lines the next. That's the other part they have to understand about memorizing a longer piece: Memorization comes and goes before it's locked in. In order to memorize something you've actually got to build in time to forget and remember it again. Memorizing lines is exactly opposite from memorizing vocabulary words for a test. While a pretest cram can keep those words front and center until the test gets turned in, interpretively performing lines from a poem or a play requires on demand recall weeks later. No day before cram session is going to facilitate this kind of memorization. And I prove my point later in the year when we stand up and recite *Macbeth* the following April just before we start our final unit of the year, *Othello*. Even though the kids haven't practiced the poem since last fall, they remember almost all the words after the second run through. Long-term memorization does take some time, but once you've got it, you've got it forever.

When they've just about memorized the whole thing, I finally give them the poem and have them count off to form groups of three. The final part of the assignment is for them to divide up the lines in the verses and work on saying them from memory as if they are talking dramatically about their favorite recipe. I also instruct them to add to the gestures we started; ideally every line has at least one gesture. Of course, students ask if they can dress up. Yeah, fine, knock yourselves out! (It's about time those kids start entertaining me for a change!)

I always schedule the performances for Halloween or the closest school day. I don't know about your kids, but mine are pretty nutty on Halloween. Apparently the candy binge begins early and they are wired. However, since I've discovered *Macbeth*, I love Halloween. At the beginning of the period, the kids put their costumes on and we have a run-through of our performances. Then we review the good audience chart (discussed earlier in this chapter) and the performances begin, which I video-record. Afterward, the kids watch the tape, jotting down three things they did well, three things they would improve, and one thing they liked about another group's performance. And by then, the period is over! Voila!

Now, depending on where you work, some places might have some religious objections to the *Macbeth* poem and the "But it's Shakespeare!" argument just won't fly. Don't worry about it. The piece does not have to be from *Macbeth*. It only needs to meet three criteria: sixteen to thirty lines, lines rhyme, offers lots of potential for hamming it up with gestures. That's it! Pick the poem that best fits your students and have some fun with it.

Improving Oral Articulation with Tongue Twisters

After watching those *Macbeth* performances, you'll probably notice that the kids could probably be a little crisper in their delivery: tongue twisters to the rescue! Pick a tongue twister, have the students stand up, and teach it to them call-and-response style. The examples I've included in Figures 2.5 and 2.6 are short, so this should be quick. Next, have the kids say the tongue twister slowly, exaggerating the sounds in each word while also exaggerating the movements of their mouth. This should elicit some giggles. Remember we're supposed to be having fun. Then have them say it a little faster but retaining the exaggerated clarity. Now, if you can borrow the metronome from the music teacher, find the fastest tempo the class can recite to until everyone falls apart.

Now it's time to repeat the process in pairs. Ahead of time, print up slips of paper, each with a different tongue twister. Pass out one tongue twister to each pair. Have them practice their twisters in the slow and exaggerated style first, then faster, faster, faster. In the end, you can have the pairs perform before the class in various ways:

- reciting the twister together three times as fast as they can

- alternately reciting the twister to each other, increasing speed each time—sort of a duel

- teaching the twister to the class just as you did in the demonstration.

- When finished, tell the kids to hang on to their tongue twister slips because they'll be using them again later.

FIGURE 2.5 Sample Tongue Twisters

- Clarence claims clams can't clap.

- The fleas fled far from the ferret's fur.

- Harry hid from the hornets he heard humming in the hollow hornet tree.

- She sells seashells by the seashore.

- Peter Piper picked a peck of pickled peppers.

- A skunk sat on a stump and thunk the stump stunk.

- Which witch wished which wicked wish?

- If Stu chews shoes, should Stu choose the shoes he chews?

- Six slippery snails slid slowly seaward.

- The big black bug's blood ran blue.

FIGURE 2.6 Sample Tongue-Twister Poems

What a to-do to die today, at a minute or two to two,
a thing distinctly hard to say, but harder still to do.
We'll beat a tattoo, at twenty to two,
a rat-tat-tat tat-tat-tat tat-tat-tattoo.
And the dragon will come when he hears the drum,
at a minute or two to two today, at a minute or two to two.

(Above poem possibly penned by Lewis Carroll, but no one knows definitively; Carroll died in 1898.)

To sit in solemn silence in a dull dark dock
In a pestilential prison with a lifelong lock
Awaiting the sensation of a short sharp shock
From a cheap and chippy chopper on a big black block.

(*The Mikado*, Gilbert and Sullivan, 1885)

Improving Oral Interpretation

Have you ever heard a student read something aloud—like the paper they just wrote—in a complete monotone? This next exercise forces students to say the same lines (those tongue twisters from the previous activity), showing a specific emotion. It's very simple. Ahead of time, prepare a set of slips, each with a different emotion. Figure 2.7 is a great word list: You don't need to use all of these; pick the ones you like.

FIGURE 2.7

Intensity of Feelings	Happy	Sad	Angry	Confused
High	Elated	Depressed	Furious	Bewildered
	Excited	Disappointed	Enraged	Trapped
	Overjoyed	Alone	Outraged	Troubled
	Thrilled	Hurt	Aggravated	Desperate
	Exuberant	Left out	Irate	Lost
	Ecstatic	Dejected	Seething	
	Fired up	Hopeless		
	Delighted	Sorrowful		
		Crushed		
Medium	Cheerful	Heartbroken	Upset	Disorganized
	Up	Down	Mad	Foggy
	Good	Upset	Annoyed	Misplaced
	Relieved	Distressed	Frustrated	Disoriented
	Satisfied	Regret	Agitated	Mixed up
			Hot	
			Disgusted	
Mild	Glad	Unhappy	Perturbed	Unsure
	Content	Moody	Uptight	Puzzled
	Satisfied	Blue	Dismayed	Bothered
	Pleasant	Sorry	Put out	Uncomfortable
	Fine	Lost	Irritated	Undecided
	Mellow	Bad	Touchy	Baffled
	Pleased	Dissatisfied		Perplexed

continues

Figure 2.7 *continued*

Intensity of Feelings	Afraid	Weak	Strong	Guilty
High	Terrified	Helpless	Powerful	Sorrowful
	Horrified	Hopeless	Aggressive	Remorseful
	Scared stiff	Beat	Gung ho	Ashamed
	Petrified	Overwhelmed	Potent	Unworthy
	Fearful	Powerless	Super	Worthless
	Panicky	Small	Forceful	
		Exhausted	Proud	
		Drained	Determined	
Medium	Scared	Dependent	Energetic	Sorry
	Frightened	Incapable	Capable	Lowdown
	Threatened	Lifeless	Confident	Sneaky
	Insecure	Tired	Persuasive	
	Uneasy	Rundown	Sure	
	Shocked	Lazy		
		Insecure		
		Shy		
Mild	Apprehensive	Unsatisfied	Secure	Embarrassed
	Nervous	Under par	Durable	
	Worried	Shaky	Adequate	
	Timid	Unsure	Able	
	Unsure	Soft	Capable	
	Anxious	Lethargic		
		Inadequate		

Have the students get with their partner and find their tongue twister. Next pass out an emotion slip to each pair telling them to keep it facedown until you give the instructions. Once every pair has a slip, tell them to turn it over look at it, and then turn it facedown and not tell anyone else what emotion they have. Then, together they need to practice saying their tongue twister to reflect that emotion. Pairs should also figure out how they will use nonverbal communication as well: posture, facial expression, and gestures. Tell the groups their performance consists of reciting their tongue twisters three times. Each time the assigned emotion should become more intense. Give the groups a few minutes to practice and then begin the performances. Each pair performs their tongue twister three times and afterward the class has to guess the emotion.

As a variation of this activity, you can substitute one of the class poems everyone has memorized for the tongue twister. Then, instead of repeating the poem three times, instruct the pairs to increase the emotional intensity with each line of the poem.

Improving Physical Interpretation

Ever heard the phrase "actions speak louder than words"? Of course you have. And that's why students need to become more aware of the physical side of their performance. Just as the words need oral interpretation, the words also need physical interpretation as well. The next few activities help students begin to think about the physicality of interpretation.

Emotion Walk

Using your same list of emotions from the earlier activity, have students form a circle or square with enough room to walk around the circle. Tell the students that as they walk around the circle you will call out different emotions. When they hear the emotion, their walk, posture, and gestures should reflect it. For example, if you call out "happy," they should swing their arms, walk energetically, add a little spring to their step, look up and smile. If you call out "sad," their walk might turn into a slow shuffle, eyes to the ground, arms hardly swinging, every step looking like it takes effort. Once you've given the examples, go ahead and try a few out. If kids have trouble, stop, pick an emotion, and brainstorm the body language for each of the followiing headings, take a "walk" and see how the ideas work.

Eyes	Head	Posture	Arms	Hands	Legs and Feet (walk)	Energy

Character Walk

A variation of the Emotion Walk is the Character Walk. Start by having the kids brainstorm a bunch of different characters that would portray different physical styles: cowboy, ballerina, weight lifter, juggler, tightrope walker, lion tamer, rap artist, movie star, and so on. As the kids walk in the circle, call out different characters. In response, the students change their walk and gestures to fit the character. Same as before, if the students have trouble, stop and brainstorm a specific character using the headings and then try it out.

Character Sculptures

This activity works best when it is connected to a piece of text. Before moving, tell the students you want them to think about a specific character from the novel, play, short story, or whatever they're reading. Then have the students get into their usual circle and count off by ones and twos. Tell the ones to step in front of the twos so that everyone has a partner. The ones are sculptors and the twos are clay. Here are the instructions:

> "Sculptors, in the next few minutes you are going to create a statue that portrays the character we just discussed. Since art often aims at capturing a feeling or emotion, think about creating a sculpture that captures some feeling about the character. As you create your sculpture, you may not touch your partner at any time nor may you talk. In order to move your partner into 'statue' position, you must communicate by eye contact and the invisible strings that you will pull as if your partner were a puppet or marionette. Be kind to your partner and never put them in a position of discomfort. You now have two *silent* minutes to create a sculpture that reflects this character."

At the end of two minutes, call time. Tell the statues to stay frozen while the sculptors silently walk the circle in order view everyone else's creations.

After the walk, switch. Those who were sculptors are now statues and the statues get to be sculptors. You may wish to use the same character again or assign a different, equally intriguing character for the next sculpture.

Who Are You and What Are You Doing?

This is an improvisation game that combines using names and miming common physical activities. It's a standard of television improv shows and the baseline game practiced by any improv team. Playing this game offers students practice in thinking fast and creatively as they act out actions such as brushing their teeth, washing the dishes, or driving a car. Here are the steps.

1. Working with their partners, have students brainstorm common activities they do every day. Show them what you mean by starting with the three examples just mentioned. After a couple of minutes, develop a master list for the class.

2. Once the list is complete, tell the pairs to go over the lists and talk about how they would act out each of the activities. Encourage them to get up out of their seats and practice.

3. Now put the lists away and have the students form the usual large circle. Start the game by you miming in exaggerated style one of the activities off the list. Then ask the kids to guess what you were doing. Once they identify the activity, tell them that you are going to repeat it, but this time, as you are miming, the student to your right has to turn to you and say, "Who are you and what are you doing?"

4. When the student says, "Who are you and what are you doing?" you say your name but identify a completely different activity. So if you were brushing your teeth, you'd turn to the questioner and say, "My name is _____ and I'm driving my car."

5. The person who asked the question now has to drive the car until the person to his right asks, "Who are you and what are you doing?" And remember, the person answering the question always states a brand-new activity.

6. The game continues around the circle until it returns to the person who started it.

Students need to play this game a couple of times before they feel confident in their miming ability. Before the next round, which should be on a different day, have the pairs work together again to come up with some new actions that might be a bit more outlandish: body building, modeling, skydiving. This time do not make a master list. Let the actions be surprises for the rest of the class!

Co-Creating Rubrics with Students

Though most students have encountered rubrics in their school lives, few have actually used them to inform the quality of their work because typically they are not written very well. The language is vague or the bulleted phrases are reminiscent of "legalese." However, rubrics don't have to be this way and it's easy to teach students how to examine a product or performance, determine its components, and then define the attributes of quality. A good way to start is by talking about pizza. Begin by passing out a blank version of the following chart (i.e., only the top headings listed). Ask the students, "What would be the three most important components of a cheese pizza?" They will quickly settle on crust, sauce, and cheese. Tell them to fill in the three boxes under the Components heading. Then give them this next direction: You are now going to develop a rubric that would enable tasters to separate C, B, and A quality pizzas from one another. Turn to your partner and try to describe the difference in qualities for the three components we agreed upon: crust, sauce, cheese. Rather than focusing on the negatives, try to come up with descriptors that demonstrate the minimal requirements for a C with increasing quality expectation for a B or an A. Here are some types of quality attributes students are likely to suggest.

Components	C	B	A
Crust	■ Not soggy, no sauce seepage	■ Crisp	■ Very crisp ■ Golden brown
Sauce	■ Tomato flavor	■ Tangy tomato flavor	■ Subtle spicing ■ Tastes home-made versus out of a can
Cheese	■ Covers the pizza	■ Generously covers pizza ■ Goes well with the sauce	■ Not greasy ■ Stringy but not rubbery

Once students have completed the pizza rubric, they can easily develop rubrics for assessments with which they are already familiar or, if the performance is new, watching a video example is helpful. The goal is for them to envision what a good performance would look like and describe that quality in concrete ways. When co-creating a rubric, aim for simplicity. Work with only three components and aim for only one or two quality descriptors for each letter grade. Always remember that the assessments, and the rubrics, are works in progress. As students gain familiarity and proficiency with a specific type of performance, the rubrics can be revisited and refined. Ask the kids if there is another component that needs inclusion or a bit of descriptive language that's missing or unclear. The more they talk about the rubric, the more they will internalize a vision of quality and infuse it into their performances.

Onward to Assessment Live!

Now that you have drawn on the insights of group dynamics, selected activities that help kids build a supportive community, polished basic performance skills, and taught kids how to think about rubrics, you're ready to move on to Assessment Live!—ten specific structures where kids can show what they know about your curricular content as they engage in a live performance.

Structures
for
Live Assessment

Academic Controversy

What Is It?

Do your kids love to argue? Mine sure do. And these days, that's a good thing. Persuasive writing has now become the most valued genre of all. Both ACT and SAT writing tests require on-demand persuasive essays, as do most high-stakes state tests all around the country. Sure, kids are occasionally asked to perform in other genres—personal narrative or informational text—but persuasion is number one. Now, wouldn't it be great if there were a fun, active, engaging way to teach argumentation, since it is the new backbone of student accountability?

Academic Controversy is conducted out loud, but builds all the skills kids need to develop strong written arguments. Originally developed by cooperative learning pioneers David and Roger Johnson (1992), Academic Controversy is unlike a traditional debate, where participants focus on just one side of an issue. This model forces students to closely examine and argue both sides (see Figure 3.1). And, as the arguments conclude, students drop their positions, consider all information and points presented, and do their best to

FIGURE 3.1 Academic Controversy Steps Preview

1. Prepare Positions.
2. Advocate Positions and Listen to Opposing Arguments.
3. Prepare Refutation.
4. Structured Refutation.
5. Reverse Perspectives and Prepare New Positions.
6. Advocate New Positions and Listen to Opposing Arguments.
7. Synthesis: Partners drop positions and come up with the best possible solution to the problem.

come up with a viable solution to the problem. Thinking through both sides of an issue: What could be better practice for those ubiquitous persuasive writing assessments or well-supported formal papers?

Academic Controversy is collaborative in nature—kids are constantly working with multiple partners. In addition to increasing the fun factor, working with several other students enables kids to gather and challenge a wider range of ideas than if they just worked through the preparatory steps on their own. In addition, teaching students how to collaborate just makes good academic sense. A summary of research published in May of 2008 by the Consortium on Chicago School Research revealed that students who regularly helped each other learn did better on the ACT test than those who focused on ACT prep. Since the ACT measures the skills of analysis and reasoning, this makes perfect sense.

When and Why to Use It

Academic Controversy is a great learning tool because it is so engaging. Partner work requires that students review their sources and organize the information in order to make inferences and connections that will bolster their arguments. As they listen to the opposition and prepare for refutation, this talk forces them to be accountable for their reasoning and use higher-level thinking and questioning skills. It forces them to analyze and evaluate the information, synthesize new arguments or points of view, and then articulate those to a partner (Bolton, Shouse, Blackman, and Kuhnhein 2008).

Another reason to use Academic Controversy is that boys love it. They may not like writing argument papers, but that doesn't mean they don't like to argue. As a matter of fact, boys thrive on mild competition, and this model serves up exactly the right dose (Goff 2005).

Finally, Academic Controversy offers all students just the right tension and emotional intensity to jump-start multiple neural circuits so that they can recall the information much more easily later on. Emotion and memory are directly linked (Jensen 1998).

You can use Academic Controversy with almost any curricular topic where there is room for argument. For example, *To Kill a Mockingbird* is *loaded* with topics to argue:

Should Atticus have taken Tom Robinson's case?

Was Tom Robinson's decision to escape prison the right one?

Was Boo Radley better off hiding or joining society?

Did Aunt Alexandra help or hurt the family once she took up residence?

Yet Academic Controversy is not limited to language arts. Any content area is ripe for a good argument.

U.S. History: Should the colonies have fought the Revolutionary War or engaged in far less costly (both monetary and casualty-wise) negotiations?

Physical Science: What should be done with arsenic-treated wood? Remove it or leave it alone? This controversy is laid out in the chapter on Chemical Properties, page 59 of the Prentice Hall textbook *Physical Science: Concepts in Action.*

Psychology: Are dreams meaningful or are they nothing more than random bursts of neurons?

Government: Is the electoral college an important safeguard or an unnecessary hindrance in presidential elections?

Biology: When studying a unit on bacteria and viruses—should students be allowed to opt out of required vaccinations due to personal concerns or beliefs?

Math: Is it necessary to memorize times tables?

Health: Should smoking be banned from all public places including restaurants, bars, and casinos?

Culinary Arts: Is organic food really tastier and better for you than nonorganic?

Time Requirement

For the demonstration in this chapter, one class period is all that is needed. However, if you choose to add a research component, you'll need to plan for additional class time, probably two or three periods total.

Starting with the End in Mind

I do not recommend using the rubric and scoring sheet (see Figures 3.2 and 3.3) until students are familiar and comfortable with the controversy steps. However, once they have reached this point, I begin an Academic Controversy with students reviewing the rubric, emphasizing that in order to be convincing you have to execute your arguments and refutation well. Also, you've got to look the part. No matter how convincing your arguments are on paper, they won't persuade anyone unless you are enthusiastic and persuasive in your voice and body language.

FIGURE 3.2 Academic Controversy Rubric

C	B	A
Arguments & Support	**Arguments & Support**	**Arguments & Support**
▪ Three main points	▪ Three strong main points	▪ Three or more strong main points that clearly diminish arguments of opposing viewpoint
▪ Some supportive examples	▪ Consistent and convincing support details	
		▪ Vivid examples and details support and convince
Structured Refutation	**Structured Refutation**	**Structured Refutation**
▪ Clear point made in regards to a specific argument of opposition	▪ Significant weakness in argument of opposition highlighted	▪ More than one weakness highlighted
		▪ Vivid examples and details support and convince
▪ Supportive details strengthen point	▪ Convincing details create doubt	▪ Questions posed to opposition that forces explanation/defense
Synthesis	**Synthesis**	**Synthesis**
▪ Viable solution determined	▪ Viable solution determined and explained in detail	▪ Viable solution reflects the best ideas of both sides and possibly new ideas not previously presented
Controversy Performance	**Controversy Performance**	**Controversy Performance**
▪ Good eye contact	▪ Gives special attention to planning notes	▪ Highly engaged at all steps
▪ Follows format	▪ Argues enthusiastically	▪ Consistently focused on persuading opponent to change position
▪ Engaged with partners		
▪ Takes notes		▪ High energy, appropriate gestures

FIGURE 3.3 Academic Controversy Scoring Sheet

CONTROVERSY

Name _____

Viewpoint _____ **Date** _____ **Period** _____

Directions: After the controversy concludes, rate yourself in the following categories based on the rubric. Please jot down any notes about performance details you want me to notice before I assign the final grade. Do not repeat the rubric phrases. Be sure to attach your controversy notes to the grade sheet.

Category	Points	Weight	Score
Arguments & Support	1 2 3 4 5	x 2	/10
Structured Refutation	1 2 3 4 5	x 2	/10
Synthesis	1 2 3 4 5	x 2	/10
Controversy Performance	1 2 3 4 5	x 4	/20
Notes	1 2 3 4 5	x 10	/50

Total Points **/100**

May be photocopied for classroom use. © 2009 by Nancy Steineke from *Assessment Live!* Portsmouth, NH: Heinemann.

Standards Skills Students Will Practice

Reading	Writing	Speaking and Listening
■ Summarize and draw conclusions	■ Convey information via persuasive or argument structures	■ Listen and respond respectfully
■ Determine author's purpose	■ Use writing process	■ Speak clearly
■ Connect between texts	■ Organize for structural clarity	■ Share ideas, collaborate successfully
■ Make inferences	■ Research information	■ Use elements of classical speech in formulating rational arguments and applying the art of persuasion and debate
■ Recognize author's tone	■ Develop the main ideas through supporting evidence	
■ Combine information in order to synthesize new ideas	■ Evaluate research information, present in logical manner	■ Recognize the use and impact of effective language
■ Evaluate the impact of ambiguities, subtleties, contradictions, and incongruities in a text	■ Take notes from written and oral texts	■ Respond to constructive criticism
■ Recognize unstated assumptions	■ Use tone and language appropriate to the audience and purpose	■ Deliver impromptu and planned oral presentations
■ Synthesize information from multiple sources	■ Use precise language	■ Present orally an original work supported by research
	■ Determine points of view, clarify positions, make judgments, and form opinions	

Using the Controversy Scoring Sheet (see Figure 3.3) is tricky because student pairs will be arguing simultaneously and it will be difficult for you to hear every bit of every argument from every pair. However, as they argue, monitor the room with a seating chart in hand, taking notes on performance strengths and weaknesses. After the controversy concludes, students complete the scoring sheet and attach their notes. Then you compare their scoring against your own notes and make any necessary point adjustments.

Getting Ready

Before delving into a topic that needs some serious research, it's best to start with an argument that students might have already had. A controversy most parents and their children encounter is whether a teen should have her own car once she gets her license. Despite climate change and the cost of gas, kids still dream of the total independence their own car will bring to them. And, believe it or not, this topic can create a heated debate with students even in sixth grade, maybe because these days they dream young or because they've already witnessed this argument via an older sibling. The key to a good Academic Controversy is to follow all of the steps in the most collaborative way possible. For this example, the topic of owning a car will be used as the steps are explained. You'll notice that the kids move through the steps rather quickly. Rushing the work eliminates much of the off-task activity that occurs when students are "done" and waiting for the next step. Also, in the beginning, when students are novice arguers, they will need less time. Of course, as they practice with this model and gain proficiency, students will eventually be asking you for more time to argue. But remember to budget the time carefully, for the strategy will lose much of its momentum if it is not completed within one class period.

Going Live

Step 1—Prepare Positions

As students move through the controversy steps, they will have two partners: an *argument partner* and a *planning partner*. If you have an even number of desks from front to back and side to side, the easiest and quickest way to facilitate smooth transitions between partners is for students to sit next to their argument partner with their planning partner directly behind them. As the diagrams in Figures 3.4 and 3.5 indicate, as students plan or argue, they will only need to turn around or turn to the side. No one needs to get up at all. The A's and B's indicate the two opposing viewpoints and are assigned by rows.

FIGURE 3.4 Seating Diagram—Planning Partners

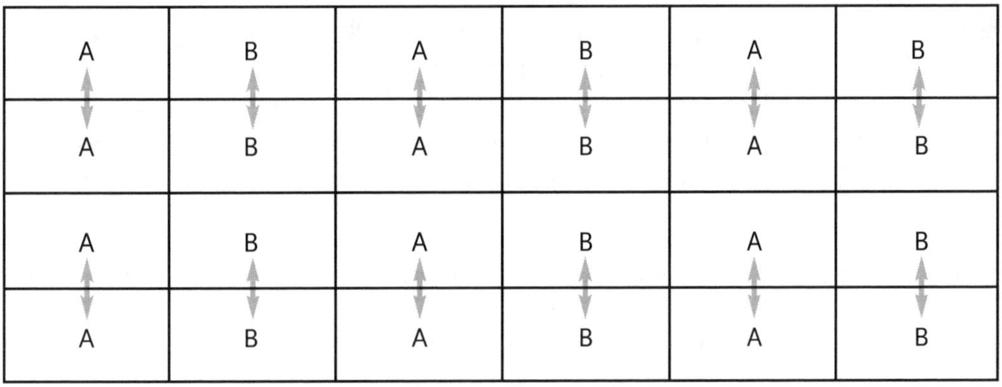

A ↕ A	B ↕ B	A ↕ A	B ↕ B	A ↕ A	B ↕ B
A ↕ A	B ↕ B	A ↕ A	B ↕ B	A ↕ A	B ↕ B

FIGURE 3.5 Seating Diagram—Argument Partners

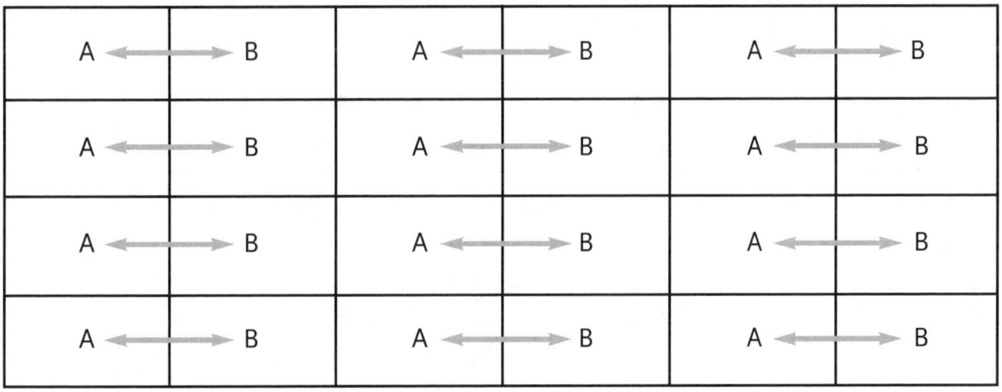

A ⟷ B	A ⟷ B	A ⟷ B
A ⟷ B	A ⟷ B	A ⟷ B
A ⟷ B	A ⟷ B	A ⟷ B
A ⟷ B	A ⟷ B	A ⟷ B

Now assign them their positions.

A: Once I have my license I should have my own car.

B: Once you have your own license, you do not need your own car.

Position A represents a teen who has recently gotten his license. Position B represents that teen's parents. Also, make it clear that if anyone is not arguing her preferred position, she shouldn't worry about it since later on everyone will switch. At this point, students turn around to their planning partner, a person who has been assigned the same position. If your desk rows are aligned, this is a snap and the kids will just turn around and find nearest person that is the same letter as them.

Once they've identified their planning partner, give students about five minutes to begin making a list of reasons why their position is the correct one. Remind students that they need facts or examples to back up each of their reasons. After all, without strong details, unsupported claims are not very convincing. Once students finish brainstorming reasons and support, give them an additional minute to rank their reasons from most to least convincing. Finally, tell them to thank their partner for all the help they gave them and now turn back to their argument partners. Figure 3.6 is a sample of what one planning pair came up with.

FIGURE 3.6 Argument Preparation Example, Position A (Teen)

DEVELOPING YOUR SIDE'S ARGUMENTS

Position A: *Once I have my license I should have my own car.*

Position Reasons	Support Facts and Specific Examples	Rank
Having my own car will save you time and make your life easier.	■ You won't have to pick me up from sports practice. ■ I can run errands (grocery, pick up little brother from soccer) for you.	2
Having my own car will make me more responsible.	■ I'll have to be careful and follow rules because if I get a ticket I could get my license suspended until I'm 18. ■ I'll have to get a job in order to help pay for the maintenance, gas, and insurance.	3
My social life will improve.	■ I can see my friends whenever I want rather than waiting for you to drop me off and pick me up. ■ Dates are a drag when someone else has to drive you	4
You'll have more control over me. If I don't toe the line, you can take the car away.	■ I'll have to maintain a C average. ■ I'll have to be home by the curfew you set. ■ I'll keep my room clean and hang up my clothes.	1

Step 2—Advocate Positions and Listen to Opposing Arguments

Planning completed, now students turn to their argument partner, the classmate sitting next to them with the opposing position. In a moment, the students will take turns arguing their position, but before any arguing begins, tell them that when it is not their turn to argue, they can only listen and take notes (see Figure 3.7, and an example in Figure 3.8). Explain that taking notes on the opposing argument is required for two main reasons:

1. Jotting down weak or erroneous reasons will enable you to more incisively refute the opposition. If you do not know the other position, you cannot challenge it effectively.

2. Later on, you will have to reverse roles and argue the opposing viewpoint. Your notes will come in handy when you prepare your new position.

Now it is time for the A's (teen drivers) to begin stating their reasons for getting a car. Remind the B's to listen carefully and take notes. Use a stopwatch and tell the A's they have one minute to convince their parents they need their own cars. When the minute is up, call time, wait for everyone to stop talking, and then tell the B's (parents) that it is their turn to convince their teens that they don't need their own cars. Remind the A's to remain silent, listening carefully and taking notes. Run the stopwatch for one minute and then call time.

Step 3—Planning for Structured Refutation

After these opening arguments, students need to turn back to their same planning partners to compare notes and develop a game plan. Which opposing arguments were the weakest? How can they exploit these while refocusing the opposition on why their best reasons make so much sense? Also, they need to predict which parts of their own arguments are weakest to attack and develop a strategy for defending them. Typically, this is the part of the controversy structure with which students will have the most trouble, probably because it requires quick thinking and articulate speaking. Giving students the opportunity to slow down and rehearse with someone else helps them better understand what is expected during Structured Refutation (discussed in the next section) as well as improve the discussion itself.

FIGURE 3.7 Listening to Opposing Arguments

LISTENING TO OPPOSING ARGUMENTS

Position Points	Weakness	Rank

May be photocopied for classroom use. © 2009 by Nancy Steineke from *Assessment Live!* Portsmouth, NH: Heinemann.

LISTENING TO OPPOSING ARGUMENTS

Position Points	Weakness	Rank
Having your own car will save me time and make my life easier.	■ I don't mind driving you around. ■ Every time you are out in the car, I will worry and that will make my life harder. Teens get in accidents all the time!	4
Having your own car will make you more responsible.	■ Considering the price of gas, you will need to quit school in order to make enough money to pay for a car. This is going to cost a lot more than what you can afford and I'm going to have to make up the difference.	1
Your social life will improve.	■ Your social life is fine as it is. Plus, I know that you will not just be hanging out with your friends at someone's house; you'll be driving around, distracted. That's dangerous!	2
I'll have more control over you. If you don't toe the line, I can take the car away.	■ If you goof up and I take the car away, you are going to argue and pout. Either way you having a car is going to make my life more difficult!	3

Step 4—Structured Refutation

Now, it's time for students to turn back to their argument partners for a second stage of controversy. The difference between this step and the first round of arguments, which only required silent listening and note taking, is that Structured Refutation allows the two sides to interact, giving them two or three minutes to question or cast doubt upon their opponent's flawed arguments as they follow these Refutation Rules.

1. Take turns pointing out a weak argument and then allow the opponent to defend. Rather than arguing back and interrupting (this is not like Tucker Carlson's old show *Crossfire*), ask clarification questions or request a hypothetical example. Try to stump them.

2. Once one opponent has pointed out a weakness and allowed for rebuttal, it is the other partner's turn. One partner should not be allowed to monopolize the entire refutation segment.

3. Criticize ideas, not people.

See Figure 3.9 for a sample of how this would sound.

Let students begin their refutation and monitor them carefully. If you see discussions degenerating into argument without listening, call time and get a couple of student volunteers up front for a quick fishbowl demonstration. Don't be afraid to coach and offer suggestions on how to respond. Sometimes it's helpful to stop the class and brainstorm a list of starter questions or statements that can begin a refutation (see Figure 3.10). Once students understand that their refutation is not talking over and interrupting one another, give them another couple of minutes to try again.

Step 5—Reverse Perspectives and Prepare New Positions

It's time for the kids to argue the other perspective. Once again, have students turn back to their planning partners to rehearse their new positions. Since they've already talked about the opposing viewpoint as they prepped for the refutation segment, it shouldn't take them more than a couple minutes to organize their new arguments. Encourage them to not just repeat what they've heard before but improve upon it.

FIGURE 3.9 Refutation Transcript Excerpts

Teen Refutes Parents	Parent's Rebuttal
How can I ever save enough money to help pay for the gas and insurance unless I get a job? For me to get any kind of job, I would have to have a car to get there. Give me some examples of places I could work if I didn't have my own car.	First of all, I think you should start saving all the money your relatives give you at Christmas and for your birthday. If you really wanted a car, you would not be blowing all that money on clothes and video games. Second, I know a couple of neighbors within walking distance who would love to have some help with yard work, dog walking, and shoveling snow in the winter. Let's see how hard you work and save for the next six months and then we can talk about your own car.

Parent Refutes Teen	Teen's Rebuttal
How can you claim having a car will make you more responsible? Your grades are low and some of your teachers complain that you are easily distracted. I worry that you'll be distracted when you drive.	I know I've made some mistakes, but I really want my own car and that is real motivation. Having a B average will give me lower insurance rates and I know I can keep a B average if I just do all my work. Don't worry about me being distracted when I drive. Remember that I can only have one friend in the car or else I'll get a ticket. I'll even let you pick which friends I can drive around and if you catch me with someone you don't approve of, you can take the car away.

FIGURE 3.10 Refutation Starters

If this happened, did you ever think about . . . ?

What if . . . ?

Do you have a plan for . . . ?

Have you considered . . .?

I hear what you're saying, but . . .

I actually checked this out and . . .

I understand your point, but what will you do when . . . ?

I agree with you on this point, but as for your other argument I disagree because . . .

Step 6—Prepare and Advocate New Positions and Listen to Opposing Arguments

Preparation partners meet one last time to organize their new positions, then return to their argument partners for the final round. Just as in Step 2, the A's (teens) will have one minute to state and support their best reasons and then the B's (parents) will have their minute. Just like the last time, non-arguers must listen respectfully and add to their original notes. Though this step seems a little anticlimatic after a particularly rousing round of Structured Refutation, it's important for students to understand and take both sides of a position. Effectively arguing the opposing viewpoint proves that they were listening and taking notes earlier. Also, it's great whenever a "new" teen or parent comes up with an argument that the original position owner never used.

Step 7—Synthesis

This is the payoff: partners drop advocacy and find an answer. They are no longer teens or parents; they are two rational people trying to come up with the best solution that addresses the concerns of all. The *best* ideas from *both* sides are incorporated. Or a solution might be based on a completely new position. Give the argument partners a few minutes to review their notes and brainstorm a solution. Finally, go around the room and hear from each pair. As unreasonable as kids can be at times, I bet you will hear very few students conclude that their own new car (no strings attached) is the best solution!

Refinement Tips

It's best to make sure that students truly understand and internalize the Academic Controversy steps before moving on to more challenging topics or attaching grades to this assignment. Let students practice with other topics that do not require additional research. Retired writing test prompts are a good source: Should schools adopt uniforms? Should high school be lengthened to five years? Should the cafeteria quit selling its mystery meat and become a food mall with franchises? Or have students brainstorm a list of school- or student–life-related topics that would be interesting to argue.

Rather than always just preparing in partners, it's okay to complete the preparation as a whole class. Let partners brainstorm reasons and support for a position but then open it up to the entire class and work together to complete the ultimate list of reasons and support. This will give you a chance to coach, prod, and model when the kids fall short on the specific details. In writing assessments, this lack of specificity is what most student prose lacks. Go ahead and plan both sides in this manner, but then let students move through the active part of the model since writing notes down is very different from having to articulate those notes orally.

In addition to allowing students to gain confidence and skill in Academic Controversy, easier topics also enable you to subtly introduce some craft lessons such as when and how to use transition words. Though in writing we strive for more sophisticated transitions between paragraphs, following the organization of a speech is much easier when the speaker uses clear transition words. Another craft for this stage of student work with Academic Controversy is the use of persuasive techniques and devices. Understanding the power of emotional appeals or loaded language will enable them to become craftier in their arguments as well as more sensitive to the hidden powers of persuasion that surround them in the media.

Adding a Research Component

Once students have mastered the steps of Academic Controversy and articulating a strong case with specific reasons and support, they're ready to tackle some meatier issues via guided research. One of the best investments a teacher can make is to buy a subscription to a respected daily paper that also offers free online archive access. Try to get into the habit of reading the paper every day or at least catch up on the weekends. Be on the lookout for articles that would be good fodder for controversy. The nice thing about newspapers is that they are supposed to be objective. Even with an evident bias, the typical article will still at least give lip service to both sides of an issue. When you find good controversy articles in the paper, go online and save them. If they're too long, go ahead and abridge them since one-page articles work best for in-class controversies.

Start the in-class controversy by passing the article out and pointing out the A and B positions. Tell the kids to look for arguments on both sides and mark up the text. Underline the arguments and code them *A* or *B*. Then go ahead and follow the normal controversy steps, but encourage students to try to think of additional reasons and support to the ones mentioned in the article. As students gain skill with this kind of research, expand the resources either having each prep partner read a different article on the same topic or having both partners read two or more. Also, as long as you are working with multiple articles, go ahead and teach them how to document their research with a works cited page since they'll need it anyway when doing that required research paper unit!

Assessment Live!

Of course it is impossible for one teacher to assess a class full of students as they engage in a vigorous Academic Controversy. With a class of thirty students, you'll have fifteen simultaneous arguments occurring if everyone is fully engaged. But think about that scenario. Is it such a bad thing if an entire class is fully engaged in honing the skills necessary to get a 5 or 6 on the writing portion of the ACT test? Also, just because you can't assess everyone easily, it doesn't mean students cannot assess themselves. After a couple of controversy run-throughs, have them rate themselves on a scale of 1 (low) to 5 (high) on each step in the model along with a sentence or two explaining the rating (see Figure 3.11). Taking note of their strengths and weaknesses, students then choose something to improve for the next controversy and list some specific actions they can take to ensure that refinement occurs. And once students are focused on how to successfully argue, go ahead and introduce the rubric and the scoring sheet (see Figures 3.2 and 3.3).

FIGURE 3.11 Controversy Skills Checklist

CONTROVERSY SKILLS CHECKLIST

Body Language

_____ Sitting Next to Opponent

_____ Leaning Toward Opponent

_____ Eye Contact/Focus on Opponent

_____ Energy/Enthusiasm in Discussion

Arguing Positions

_____ Position Points Clearly Organized

_____ Specific Facts/Examples Back Up Points

_____ Points Argued Forcefully and Persuasively

_____ Taking Notes on Opponent's Arguments

Structured Refutation

_____ Taking Turns

_____ Asking Questions or for Proof, Facts, or Examples

_____ Defending Position with Facts, Examples

_____ Refuting a Specific Reason Posited by Opponent

_____ Criticizing Ideas, Not Individuals

Reverse Perspectives

_____ Arguing Opponent's Position as Forcefully as Your Own

_____ Arguing Reflects Careful Listening and Note Taking

Another way to add rigor to controversy planning and execution is to have a few pairs perform for the entire class, after the first round has been completed. Tell students that *everybody* will have to perform eventually and keep it as a participation/check–off-style grade that won't be added in until everyone has gone. You can decide on whether to pick volunteers or choose performers at random. Rather than having audience members rate performers against the rubric, give each observer two index cards. Put one partner name on the red line of each card. As the students perform their Academic Controversy to the class, audience members should observe for two pieces of feedback:

What was something the students did well during their arguing and structured refutation?

What is something the students could improve in the next controversy?

The positive feedback goes on the lined side and the improvement goal goes on the blank side of the index card. Each student observer also legibly signs his name on the blank side. Having to sign the cards and thus own the feedback keeps audience members honest and helpful. Once all members of a class have performed, it doesn't mean the performances are over. In the next round, pair A's and B's randomly. By this time, students should be skilled at controversy and ready for the curveball a new partner might throw in the form of some fresh arguments.

Of course, the ultimate assessment is when a rehearsed Academic Controversy is turned into either a written outline or a full-blown persuasive or argumentative essay. In that case, enjoy your weekend's worth of reading and be sure to use your favorite writing rubric.

Predictable Problems

First, anticipate that students will have their biggest problems with developing good, supportive details and creating lively but thoughtful refutation. Developing these skills will take repeated practice, coaching, and modeling. Don't be afraid to back this work up with well-chosen mentor pieces or mentor video clips. Pay attention to the opinion pages in that newspaper you subscribed to as well the columnists who regularly write for *Time* and *Newsweek*. And remember to take a daily look at *USA Today*. A different debate is featured every day on the opinion page. These debates argue two sides, each with their own article. The December 12, 2008, debate argued whether or not the United States should continue to employ the services of private military contractors. These written pieces can serve as great models when it comes to organizing an argument, developing reasons with specific details, and addressing the opposition.

Also, given the preponderance of opinion shows on Sunday morning (*Meet the Press, Face the Nation, This Week with George Stephanopoulos*) as well as the evening shows available on CNN, MSNBC, and Fox, it's not too hard to find some good examples of well-executed refutation (along with "how not to argue" shout fests) as long as you're willing to record a couple of shows and find the best clips.

In terms of classroom management, remember to keep the time short for each step. Don't give students more than one minute to argue their position until you are confident that they can really use more than one minute. (Finishing an argument with time to spare frees up time for throwing something across the room!) Also, as you monitor, if kids finish before their sixty seconds are up, tell them to keep repeating their arguments until time is called.

Finally, as you monitor groups, you need to develop some way to keep track of who is supposed to be arguing at any given time in each pair. As I mentioned earlier, having the desks in rows and assigning position by rows is very efficient. Also, if you want to make the change of positions in step 4 even more dramatic, have the pairs switch seats. That way the odd rows are still the A position and the even rows are still B's. However, your particular room or furniture situation may not lend itself to this. In that case, different colored tags are the answer. Using two different colors, have students tape a colored sticky note or index card to their right shoulder, each color indicating a specific position. When they switch positions, they trade colors. Like changing seats, the color switch is a good visual cue that each student is in a new role. The downside of the sticky notes and index cards is that they tend to fall off unless you have some sort of miracle masking tape. Also, passing the tape around and waiting for everyone to rip a piece off wastes some time. The deluxe tag solution is to get your school to buy you a set of plastic clip-on name tag holders. Put the colored index cards in the holders and you are set for life as long as you remember to get them all back after each controversy has concluded!

QUICK GUIDE: Academic Controversy—Arguing for Fun

1. Prepare Positions (planning partner)

2. Advocate Positions (argument partner)

3. Prepare Refutation (planning partner)

4. Structured Refutation (each partner identifies the opponent's weakest argument and picks it apart in turn)

5. Reverse Perspectives and Prepare New Positions (planning partner)

6. Argue New Positions (argument partner)

7. Synthesis (argument partner)—Drop Advocacy (create a new solution that incorporates the best points and ideas from both sides or come up with a completely new position; go around the room and hear each pairs' final solution and ask them how they ultimately arrived at this position)

8. Self-evaluate Performance (use rubric and scoring sheet; discuss how next arguments could be refined; set improvement goals)

Book Buddy PowerPoint

What Is It?

How many bad PowerPoint presentations have you seen? Quite a few? Me too. In teacher workshops, as well as countless business and community settings, so many presenters seem to think that jam-packing screen after screen with text in bullet points will guarantee effective communication. Then they stand with their backs to the audience, reading the words aloud from the screen, while viewers are expected to follow along on a miniature printed version. I mean snoozeville. Back in the old days, when kids gave traditional "no tech" speeches, they might have read off their index cards but at least they were facing the audience! Sometimes it seems like this particular "powerful" technological tool is almost designed to yield dull, dry, sleep-inducing deliveries.

Given the mind-numbing nature of so many of these presentations, I didn't consider using student PowerPoint performances until one of my students suggested a project: let two kids read the same book of their choice and do a PowerPoint presentation for the class. It sounded okay, but wanting to avoid slide after slide of dreary bullet points, I decided to outlaw them. Instead, I asked the kids to prepare a read-aloud from the text and use graphics or illustrations on the slides to enhance the meaning of that performance. The point was for kids to show that they had thought carefully about their chosen book and used the PowerPoint as a visual enhancement, not the main event. I was happily surprised by the results and have been tweaking this idea for several years.

It turns out PowerPoint is just a tool like any other; most people simply use it incorrectly. This Assessment Live! project brings out the best in the medium; kids work with a whole new set of rules that bring PowerPoint to life. And the final projects result in anything but audience anesthesia; they engage, provoke, and persuade.

Maybe you have also been wary of the PP bandwagon. But give it another look. And if you're not a PowerPoint user yourself, don't worry about it. Most students these days are PowerPoint pros, apparently having honed their skills way back in elementary school.

When and Why to Use It

We know from extensive recent research that kids need to read *a lot* to improve their reading skills—as well as to become committed lifelong readers (Allington 2001). In fact, kids need to read far more than just the amount of text we assign in school, in English, science, social studies, and the rest. They need to read "widely and wildly," as Shelley Harwayne puts it. So today, many teachers are finding ways to stimulate and structure kids' independent reading of whole real books. There are several delivery systems for this added reading. Sustained Silent Reading is a key component of many Language Arts classrooms, typically offering students 15 minutes of daily reading time in books that hopefully are continued after school. Literature Circles or book clubs are a bigger commitment, helping kids form into small, self-chosen reading discussion groups that read outside class but meet to discuss their books at school. Even content-area teachers, in their quest to move toward a more balanced diet of reading, are embracing the independent reading of trade books. *Subjects Matter: Every Teacher's Guide to Content-Area Reading,* by my colleagues Harvey Daniels and Steven Zemelman (2004), lists 150 nonfiction books that have been popular with middle and high school kids.

We teachers usually provide these choice reading opportunities for two reasons: one to increase diverse reading experiences and increased reading proficiency; two, to get students interested in our content-area subjects, something textbooks fail to do. The problem with this kind of reading, though, is how do we assess it? Clearly, traditional book reports won't work. Ideally, the assessment should not just demonstrate that the students thought carefully about their book, but also create a social event that might persuade other students to read the book as well.

The Book Buddy PowerPoint is a perfect performance assessment to culminate this kind of choice reading. Typically, two students agree to read the same book together, create a read-aloud and PowerPoint presentation about that book, and present it to the class. The catch is that the students are forbidden from following the conventions that make PowerPoints deadly: excessive bullets and heavy text loads. The emphasis is on headings and representative graphics while the text comes from an oral presentation that *cannot* be read from the screen! This presentation is a great alternative to the traditional book report because it incorporates collaboration as well as a way for students to share their books with the class. Plus, since students work in pairs, the performances take half the class time it would take to present if each student were working individually.

Standards Skills Students Will Practice

Reading	Writing	Speaking and Listening
■ Interpret and evaluate the impact of ambiguities, subtleties, contradictions, ironies, and incongruities in a text	■ Use precise language	■ Use appropriate rehearsal to achieve command of the text, and skillful artistic staging
■ Analyze interactions between main and subordinate characters in a literary text	■ Revise writing to improve the logic and coherence	■ Recite poems, selections from speeches, or dramatic soliloquies with attention to performance details
■ Evaluate the qualities of style	■ Draw comparisons between specific incidents and broader themes	■ Listen respectfully and responsively
■ Analyze characteristics of subgenres (e.g., satire, parody) that are used in poetry, prose, plays, novels, short stories, essays, and other basic genres	■ Take notes from written and oral texts	■ Apply delivery techniques such as voice projection and demonstrate physical poise
■ Recognize unstated assumptions	■ Write for real situations	■ Use nonverbal communication techniques to help convey a message
■ Recognize and analyze the relevance of literature to contemporary and/or personal events and situations	■ Use electronic formats	■ Recognize the use and impact of effective language
■ Share reading experiences with a peer or adult	■ Evaluate research information present in logical manner	■ Respond to constructive criticism
■ Engage in a variety of collaborative conversations		■ Determine points of view, clarify positions, make judgments, and form opinions
■ Read with fluency		■ Deliver impromptu and planned oral presentations
■ Explain and justify interpretation		■ Present orally original work supported by research

Time Requirement

If the preliminary Internet research and the later PowerPoint presentations are pursued during class time, you will need to allow five to six class periods once partners have finished reading their books independently or during SSR. However, if you can depend upon your students to work together outside of school without your direct supervision, the class time used can be cut in half if you are only watching the final presentations, which last about five or six minutes apiece.

Starting with the End in Mind

The rubric shown in Figure 4.1 describes quality expectations for the content components of the presentation as well as for the performance aspects. Also, as in all of the rubrics presented, the criteria for a C is considered minimum expectations. For a B or an A, presentations should have hit all of the marks in each grade category.

The scoring sheet (see Figure 4.2), filled out by students and reviewed by you, is based on the audience review sheets, presentation notes and passage script, and the students' perception of their own performance.

Getting Ready

The Book Buddy project is probably not something to undertake in the beginning weeks of a class. In fact, it draws upon many skills that will have been developed in other Live Assessments, particularly Readers Theatre. Also, since partners will need to agree on a title and then work closely together over a period of weeks, it's best to wait until students have gotten to know each other well and read a few choice books in your content area. About three to four weeks prior to creating the PowerPoint presentations, students pick their partners and negotiate a book that both will read. This book could be a title that one partner is recommending to the other; it could be a title that both partners have had on their reading lists and wanted to read; it could be a title chosen from a content-area list that the teacher has created. I always stipulate the title be one they are reading anew and that the class has not already heard about in a previous book project. Though I encourage students to check books out from the school library, they are free to look in other places, such as the public library or bookstore. Once partners and books are picked, students make their partnerships official by writing their names and book title on an index card and turning it in to me so that I can keep tabs on the reading and the projects. Then the book buddies have about four weeks to read the book before the actual project commences.

FIGURE 4.1 Book Buddy Rubric

C	B	A
Author Study ■ General information presented	**Author Study** ■ Some focus on writing process	**Author Study** ■ Writing process fully researched and connected with book
Plot, Characters, & Conflict ■ General information presented	**Plot, Characters, & Conflict** ■ Plot and characters described in enough detail so listener could decide whether to read book ■ Types of conflict clearly defined	**Plot, Characters, & Conflict** ■ Plot, character, and conflict explanation well organized and easy to follow
Connection ■ General information presented	**Connection** ■ Specific comparison between book incident and outside connection	**Connection** ■ Discusses how this connection helped readers understand the story
Passage ■ Introduction given before reading ■ Both partners read	**Passage** ■ Reading uses two voices and choral parts	**Passage** ■ Thorough and thoughtful interpretation, should be evidenced by script notes
Conclusion ■ Three reasons given for rating	**Conclusion** ■ Specific book details connected with each reason	**Conclusion** ■ Three reasons explained thoroughly and well supported with text details
Presentation Skills ■ Consistent eye contact ■ Easily heard ■ Good posture	**Presentation Skills** ■ Seldom looks at notes ■ Enthusiastic ■ Good pace—Speaking is not too fast nor too slow	**Presentation Skills** ■ Presentation mostly memorized ■ Truly persuasive—clear speakers thought book was good and they want others to read it
PowerPoint Slides ■ Outline followed, no missing slides	**PowerPoint Slides** ■ Slides complement explanations	**PowerPoint Slides** ■ Creative but does not detract from speakers

FIGURE 4.2 Book Buddy Scoring Sheet

BOOK BUDDY

Name _____

Book Title _____ **Date** _____ **Period** _____

Directions: After reviewing your audience feedback, rate yourself in the following categories based on the rubric. Please jot down any notes about performance details you want me to notice before I assign the final grade. Do not repeat the rubric phrases. Be sure to attach your final reflection, presentation notes, and your book passage script. Turn in your sheet with your partner's.

Category	Points	Weight	Score
Author Study	1 2 3 4 5	x 3	/15
Plot, Characters, and Conflict	1 2 3 4 5	x 2	/10
Connection	1 2 3 4 5	x 2	/10
Passage	1 2 3 4 5	x 4	/20
Conclusion	1 2 3 4 5	x 2	/10
Presentation Skills	1 2 3 4 5	x 5	/25
PowerPoint Slides	1 2 3 4 5	x 2	/10

Total Points **/100**

I encourage all students to work with a partner, but it's a guarantee that one or two will prefer to work alone. Rather than forcing kids into a shotgun partnership for which they are not ready, I allow these singletons to work on their own. Very few choose this option.

Researching the Author

While students are in the midst of reading their books, we spend one day in the computer lab researching the authors of the chosen books. I specifically have kids focus on how the authors find their book ideas and what kind of process they follow when writing a book. I also tell students to look for photos of the author and save them on their H drives (the personal memory space connected to the school file server) or flash drives. Each partner must find three different author sites and print out the information. Together book buddies then have six different sources. The following day we spend some time in class reading the author info, underlining bits that seem interesting or that explain how the author undertakes the writing process. Later in the period, partners get together and share what they've underlined about the author and connect it to their books.

Choosing and Cutting a Passage to Read Aloud

During this time I show students how to choose a passage to read aloud, something from the book that is only a page or two that grabs the attention of potential readers. Also, since both partners will be required to read aloud, I use the techniques outlined in the chapter on Readers Theatre (pp. 116–129) and demonstrate how buddies can split the text up into two voices in order to make their reading more dramatic. I start by passing out a reading I've prepared that illustrates how to cut a text in order to make it more concise and dramatic. I ask for student volunteers to read the script aloud both ways. Afterward, we talk about how that passage piques interest in the book and I explain my decisions for cutting parts out of the original text so that the scene is shorter and sharper. Students always like the shorter version better because it concentrates the drama. And I also point out that the read-aloud needs to be G-rated, which is another reason cutting might be necessary.

Next, I give students a second handout with the same passage (see Figure 4.3), but this time the text includes the full scripting (scene introduction, two voices, interpretation notes) in addition to the original cuts. Look carefully at the student example for *Stick Figure* shown in Figure 4.3: the parts crossed out are editing cuts, and the remaining lines have been divided into speaking parts (one speaker with single underline, the other with double underline, and the choral part at the end with a dotted line), with interpretation notes handwritten in.

FIGURE 4.3 Prepared Read-Aloud Script—Example of Full Scripting

Stick Figure by Lori Gottlieb

"Shereen's Jeans," pages 181–182

Scene Introduction:

Shereen is one of the patients in a hospital for anorexics. Even though her life is

threatened by her refusal to eat, Shereen's body image is so distorted that when she looks

in a mirror, she only sees herself as fat. When we read this part of the book, we really

wondered if Shereen would recover since her doctors are unable to get her to understand

what danger she is in.

~~When Dr. Gold came into my room, I asked him why they weren't putting The~~

~~Tube down Bonnie's throat because of how little she eats. But~~ Dr. Gold said that one of

my problems is that I worry too much about what everyone else is doing when I should

be focusing on myself. That's why he's decided to film me. ~~It's this new plan he has so I~~

emphasize

~~won't have to get The Tube.~~ Dr. Gold wants me to take a good look at myself instead of

worrying about what everyone else sees. I told Dr. Gold that I already spend hours   *Frustrated — why doesn't he get it?*

looking at myself, which is why // I know // I'm fat. But he said he feels I'll see myself

better in a film.   *PAUSES*

Dr. Gold explained that they'll film me tomorrow, but they'll be careful to block

out my face so I can be used as a "case study" for other doctors to watch. Then he said

emphasize

that I'm an "excellent case," which is why they picked me in the first place. I guess that   *pleased —*

means I'm an excellent dieter. I was thinking about how it means I'm the best dieter at   *she's succeeding!*

---

continues

REALLY excited!

my school, and I'm probably the best dieter in the country, maybe even in the world! I

mean, I must be, because they want to make a *movie* of me. I was pretty excited about it, *THRILLED, DELIGHTED*   *She's going to BE A MOVIE STAR!*

but then I thought that maybe the doctors watching my film would have seen thinner

anorexics than me. That's because I remembered the pictures Dr. Katz showed me before

I came to the hospital.   *Worried she won't be good enough, thin enough*

The last time I went to Dr. Katz's office, he showed me pictures of all these bony   *sound really bored*

looking women that had the words, "Anorexic Female" written underneath. The reason

they had to write the word "female" is because these women didn't look much like

women. They looked more like the big skeleton that hangs in the corner of our science

classroom, ~~and I have no idea if that skeleton is supposed to be a man or a woman. I~~

~~always thought there was something wrong with it, because whoever made it put two~~

~~bones connecting each ankle to each knee, and I was almost positive there was only one~~

~~bone going between your ankle and your knee. I figured the school bought a broken~~

~~skeleton on sale or something because they're always telling us not to waste our supplies.~~

~~In the pictures in Dr. Katz's book, though, I saw that humans really do have two~~   *Kind of laughing—*

~~bones right next to each other between the ankle and the knee.~~ I guess Dr. Katz figured   *Katz is such a dork!*

that the pictures would scare me into eating, because he kept looking at my face to see if I

was getting grossed out. ~~But when I told him how neat it was that humans actually do~~

~~have two separate bones in the bottoms of our legs, even though it looks like only one, he~~

~~just blew all this air out of his mouth and said my brain wasn't working right because I'm~~

~~so malnourished. The truth is, my brain wasn't working right because of his smelly~~

~~breath.~~

PAUSES

emphasize

Anyway// that's why I figured Dr. Gold made a big mistake calling me an "excellent

case." // I mean, // if that's what a real anorexic looks like, I'd be a pretty bad example. So

Scornful

I decided not to eat anything until after the filming tomorrow. Not one bite.

Say last part together — Sound excited, happy to have a concrete goal

---

Now I enlist my best, most dramatic reader to be my partner and the modeling begins. I start with a short introduction so that students understand the book and the passage, and then we read it aloud. Finally, we talk about the interpretation notes and how to determine pacing, emotion, and pauses when reading aloud, skills that were explicitly taught and rehearsed in the Readers Theatre and Tableaux assessments. The next day, I pass out a different passage, one from a book most students are familiar and have them work with their partners at cutting and scripting. Then we take a few volunteer partners willing to read aloud to the class. The students find it interesting that different groups cut and script different ways even though everyone started with the exact same passage.

Preparing the Presentation

On the day students should have finished their books, I hand out three blank forms: a two-column Book Buddy script, the Book Buddy rubric, and the score sheet. When looking at the score sheet, I emphasize that 65 points out of 100 are awarded for the quality of their presentation content, so it's most important that they do a good job planning their scripts and their read-aloud, mentioning that some extra snazzy PowerPoint slides will add to the presentation, but having solid content is what will really enhance their grades!

After the rubric review, partners use a copy of the book and the author information collected earlier to write their script. For their Book Buddy script (see an example in Figure 4.4), students need to determine what will be said and who will say it. I require

FIGURE 4.4 Brenda and Romy's Book Buddy Script Notes

Author Study
Looking for Alaska by John Green

Partner 1 Notes	Partner 2 Notes
■ Started writing for teens after he was a year out of college and he lived in Chicago. Now he lives in New York with his wife and his dog. ■ While living in Chicago, he worked for *Booklist*, a book review journal. ■ His boss at *Booklist*, Ilene, wrote children's books that inspired him to write for teens. ■ One of the YA books that inspired his own writing was *The Perks of Being a Wallflower* by Stephen Chbosky.	■ John Green doesn't really know how he gets his ideas; he always starts with a person. ■ He uses his experiences to help him write his books. For example, he got the ideas for *Looking for Alaska* when he was at a hospital. It got him thinking about life and death. ■ The part of the writing process that stands out to him is revision. He spends a lot of time revising what he writes.

Plot (Fiction) or Premise and Main Points (Nonfiction)

Partner 1 Notes	Partner 2 Notes
■ In the "Before" part of the book, Miles talks about how his life is boring and he is going to seek the "Great Perhaps" at his new boarding school in Alabama. He meets Chip, his roommate, who introduces him to his beautiful female friend, Alaska.	■ In the "After" part of the book a tragedy occurs and the characters that remain are left trying to understand what happened.

Characters (Fiction) or Key Players (Nonfiction)

Partner 1 Notes	Partner 2 Notes
Miles ■ The protagonist, a 15-year-old loner but the kind of teen that parents and teachers would call "a good kid." ■ He's sort of an idealist, but his hobby is kind of weird: collecting people's last words.	Alaska ■ Leader of the group and subject of the book. ■ Curvy, petite, drop-dead gorgeous. All the guys are in love with her.

FIGURE 4.4 **Brenda and Romy's Book Buddy Script Notes,** *continued*

Characters (Fiction) or Key Players (Nonfiction), *continued*

Partner 1 Notes	Partner 2 Notes
■ Physically he's "chicken-leg" skinny.	■ Creative, free-spirited, loves to read books, yet underneath she is seriously unhappy.
Colonel	
■ A short, stocky kid from a poor background.	**Lara**
■ He's attending this expensive private boarding school by earning a scholarship. He has worked his butt off and he is "mad" smart.	■ Sweet, mild-mannered.
	■ Miles' first girlfriend; Alaska introduced them.
Takumi	
■ Soft spoken, a good rapper.	

Conflict (Fiction) or Problem (Nonfiction)

Partner 1 Notes	Partner 2 Notes
Side note: There's an ongoing conflict between the kids who stay at school and those who are rich and have enough money to travel home every weekend. These "richies" are called Weekend Warriors.	**Internal Conflict:** Miles and Colonel blame themselves for the tragic event we mentioned earlier.
	External Conflict: The four main characters, under Colonel's direction, pull off a series of pranks aimed at the Weekend Warriors.

Connection

Partner 1 Notes	Partner 2 Notes
Personal Connection: When my older sister was a sophomore, a girl in her English class committed suicide. My sister couldn't believe it. She had just talked to her the day before and now she was gone forever. Everyone who knew her was shocked and kept wondering what they could have said or done differently to keep	**Book Connection:** I read another book called *As Simple as Snow*. Though the plot was different, two of the characters were very similar to Miles and Alaska. In *Snow* the boy's life is rather uncomplicated until he meets his girlfriend. Like Alaska, this girl is very smart but also very unpredictable. The

continues

FIGURE 4.4 Brenda and Romy's Book Buddy Script Notes, *continued*

Connection, *continued*

Partner 1 Notes	Partner 2 Notes
their friend from making such a terrible decision. Everyone who knew her felt guilty that if they had only been paying better attention this wouldn't have happened. This is exactly how the characters in the book feel when Alaska dies, except they feel even worse because they possibly could have prevented the "accident."	safe thing for the boy to do would be to distance himself, but he is attracted to her scary edginess because it is so unlike himself. I think this is what attracts Miles to Alaska as well; she is the opposite of him in many ways.

Passage Setup

Partner 1 Notes	Partner 2 Notes
(Page 5, starting with third paragraph) **Setup:** This is in the beginning of the story. Miles is just about to leave for boarding school after a rather unsuccessful going-away party—only two kids show up—so it doesn't appear that he is going to miss anyone when he leaves. But his mother doesn't want him to go and keeps asking why he wants to leave. This is his explanation to his parents.	**Why We Picked It:** In this passage, Miles introduces the reader to his idea called "The Great Perhaps," the idea that you've got to search for new experiences and opportunities or just fall into a rut and always wonder what might have been. Miles refers to "The Great Perhaps" throughout the entire novel.

Conclusion—Rating and Explanation

Partner 1 Notes	Partner 2 Notes
1. Events in the book are believable, realistic: most teens encounter drinking, smoking, and depression. Author doesn't preach or glorify, just treats these things as part of life. 3. The characters are believable. They didn't seem like someone's image of teens; they seemed like actual teens, people you might know.	2. This book has everything you'd want in a novel: love, death, practical jokes, a plot, and characters you can believe in.

that both partners speak equally and that their scripts be complete, with both partners writing down everything, not just what they will say. On the second day of work, students must bring in two photocopies of the read-aloud passage. Though partners need to finish their scripts, they also need to work on cutting and scripting their passage. I remind them to use the *Stick Figure* script (see Figure 4.3) as a model for this.

Once cut, the scripting requires that they plan how they will share and interpret the text. Students first must determine how they will divide the reading. Though they may want to just split it in half ("I'll read the first three paragraphs and you read the last four"), I encourage them to find a way to read the piece in two voices, more in the style of Readers Theatre. Once again, the *Stick Figure* script demonstrates this well and I encourage them to return to it. After they've worked out their parts, they need to discuss their oral interpretation and mark the text, thinking about what words to emphasize, where to pause, what lines denote what emotions, places where the delivery should become louder or softer.

Finally, now that the students know exactly what they will be saying throughout their presentation, it's time to go back to the lab to create the PowerPoint. This time I have students sit next to their book buddies and I make both of them create and consistently save identical files, so even though they are working together they both have their own PowerPoint presentation. That way, if one buddy is absent on a lab day, the other can continue working. Also, when both partners have to create files, they are both busy working rather than the alternative: one partner working while the other just watches. Finally, it is almost always the case that one partner knows more about PowerPoint than the other. By having them both create files, the PowerPoint experts improve their partners' skills when they have to walk them through a new step. As they create their PowerPoint, they follow the slide outline (see Figure 4.5) and their notes so that the images really fit their script. You can never remind students enough that the PowerPoint is not the main act; it is only a visual enhancement of their scripted material.

Of course, the PowerPoint slide outline is not locked in stone—You'll want to change the script and slide outline to fit your own personal assessment needs and students should have some freedom to add some extra slides as long as they aren't loaded with text and bullet points.

Though the described example best fits a novel or memoir, the presentation can be easily modified for a nonfiction book. Here's how:

Plot becomes **Premise** and **Main Points**

Characters become **Key Players** (and those key players might be people, animals, bacteria, etc.)

Conflict becomes **Problem**

FIGURE 4.5 PowerPoint Presentation Outline

Book Buddy Slide Outline

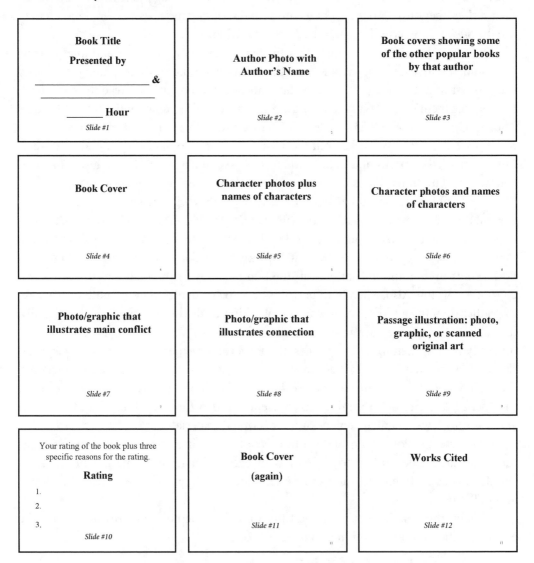

Once done, each group should print out three copies of their PowerPoint presentation outline: one for you and one for each partner. Make sure they print handout style; otherwise, they'll waste oodles of paper. If the kids print six slides per page (see the Figure 4.6 screen shot), they'll only use two or three sheets per presentation copy.

FIGURE 4.6 PowerPoint Presentation Setup for Six Slides per Page

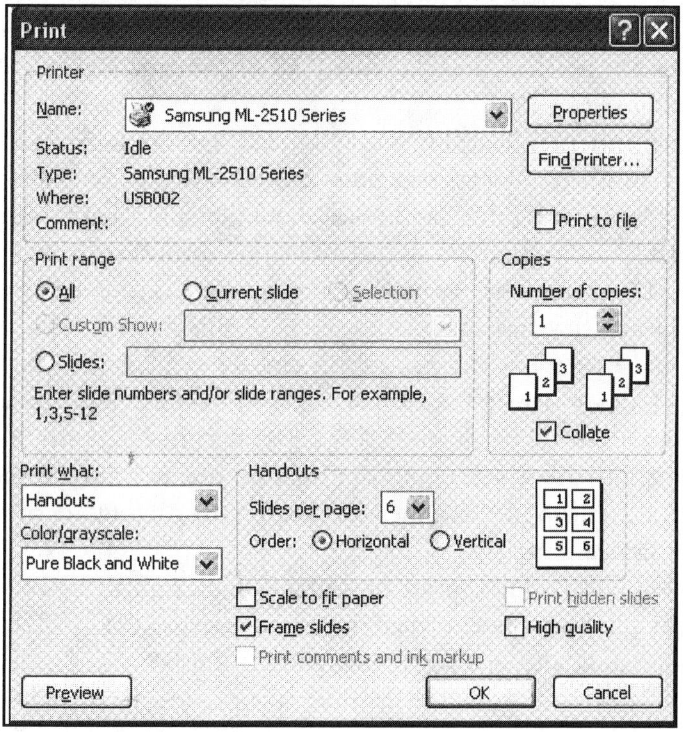

Assessment Live!

With the notes written, the passage cut and scripted, and the PowerPoint printed out, it's time for some run-throughs. The day before the presentations begin, partners spend time practicing in class with four goals. One: be able to say as much as possible without looking/reading their notes. Two: speak confidently and clearly and know what each other is going to say. Three: know the passage and be able to read it fluently and dramatically. Four: know what PowerPoint slide goes with each part of the script. As students practice, I monitor and jot notes. I award points for sustained practice and I keep reminding them of how important rehearsal is. If time permits, groups can team up and practice in front of each other in order to get some useful feedback based on the rubric.

On the day the performances begin, I remind the presenters to be enthusiastic. Their job is to share a book they enjoyed and really sell it to other potential readers! Usually we listen to about six presentations during a class period. The presentations run about five minutes apiece and though you could probably fit a few more into the period, I don't recommend it. Even when the students are coached to be as lively, informative, and energetically entertaining as possible, hearing more than six presentations in a day diminishes their individual impact.

Each performance is evaluated by me and the kids in the audience. I use the rubric introduced in Figure 4.1. Students take notes on each book presented by writing down the title, author, presenters' rating, and notes about plot and what interests them about the book. Students also complete a simple evaluation form that the book buddies pass out (see Figure 4.7). Before they begin their presentation, it is presenters' responsibility to make sure the audience has their names and book title written down. Afterward, presenters collect the evaluations and hand them directly to me. Just in case an insensitive comment might appear, I read the evaluations before returning them to the students. Also, I emphasize before we begin (and every day of the presentations) that the audience members' evaluations are worth points and that no points will be earned for writing comments that are unhelpful. Once they are clear on the concept, most students fill out useful, accurate evaluations.

I encourage Book Buddies to jot presentation notes on their scoring sheets (see Figure 4.2) right after they present when their memories are the freshest, but we do not finish the scoring until after the last presentation is finished. That's when I return the audience evaluations to the groups. Pairs finish their scoring and complete a reflection based on their own perceptions as well as the evaluations of others (see Figure 4.8).

Predictable Problems

With any presentation, there will be a whole range of performance levels from reluctant performers to those destined for Broadway, but the more students practice the better the performances will be. This is doubly true for the read-aloud portion. It takes significant practice for a read-aloud to reach true interpretation.

I seldom find any problems with the PowerPoint slides. It always amazes me how skilled the kids are at finding just the right graphics or photographs to complement their information. But since one can find all sorts of pictures on the Internet, it's important to keep reminding them that pictures need to be school appropriate. If they aren't sure, they should ask. Also, as they are putting their slides together, discourage them from using all of those slick features like pictures that slide in one at a time or graphics that spin or move around the frame. Though fun to play with, in reality those special effects distract the audience from the presenters.

FIGURE 4.7 Audience Evaluation

Name _____ **Date** _____

BOOK BUDDY POWERPOINT PRESENTATION

Names of Presenters _____

_____

Book Title _____

Rating Scale 1 = Poor   5 = Very Good

Book detail explanation (author, character, connection, etc.)   1   2   3   4   5

Well-practiced, dramatic read-aloud   1   2   3   4   5

Well-practiced speaking—did not read off notes   1   2   3   4   5

Something you liked about presentation _____

_____

_____

_____

Something the group could have done to improve presentation _____

_____

_____

_____

FIGURE 4.8 Book Buddy Reflection Form

Name _____ **Date** _____

BOOK BUDDY POWERPOINT PRESENTATION

Book Title _____

If you had to do another partner project, what are three things you would do differently so that you and your partner are better connected as you work and more practiced when you present?

1.

2.

3.

As you look at your audience evaluations, what were the three "positive" comments that seemed to be repeated the most?

1.

2.

3.

As you look at your audience evaluations, what were the three "improvement" comments that seemed to be repeated the most?
1.

2.

3.

Variations

Though the project just described focuses on a mutual book, this project lends itself to any kind of group investigation and reporting out. And, instead of the read-aloud, students might write their own original piece, which would lend itself to oral interpretation. Or, depending on the topic, the read-aloud might be eliminated. In either case, students would follow the preparation steps similar to those described earlier and reviewed in the following Quick Guide. Bottom line: remember that the PowerPoint is only there to enhance the message and keep the audience engaged. No bullet points!

QUICK GUIDE: Book Buddy PowerPoint

1. Tell students that this project will involve reading the same book and creating a crafted read-aloud and a PowerPoint presentation, so they should choose a partner who has some knowledge of PowerPoint and similar reading tastes.

2. Partners meet and brainstorm a book for both to read: a title that one partner is recommending to the other; a title that both partners have had on their reading lists; a title chosen from a content-area list that the teacher has created. It must be a title that the class has not already heard about in a previous book project. Set a deadline for book acquisition.

3. Take the class to the library for books. Make it clear that it is the pair's responsibility to find their chosen title if it is not available in the school library. If necessary, allow partners to renegotiate choices based on availability.

4. Set a "Books Finished" deadline as well as a "Photocopy" deadline for the selection students will read aloud.

5. Reserve three days in the computer lab if students are going to complete the author research and PowerPoint slides during class time. Remember that the author research needs to occur while students are still reading their books but the PowerPoint work is done after the scripts and read-aloud are planned.

6. The day before the computer lab, outline the assignment components and show an example PowerPoint Book Buddy slideshow. Remind them that their slides need to complement their scripts. Also, no bullet points!!

7. Assign partners to sit at computers next to each other. Both partners create the same PowerPoint simultaneously so that each gets to learn new program skills as well as have a copy of the file just in case their partner is absent during a lab day.

8. When the presentation is complete, students print out a thumbnail slide-show and turn it in to you.

9. On "Photocopy" deadline day, show students how to cut the passage and script it Readers Theatre-style.

10. Give students ten minutes of practice in class for two days and then begin the presentations.

11. As Book Buddies present, the audience listens and takes notes on the books as well as the presentation. Afterwards, buddies receive their student feedback sheets and complete a final reflection.

12. If your independent reading component continues, students take their Book Buddy Book lists to the library and check out one of the books or get some other great recommendations from their fellow book connoisseurs.

Found Poetry

What Is It?

The lines for a found poem originate from a piece of text, published or original. Instead of writing the poem from scratch, the poet finds lines in that text that he can rearrange, reshape, and revise so that an informative and energetic poem results. The following example poem was excavated, conceived, and created from a section of a science textbook.

The Scientific Method
Goal
To solve a problem
Or better understand an observed event
The Scientific Method

Investigations begin with observations
When you walk in the rain, you get wet
When you run in the rain, you still get wet.

And observations end with a question:
How does speed affect how wet you'll get?
The Scientific Method

Think you might stay drier if you run versus walk?
This hypothesis needs testing with an experiment
A controlled experiment
Those variables of speed and rain need to be controlled!
The Scientific Method

Find two men: same height, same weight
Both wear exactly the same clothes

Wait for a heavy rainstorm
On your mark, get set, go!
One strolls, one sprints, same distance
Collect the data—interpret the results
The Scientific Method

What did the experiment data reveal?
If you run you'll stay 40% drier!
Scientific evidence supports your hunch
Better to run than walk between the raindrops
Repeat the experiment
Find consistent results
Voila!
A well-tested explanation—
A scientific theory is born!
The Scientific Method

The easiest way to create a found poem is to use lines from an existing piece of text: novel, textbook, newspaper story, pamphlet, speech, dictionary definition, you name it! And this format is equally useful for fiction or nonfiction text. However, just copying down some lines from a textbook doesn't make poetry. In order to create engaging poetry, students must carefully read and reread the text under study, pulling strong or important lines from the original source and then arranging and manipulating the lines in a way that creates nonrhyming poetry that targets key concepts. Writing a found poem requires students to think well, think hard, and think in new ways. A great poem is the combination of successful conceptualization combined with synthesis. The writer is not just copying lines but arranging and revising in ways to create something brand new. Take a look at "The Scientific Method." For the most part, this poem only uses existing lines from a science textbook's explanation, but a few original lines are there as well. In order for the textbook lines to create poetry, this writer had to dip into her writer's toolkit and add the lines that turned the prose into flowing, engaging poetry. This mixing of found and self-created lines is part of what makes found poetry creative and fun.

But free-verse poetry can also arise from original prose written by your students in the form of a reader response, reaction to a prompt, or a journal or letter written from an alternative perspective: another person, fictional character, historical figure, or scientific concept. Found poetry made from such original, alternative-perspective prose combines a powerful writing-to-learn tool with engaging publication that concludes with a planned poetry performance. This writing makes students review the material, reinvent it in the context of a new perspective, and ultimately distill their prose into the essence of poetry. This assessment makes kids think twice as hard as they revisit, rethink, and re-envision the content in order to move towards synthesis, their creation of an entirely original piece.

When and Why to Use It

Found poetry is most useful when you want students to reread some vital text and think about what's most important. Rather than having students write boring summaries in their own words, students must use the existing text as a cornerstone for creating something new and fresh: a piece of text that captures what's important yet entertains an audience while helping them remember essentials of what's been studied.

After finishing a unit, chapter, or novel, students can skim their books and notes, brainstorming a list of key concepts. Then students choose different ones from the list and create found poems. The performance results in a dramatic review before a test or a final assessment in lieu of one.

Another application of found poetry is to help kids sit up and pay attention when you show a video. Rather than nodding off, students need to watch closely, jotting down quotes that jolt, details that surprise, moments that must be remembered. Afterwards, students begin with a written reaction using their notes and then reread their reaction to capture lines for a found poem.

While directly pulling lines from an existing source is the easiest way to create a poem, perhaps the most challenging kind of found poetry (and the one described in detail in this chapter) is created when students use lines from their own original pieces of prose writing. Dramatic, riveting pieces of found poetry are guaranteed when students write letters or journals from an alternative perspective. As students take on the persona of fictional characters, people from history, scientific principles, or even inanimate objects, they are forced to step outside of themselves and imagine how others might be affected by historical events or scientific theories. Students are challenged to think more deeply about the information in a new much more personal, creative way.

Time Requirement

One to two class periods for writing and performing is appropriate. Add additional periods depending on how long it will take you to move through the source material the writing is based upon.

Starting with the End in Mind

The best found poetry is created from original student prose that reflects deep thinking about content information in a personified way. Students begin by writing an alternative-perspective journal and then work with others to pull and revise their best, most powerful lines into a subject matter found poem with impact. Students will need to consider the rubrics shown in Figure 5.1 when writing their journal pieces, Figure 5.2 as they transform their prose into found poetry, and Figure 5.3 when they perform before an audience.

While the creation and performance of poems can be spontaneous (as you'll see later in this chapter), groups can also collaborate in creating and presenting poems. The rubrics shown in Figures 5.2 and 5.3 define the quality for these polished found poems and their performance.

FIGURE 5.1 Alternative-Perspective Writing Rubric

C	B	A
Role	**Role**	**Role**
■ Point-of-view, descriptions, and details were consistently in character	■ Logical extensions and imagination evident ■ Describes interpretations of what was seen and witnessed	■ Extensive use of sharp imagery and description ■ Reader can feel the emotions and identify with the character
Fact Integration	**Fact Integration**	**Fact Integration**
■ Two to three clear recognizable facts from source material	■ Four or more clear recognizable facts from source material ■ Clear indication that writer returned to notes/text	■ Consistent integration of facts from source material throughout entry

May be photocopied for classroom use. © 2009 by Nancy Steineke from *Assessment Live!* Portsmouth, NH: Heinemann.

FIGURE 5.2 Found-Poetry Rubric

C	B	A
Role	**Role**	**Role**
■ Point-of-view, details are consistently in character	■ Imagination evident ■ Describes what character has seen and witnessed	■ Extensive use of sharp imagery and description ■ Reader can identify with the character
Fact Integration	**Fact Integration**	**Fact Integration**
■ Two to three clear recognizable facts from source material	■ Four or more important facts	■ Consistent integration of facts throughout entry
Poetic Format	**Poetic Format**	**Poetic Format**
■ Eight lines ■ Line order makes sense ■ Free-verse format	■ Over eight lines ■ Strong line beginnings and endings ■ Nonessential words cut	■ Extensive revision evident ■ Precise, sharp word choices

FIGURE 5.3 Found-Poetry Performance Rubric

C	B	A
Posture and Eye Contact	**Posture and Eye Contact**	**Posture and Eye Contact**
■ Some eye contact ■ Uses confidence stance	■ Establishes eye contact with everyone in the room during the presentation	■ Displays a relaxed confidence in body posture
Clarity and Volume	**Clarity and Volume**	**Clarity and Volume**
■ Can be heard and understood	■ Crisp diction, loud enough to be heard	■ Volume is varied for word emphasis
Interpretation	**Interpretation**	**Interpretation**
■ Voice reflects emotion behind words	■ Important words emphasized	■ Lines read with energy ■ Facial expression reflects emotion behind words

FIGURE 5.4 Found-Poetry Scoring Sheet

FOUND-POETRY PROJECT

Name _____

Topic and Role_____ **Date**_____ **Period** _____

Directions: Referring back to the rubrics for the journal, found poem, and performance, rate yourself in the following categories. Please jot down any notes about details you want me to notice about your writing and performance before I assign the final grade. Do not repeat the rubric phrases. Be sure to attach your journal and found poem. If you are working in a group, turn in your sheets together.

Category	Points	Weight	Score
Journal: Role	1 2 3 4 5	X 2	/10
Journal: Fact Integration	1 2 3 4 5	X 2	/10
Found Poem: Role	1 2 3 4 5	X 2	/10
Found Poem: Fact Integration	1 2 3 4 5	X 4	/20
Found Poem: Format	1 2 3 4 5	X 2	/10
Posture and Eye Contact	1 2 3 4 5	X 2	/10
Clarity and Volume	1 2 3 4 5	X 2	/10
Interpretation	1 2 3 4 5	X 4	/20

Total Points   **/100**

Standards Skills Students Will Practice

Reading	Writing	Speaking and Listening
■ Interpret and evaluate the impact of ambiguities, subtleties, contradictions, ironies, and incongruities in a text	■ Use precise language	■ Assess how language and delivery affect the mood and tone
■ Read, view, and interpret texts and performances in every medium	■ Develop the main ideas through supporting evidence	■ Listen respectfully and responsively
■ Recognize unstated assumptions	■ Synthesize information from multiple sources	■ Apply delivery techniques such as voice projection and demonstrate physical poise
■ Share reading experiences with a peer or adult	■ Revise writing to improve the logic and coherence	■ Recognize the use and impact of effective language
■ Engage in a variety of collaborative conversations	■ Use tone and language appropriate to the audience and purpose	■ Determine points of view, clarify positions, make judgments, and form opinions
■ Read with fluency	■ Take notes from written and oral texts	■ Deliver impromptu and planned oral presentations
		■ Present orally original work supported by research

Getting Ready

As mentioned earlier, students begin this version of found poetry by creating a journal or letter grounded in the content studied but written from an alternative perspective. Once completed, students choose their best lines, transforming that text into found poetry. The most gripping student writing will emerge when they study a text that has a strong hook and an emotional wallop. Look for a story that gets the blood boiling. The text (fiction or nonfiction) might be a short reading, a strong graphic image (painting, photograph, sculpture), a song (be sure to provide written copies of the lyrics for students to use as they listen), or a film.

How Alternative-Perspective Writing Becomes Found Poetry

Jim Gaither, a middle school social studies teacher at Woods Learning Center in Casper, Wyoming, often uses alternative-perspective journals when viewing videos. A favorite of Jim's is the second episode of the National Geographic series called "Guns, Germs, and Steel," based on the book by Jared Diamond. This installment discusses the contact and subsequent conquest that occurred when the Spanish met the Inca. Rather than being passive observers, Jim asks his World Geography students to funnel the information into specific viewpoints. After viewing, half the students write letters from the point of view of the Spanish, and half write from the perspective of the Inca, each group examining the advantages and disadvantages both cultures brought to the conflict, experiences that ultimately determined the outcome. Before the students write, Jim gives them the following prompts.

Letter Prompts for Spanish and Inca

You are there . . .
The Incas, your people, have lived in a successful culture for centuries, yet, in several months time, has faced virtual devastation at the hands of Spanish conquerors. Write a letter to future generations that examines the advantages and disadvantages your culture brought to the conflict. Acknowledge the atrocities your people endured but also encourage future generations to feel hopeful and strong.

You are there . . .
You are a Spanish conqueror. The Incan society you have just discovered offers a wealth of gold and slaves. With their simple weapons and primitive beliefs, these people can be easily defeated. Write a letter to future generations that examines the advantages and disadvantages your culture brought to the conflict.

As evidenced by their letters (see Figures 5.5 and 5.6), it's readily apparent that these students did not put their heads down during the video. They were paying attention to the details and imagining how the same story might be told differently depending on whether you were an Inca or a Spaniard.

Though alternative-perspective journals could become a major writing assignment carried through several drafts (and assessed using a rubric similar to the one in Figure 5.1), Jim chose to use this activity in a more informal writing-to-learn way; he only gave

FIGURE 5.5 **Letter from Spanish Viewpoint**

I am a proud Spaniard in the year 1533. We had been on a long journey when we started to see small villages of Incas. Before long we came upon the palace of Atahualpa; our job was to conquer. Yet there were thousands of them and only about 200 of us, but we knew we had to do it. At first they thought we were gods. But Atahualpa knew we weren't gods, so he planned a surprise attack, but he chose to give his soldiers no weapons to try to make us think they were our allies. But unknown to him we also planned a surprise attack! The Incas sat waiting for us in the palace, so we sent out our priest to tell Atahualpa to turn to Christianity, but Atahualpa dishonored us by throwing the bible! So we attacked. It wasn't a very long battle since the Incas had no weapons. Not a single drop of Spanish blood was shed that day. We took Atahualpa prisoner and took all his gold then killed him when it was all gone.

Sincerely,
Sage, a proud Spaniard

FIGURE 5.6 **Letter from Incan Viewpoint**

I am a proud Inca. I wrote this letter to future generations so they would know exactly what happened in the year 1532. One year ago, we saw the Spaniards riding on weird, huge four legged animals. Our ruler, Atahualpa, was not concerned; he believed they were not gods, but humans. But still we did not want them near us, so he planned to scare them with our numbers. He did not want to kill them, but make them leave out of fear. We were foolish; we did not notice their weapons. We invited them to our town. Thousands of us were in a huge square. Atahualpa told us not to bring our weapons. We went unarmed. Pizzaro and his men came armed. They attacked us, slashing and trampling thousands of us. Then they captured Atahualpa. Without a ruler, the survivors ran. We hid in the hills. We thought we survived but we hadn't. Thousands of us got a weird disease. Soon everybody had it. Soon almost all of us were dead. We shouldn't have invited the fake gods into our land. We should have been armed. We gave them their victory. And when we escaped, we should have left the sick alone. One mistake caused thousands of deaths. But we are not defeated. No, we're not the great empire we were before. But the few survivors, one of them myself, have preserved our language and beliefs. I am sure that our heritage and culture will always be here. Maybe one day we will be a powerful empire again. Maybe next time we will fight for our land.

Sincerely,
Ryan, a proud Inca

the class ten to twenty minutes for the writing. Once finished, he encouraged them to look over their video notes so that the letters were grounded in fact, but reminded them to make the letters personal, including reactions and feelings in order to get the reader to identify with the writer.

Using their own letters, Jim then led his students through the steps described in the following section to some powerful found poetry based on the video they had watched.

Creating Found Poetry: Finding Powerful Lines

When students finish their pieces, have them quickly proofread in order to correct any glaring errors. Tell them to just focus on the things that might confuse a reader. Then they should trade with a partner, who reads the story and underlines the most powerful lines, looking for five to ten lines/sentences. Trading back, owners take a look at what their partners chose and see if they agree. If they don't, they should double underline the lines/sentences they liked most.

Now it's time for some revision. First, students rewrite their most powerful lines/ sentences on the reverse side of their paper. Then you need to give a really quick miniles-son on free-verse poetry:

1. From your powerful lines/sentences, you are going to create a piece of free-verse poetry, poetry that conveys a strong emotion and message but doesn't have to rhyme.

2. First, take a look at the lines/sentences you copied and draw lines through all of the nonessential words: *if, and, but, it, is.* Look for words that have little or no meaning. Remember that sentence fragments are okay in poetry.

3. Second, look at each word individually. Wherever you can, replace weak words with stronger, more powerful and precise ones. Words that create a picture.

4. Now check the line starts and endings. Make sure your line starts grab attention and the line ends finish with an action verb or visual image.

5. Make sure none of your lines is too long. A typical free-verse poetry line is no more than eight words in length. If you need to, cut words or rewrite the line.

6. Finally, rewrite your lines in the order that makes the strongest poetic statement.

7. Pair up and practice reading your poem to your partner. Decide which words you really want to emphasize and drive them home. Work to leave an emotional impact on your listeners.

Here are the finished poems in two voices that originated from the students' Spanish and Incan letters. Notice how students have revised and altered their lines rather than just recopying what they originally wrote. Though the directions suggest six to eight lines, these students chose to write longer poems since they had trouble deciding what to cut—it's such a tragedy to have an abundance of great material! More important, check out the content information and the human context. These poems pack an emotional wallop, exactly what kids' brains need if we want them to remember how exploration and colonization led to the decimation of indigenous peoples (Sylwester 1995).

Found Poetry from Inca Perspective
The fake gods came atop four-legged giants
Spaniards
We were foolish
We invited them to our town
We did not notice their weapons
They attacked
Slashing and trampling thousands
Our ruler, Atahualpa, captured
Survivors ran and hid in the hills
We survived but disease struck
We should have left the sick alone
One mistake caused thousands more deaths
We gave them this victory
But we are not defeated
One day we will again be a powerful empire
Next time we will fight for our land

Found Poetry from Spanish Perspective
I am a proud Spaniard in the year 1533
Ending a long journey
Our job was to conquer

Standing in the palace of Atahualpa
Thousands of Inca met us
We offered Christianity
Our job was to conquer

Planned a surprise attack
But his soldiers had no weapons
Two hundred Spaniards against thousands
We attacked
Our job was to conquer

It wasn't a very long battle
Not a single drop of Spanish blood was shed
We took Atahualpa prisoner
We took all his gold
Then we killed him when it was all gone.
Our job was to conquer

Assessment Live!

Even though all students started by watching the same video, the finished pieces capture important information in a memorable and highly personal fashion. Each poem is unique. But we are just getting started!

Now you potentially have 150 great poems and the question is this: How can you turn these poems into an engaging performance that deepens the kids' understanding of the subject as well as celebrates some great authorship—versus you taking home all of those poems to grade in the silence of your study? Here's the answer: Rather than presenting 150 individual poems, students work together to combine their best lines with other class members in order to create brand new poems!

Creating Found Poetry with a Group

1. Once students have finished their poems, have them trade with a partner. Each partner reads the poem, underlines the *one* most powerful line, and then passes it back. Writers take a look at the feedback but have the option to choose that line or a different one.

2. Next, the writer takes that one line and sees if he can make it even better: shortening the line to eight or fewer words, rephrasing, substituting more powerful words.

3. Then, on index cards, students write their first and last names at the top and then their absolute best line below.

4. Now ask for six to eight volunteers to step up to the front of the room with their cards and stand in a straight line. Starting with the first student on the audience's left, each student, in turn, clearly reads her line aloud while the class listens carefully. Then, tell the class that the volunteers are going to read their lines again, but this time you want the audience to think about what order the lines should really go in. Which lines seem to go together? Which line should be first? Which line should be last? After the next reading, take suggestions from the class, have the volunteers reposition themselves, and then read the poem again. Repeat this process a couple more times. For an eight-line poem, it takes about three revision readings to get the poem set.

5. Once the audience thinks the lines are in exactly the right order, have the volunteers read the poem again and tell the audience to think about how each line should be interpreted. Listeners should think about volume, pace, pausing, emotion, and also if any of the lines really need to be emphasized by reading them twice or repeating them elsewhere in the poem. Let the audience give the readers their suggestions and then read it full throttle, energy and emotion dialed up to ten.

Though this might seem a bit haphazard, you'll be surprised how many times the class ends up with a poem that just knocks everyone's socks off. Of course, the performances and live revision are not completed until all students have had a chance to participate in a found poem. After each rousing round of applause, remember to have the kids put the final order number on their cards before turning them in to you. That way your class can savor the poem further when you type them up and post them on your classroom bulletin board or blog.

Later on, when students are honing individual pieces, remind them of this assessment and how it demonstrated the value of rewording, rephrasing, and rearranging in order to create writing with greater impact.

Found-poetry performances can serve as summative assessments or formative ones. If formative, this writing-to-learn activity should not face the same kind of scrutiny a summative assessment would, since the goals of writing to learn are to get kids to think about the material studied and experiment with new skills (taking an alternative perspective, creating free-verse poetry, participating in a poetry performance). Very often these kinds of activities only get points for completion or participation. On the other hand, if you are using found-poetry performances at the conclusion of a novel or unit, the stakes are higher and the rubrics in Figures 5.1, 5.2, and 5.3, and the scoring sheet in Figure 5.4 will prove useful.

Predictable Problems

The first time you try this assessment strategy, your students may be a bit confused at each step. Their alternative-perspective letters may look more like summaries. Their powerful sentences may be long, unwieldy, and unpoetic. Rather than throwing themselves into the physical revision of the found poetry, they won't quite understand the idea of moving people around. That's to be expected; much of this is due to inexperience. When you try this strategy a second time, the process is likely to be far more smooth and successful. However, if students still have difficulty with the various steps, here are some tips.

- Seeing an event from an alternative perspective: Read aloud an example. This model might be from a former student, an example you wrote, or an existing book. The best book model I've run across is *Encounter* by Jane Yolen. It tells the story of Columbus' discovery of the New World, but from the perspective of a young Taino boy who witnesses his civilization's destruction. As students listen to this boy's story, solely from his perspective, of the callous destruction of his people fueled by conquistador greed, the story automatically creates a visceral reader response. The point of view jars listeners and afterwards students totally understand how circumstances have completely different interpretations depending on who is telling the story. *Encounter* is a picture book, only thirty-two pages long, so it can be read to a class in less than ten minutes.

- Creating poetic lines versus long sentences: Show students some examples of free-verse poems and mark them up, noting their use of the free-verse conventions mentioned earlier in the poetry minilesson. Also, a poetry book that actually incorporates the use of found poetry is called *In Evidence: Poems of the Liberation of Nazi Concentration Camps* by Barbara Helfgott Hyett. These poems are based on taped interviews of American liberators and the poet worked to change their words as little as possible. The collection is excellent but at times disturbing. However, as long as students are old enough to understand the Holocaust, the collection contains entries suitable for younger and more mature audiences. Though this book is out of print, Amazon.com shows used copies available.

- Students have no suggestions for the physical revision: If no one has any suggestions, just say, "I don't think this poem is perfect yet; let's hear the lines again and listen for which ones seem to go together." Just have the volunteers stay in place and read through their lines two or three more times. If students still have no suggestions, give them one of yours (by this time you will have rewritten the whole poem in your head and know exactly how it should go!) but hold back on the others. Tell the kids to listen to how the poem changed when the line moved. Read through the poem again and open up for suggestions on which other lines go together. By this time, students should have some suggestions. Make the changes, read it again, ask them if the lines at the beginning and end are in the right spot. Students will begin to own the physical revision, but it will take some patience on your part. Be sure to bite your tongue when they make decisions different from your own.

Variations

Another writing-to-learn way students can put together a "class" found poem is through the improvisation game called "String of Pearls." Have students look carefully at their lines and decide if they think theirs would make a really good first or last line. Have first and last line volunteers step up to the front and read. From there, other volunteers step up, placing themselves where they think their line should go between the first and last lines. And like the previous version, members of the audience can give revision suggestions. However, this time the steadfast rule is that the beginning and end lines cannot move.

QUICK GUIDE: Found-Poetry

1. Each student writes a letter or diary entry from the perspective of a specific historical or fictional character. Students should all write from the same perspective or from two different perspectives if there is a relationship connection (Spanish conquistador and Inca, mother and daughter, etc.).

2. Trade letters with a partner. Partner reads silently and underlines the most powerful sentences/lines.

3. Partners trade back and reread their own letter, looking for other powerful sentences/lines and underlining them twice.

4. Writers pick six to ten of their best sentences/lines and rewrite them on the back of the paper.

5. After a quick minilesson on revising free-verse poetry, students revise their sentences/lines on the paper, re-order the lines for greatest impact, and rewrite the finished poem on a clean sheet of paper.

6. Students trade their finished poems with a partner who once again finds the most powerful line.

7. Using that line or another, each student revises that one line and then copies it on to a note card.

8. In groups of six to eight, students come to the front and read their lines to the class. Listeners revise the poem, telling students where to move within the lineup to make new versions.

9. Once revision is set, the poem is read a final time with as much emotion as possible. Remember to have students put the final order number on their cards so that the poems can be recorded. Later on, when students are honing individual pieces, remind them of this assessment and how it demonstrated the value of rewording, rephrasing, and rearranging in order to create writing with greater impact.

10. After hearing the pieces, take the opportunity for students to voice what they learned or were reminded of as they reviewed the material through their found poems.

PostSecret Project

What Is It?

Perhaps you have seen the PostSecret books compiled by Frank Warren. Anonymously, people send in artfully decorated postcards with messages that bare their souls and innermost secrets which range from humorous to embarrassing to completely inappropriate for school! These secrets, never previously revealed, are told in just a few words:

- Every regret I've ever had involved alcohol.

- I have never been anyone's first choice.

- I kept the keys and visited my old apartment after I moved out.

- I'm afraid the only thing I like to do won't take me anywhere.

- I wrote it on this note so I'd never forget you said it: "You're giving yourself too much credit. No one is going to pay attention to you."—Mom

Begun in 2004, the PostSecret project continues to this day and can be visited at http://postsecret.blogspot.com. The online art installation changes its gallery on a weekly basis. This assessment is patterned after the PostSecret Project.

After finishing a unit of study, students return to their notes and text to search for a plausible yet unrevealed secret about a fictional character, an historical figure, a contemporary leader, or a personified object. After all, doesn't everyone have a secret or conflict, one that is hidden sometimes even from themselves yet drives their actions? And even though the secret is their original creation, the job has just begun because the kids need to amass multiple text support examples that make the secret realistic and believable.

Finally, once the "proof" is established, the students create posters about the secret (see the example shown in Figure 6.1), but do not give away the secret owners. On the due date, the posters are displayed and the the class has to guess which secrets go with which character.

FIGURE 6.1 Poster Example—Which Gatsby Character Has This Secret?

When and Why to Use It

As mentioned earlier, the PostSecret project is a wonderfully fun way to get kids to review notes and dig far more deeply into the text than through a traditional objective test. Also, the need for ample text support and rationale is very similar to what a traditional essay requires since students must create believable yet not easily guessed secrets held by a person—real or fictional—or a personified object. Searching for the perfect secret requires students to pore over their notes and annotations of the book so that they can defend their secret with supporting text. Furthermore, writing the secret requires precision and concision; though a secret should pack bombshell of information, it is only one sentence long! The perfect secret is a testament to higher-order thinking: synthesis. Students have to take all the evidence and then create something completely original. This assessment employs great imagination and creativity as well as several multiple intelligences: verbal/linguistic, spatial/artistic, and interpersonal. Plus, when it comes time for the exhibition, students must get up and walk around to study the art. It turns out that much of our memories are episodic, that a memory is connected to a specific time, place, smell, song, and so on. Hanging the posters in different areas of the room gets the kids out of their chairs and walking around as they study the art. The movement stimulates the brain (and replaces some chair-tipping time from the boys) and increases the chance of enhancing long-term memory via spatial connections (Jensen 1998).

Time Requirement

One and one-half periods should be sufficient. Some time is needed in one period to explain the project and then, once the unit of study is completed, an additional period for presentation.

Standards Skills Students Will Practice

Reading	Writing	Speaking and Listening
■ Interpret and evaluate the impact of ambiguities, subtleties, contradictions, ironies, and incongruities in a text	■ Use precise language	■ Listen respectfully and responsively
	■ Develop the main ideas through supporting evidence	■ Apply delivery techniques such as voice projection and demonstrate physical poise
■ Analyze interactions between main and subordinate characters in a literary text	■ Take notes from written and oral texts	
	■ Evaluate research information, present in logical manner	■ Recognize the use and impact of effective language
■ Read, view, and interpret texts and performances in every medium		■ Determine points of view, clarify positions, make judgments, and form opinions
■ Recognize unstated assumptions		
■ Recognize and analyze the relevance of literature to contemporary and/or personal events and situations		■ Deliver impromptu and planned oral presentations
		■ Present orally original work supported by research
■ Explain and justify interpretation		

Starting with the End in Mind

Distribute and discuss the rubric shown in Figure 6.2 in the beginning assignment phase. Use the scoring sheet shown in Figure 6.3 for student self-evaluation.

FIGURE 6.2 PostSecret Rubric

C	B	A
Secret	**Secret**	**Secret**
■ Makes logical sense ■ Somewhat obvious	■ Harder to guess	■ Total surprise but makes complete sense ■ Reflects creativity and imagination
Text Support	**Text Support**	**Text Support**
■ Two or three passages	■ Four to five passages	■ More than five passages found throughout text
Postcard Poster	**Postcard Poster**	**Postcard Poster**
■ Correct dimensions ■ Neat ■ Secret clearly printed and large enough to be read easily ■ Images enhance secret	■ Attention to detail ■ Cohesive design	■ Experiments with style and materials ■ Highly imaginative and creative
Presentation	**Presentation**	**Presentation**
■ Displays poster so that audience can study it during explanation ■ Explains how quotes back up secret ■ If a team, both members present equally	■ Greater elaboration on how quotes connect to secret	■ Ample text support and explanation ■ Reads quotes aloud interpretively ■ Lots of energy, keeps audience interested

FIGURE 6.3 PostSecret Scoring Sheet

POSTSECRET PROJECT

Name _____

Character _____ **Date** _____ **Period** _____

Directions: Referring back to the rubric, rate your presentation in the following categories. Please jot down any notes about details you want me to notice about your poster, support, and performance before I assign the final grade. Do not repeat the rubric phrases. Attach your annotated support text to the grade sheet and turn in your sheet with your partner's.

Category	Points	Weight	Score
Secret	1 2 3 4 5	x 4	/20
Text Support	1 2 3 4 5	x 6	/30
Postcard Poster	1 2 3 4 5	x 5	/25
Presentation	1 2 3 4 5	x 5	/25

Total Points   **/100**

May be photocopied for classroom use. © 2009 by Nancy Steineke from *Assessment Live!* Portsmouth, NH: Heinemann.

Getting Ready

Your own first step is to start visiting the PostSecret online gallery on a weekly basis and begin collecting images that you think are suitable for your class and the text you are studying. Once you've got about ten or twelve good examples, put them into a PowerPoint presentation to show your class. I strongly recommend not going directly to the website and projecting whatever you find onto the classroom screen via your LCD projector because, as I've mentioned earlier, there's a reason why these secrets are anonymous!

Explain the project, providing directions like the ones shown in Figure 6.4, and show your PowerPoint presentation as you are starting the unit of study. You'll notice in the directions that students are given a choice for working individually or with a partner. Since the creation of the art will take place outside of school, working with a partner means trading phone numbers, agreeing on when to get together, finding a place to meet, and finding transportation. If arranging the logistics is impractical for some, then working solo is a suitable option.

After the examples and explanation, give students a few minutes to find their partner if they choose to work on a team rather than solo. Pass out index cards and have the pairs or solos write their first and last names down. Collect the cards so that you can keep track of who is working with whom and who is working solo. Also, save them because you'll be passing them back later on so that students can write down their finalized secrets.

As the unit of study continues, remind students that they should begin searching for their perfect secret. After about one-third of the unit has been covered, call a fifteen-minute PostSecret meeting. By this point, students should be ready to choose an intriguing character/person/object and start brainstorming potential secrets as well as looking back through their notes and text for support. Remind students to keep track of their PostSecret evidence via sticky notes or on the page annotation if they own their books. Provide a second meeting at the two-thirds point so that students can update their support or revise their secrets. Before each meeting, remind the students to keep their ideas to themselves. Announcing their PostSecrets to the class will ruin the surprise when they present the projects.

Near the unit's conclusion, give groups another ten to fifteen minutes to finalize their secrets and their textual support. Return the name-bearing index cards to the students and have them write down the official secret as well as the character/person/object it belongs to. Do not have students pass the cards up to the front. Instead, tell them to place the cards face down. Then you can walk around and collect them individually so that the secrets stay secret!

FIGURE 6.4 PostSecret Directions for Students

Assignment

- Alone or with a partner, choose a person, character, or object from the unit of study and create a PostSecret for him or her. The secret cannot be directly stated but could be inferred from the text. The secret must be consistent with the character and as real and plausible as possible yet not easily guessed or obvious. The best secrets are a complete surprise yet make logical sense.

- As you study, look for potential secrets for your person, character, or object and mark passages that lend support to your extension. The more textual support you can find, the stronger your secret is!

- Your character's/person's/object's secret will be announced anonymously on an artfully decorated poster that replicates the look of a postcard. The "postcard" should be on one half sheet of standard poster board (22" x 28"). The postcard will measure 22" x 14".

- Also, the secret and artwork must be school appropriate. If you are uncertain about the appropriateness of a secret or accompanying artwork, check with the teacher prior to completing any work on the project.

- On the back of your poster, list all of your supporting textual evidence along with page numbers and explanation of how each quote supports your secret.

- Be sure to keep your secret and your character choice hidden from other class members. On the due date, we will be posting them and then trying to match the secrets with the characters.

May be photocopied for classroom use. © 2009 by Nancy Steineke from *Assessment Live!* Portsmouth, NH: Heinemann.

By this time, most of the kids are really into their secrets and enjoy the ritual of secret-keeping. Review the example PowerPoint one more time, answer any questions, and remind students of the due date. Students should have about a week to complete the poster since this is an out-of-class assignment and those working in pairs will need to get together on their own time. While teams are completing the art segment of the project, create a handout with the list of secrets, assigning a number to each one, and run off enough copies for everyone (see the example shown in Figure 6.5).

FIGURE 6.5 **Characters' Secrets from *The Great Gatsby***

#	Secret	Character
1	I killed a man. My weapon of choice: a bottle of whiskey.	
2	I've hurt people because they've hurt me.	
3	Women are the cause of all my problems.	
4	I wish I were part of the party.	
5	Over in Europe, I have a girl and a little baby.	
6	I'm obsessed with someone I barely know.	
7	I love my neighbor.	
8	I hired a hit man.	
9	I chose money over the life of my best friend.	
10	I accidentally killed someone during a fight.	
11	I never told him the baby wasn't his.	
12	She was pregnant, so I took care of it the only way I could.	

Assessment Live!

On the day the projects are due, attach a sticky note to each poster, labeling it with the number that corresponds to the correct secret number on the handout. Prop up the posters around the room and commence a gallery walk. Students walk around, confer with others, and try to guess which characters own which secrets, jotting down their answers on the handout. After that is done, each team gets up in numerical order and displays their poster, reveals the secret, and, most importantly, defends their rationale by reading aloud and explaining the text support they had worked on gathering throughout the unit. Students correct their guesses on the handout. It's fun to award some sort of silly, worthless prize (see what's been knocking around in your desk drawer that you no longer need or pass out "magic test answer" #2 pencils) to the kids who guessed the most correctly. Afterward, hang the artwork around your room for other classes to admire and envy. When I did this project with my juniors, it really attracted the attention of my sophomores. The first day the posters were up, the display wall drew the kids to the art like a magnet. They studied the posters and immediately asked, "What is this? Are we going to do this?" All of a sudden the sophomores were intrigued by *The Great Gatsby*. I never get that kind of response when I post essays on the wall!

This is an assignment that requires some serious thought, inference, and research. The assessment improves content memory by combining emotion with a series of information rehearsals. Plus, even though students have to do all the higher-order thinking we would normally require if they were to write an essay about a character, the kids get to present their research in a different medium, one that enables them to highlight or stretch some different multiple intelligences.

See the samples of sophisticated student work and thinking shown in Figures 6.6 and 6.7. At first glance, it might seem obvious that the character whose secrets are given in Figure 6.6 is Jay Gatsby, who was in Europe during World War I and also had a rather promiscuous youth. However, Tom Buchanan has a lot of trouble staying faithful to his wife, Daisy. And then there's Nick Carraway, who was almost engaged to a girl back in Chicago, but that didn't stop him from dating Jordan Baker—and another girl from his workplace!

In Figure 6.7, the most obvious answer is also Gatsby. After all, he was the one always seen alone at his parties. But if *party* is a metaphor for an enjoyable, invigorating life, is there really any character in Gatsby who is part of the party? Myrtle Wilson can only pretend she's wealthy, Daisy can only pretend she's happily married, and Nick can only pretend he is truly connected to anyone.

Of course, while the low art threshold "I want to write a paper" kids might be a bit hesitant about this assessment, the right-brained kids who express themselves best in non-written media will rejoice. Bottom line: giving kids the opportunity to express themselves in multiple ways enables everyone to grow. The "essay" kids need to stretch themselves and

FIGURE 6.6 Carli and Holly's Secret About a Character from *The Great Gatsby*

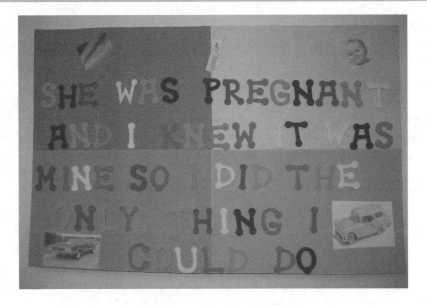

FIGURE 6.7 Maggie and Jen's Secret About a Character from *The Great Gatsby*

the "arty" kids need a chance to express themselves in ways that let them shine. Also, take note that the rubric credits inference-making, research, and artistic-expression skills equally. And the bonus is that this assessment celebrates the conclusion of the unit in a unique way.

Predictable Problems

First, keep reminding your class that the secrets need to be school appropriate even though many fictional characters are fully capable of deep dark secrets that are not. Second, some kids will complain that they can't draw. That's fine. Tell them to cut pictures out of magazines, use the Internet, or take and mount photographs. And, if they are older, tell them to go look at the examples on the website on their own time but be ready for some mature material here and there. Also, usually when students choose a partner, they tend to pick someone who complements their own talents. The arty kid who hates taking notes often pairs up with the person who loves sticky notes. But so long as both kids are using their strengths to collaborate successfully, this can prove to be more of a benefit than a problem. Remember the old saying: The whole is greater than the sum of its parts.

QUICK GUIDE: PostSecret Project

1. Show PostSecret examples and pass out directions.
2. Develop work groups—pairs or solo endeavors.
3. Meet with work group two or three times as class progresses through novel.
4. Constantly remind students that secret and postcard must be school appropriate.
5. As the unit nears completion, students comb the text for significant passages that lend support and if that support is sufficient, finalize their secrets and turn them in to you. Students have a week to organize their text support and create poster.
6. Assign numbers and type up the secrets. Run off copies.
7. Presentation day begins with a gallery walk and guessing. Students then give their presentations.
8. Award silly prizes to those who guess the most secrets correctly. Keep the posters up. On later literary analysis assignments, remind students to use the same diligent quote search and ultimate text support as they attempt to prove their points in regards to their reading.

CHAPTER

7

Readers Theatre

What Is It?

Readers Theatre is an oral interpretation strategy that requires students to decide what is most important in a piece of text and how to perform that text orally in a way that makes it meaningful and memorable. Taking an existing piece of text, students select what they think are the important lines but then they are encouraged to manipulate them, revising the wording, splitting sentences into parts, or rearranging the line order—all with the goal of creating a more dramatic, engaging reading. Once the lines are chosen, each speaking part is assigned a number. The quantity of numbers is determined by how many speaking parts are needed. If there are five kids in a group, then the Readers Theatre piece will have lines numbered 1 to 5. Also, the lines that have greatest importance or dramatic effect are marked *ALL* and are read chorally. The example of a Readers Theatre script shown in Figure 7.1 was created from sidebar text in a geometry textbook.

When and Why to Use It

Readers Theatre is a great strategy to use when you want students to review a text and to really consider what was most important about it (Frey 2007). When using a textbook as a source for Readers Theatre, a chapter can be divided into sections, each group receiving a different section. Likewise, novels can also be divided into sections. As groups perform their pieces, they demonstrate their own skill at picking out and emphasizing important text details while also providing a review of key points or incidents (in the case of a novel) to the rest of the class. And since the focus is on choosing text of greatest importance as well as manipulating the lines for greatest impact, a typical Readers Theatre script is 175–300 words in length. That final script and performance is a definitive demonstration of deep comprehension. As TV chef Rachel Ray would say in her oft repeated rhetorical question, "How good is that?"

FIGURE 7.1 Math Readers Theatre

(4 Speakers)

1, 2	From the Mud
3, 4	To the Stars
ALL	The Reach of Geometry
ALL	Since before recorded history
1	Human beings have used basic geometric principles in building and surveying.
ALL	But with the rise of civilization
2	People came gradually to recognize the power of geometry
3	As a means of controlling and explaining the world around them.
4	As Isidore of Seville tells us
1	(560 to 636 A.D.)
4	The science of geometry is said to have been discovered by the Egyptians
2	For after the Nile would flood
1	(Covering all their property with mud)
2	The Egyptians would mark off their landholdings with boundaries and measurements.
ALL	Thus giving geometry its name
1, 2	*Ge*, which means "earth"
3, 4	And *metra*, which means "measurement."
4	Later
1	(When this study had been perfected)
4	It was used to measure the expanses of
2	Sea
3	And stars
4	And air.
1	People began to investigate even the extent of the heavens
2	How far the moon is from the earth
3	And the sun from the moon
ALL	All the way to the limits of the universe.

Another great feature of this assessment strategy is that it can be executed rather quickly. Whereas regular skits require blocking, props, and costumes and often stray from the original text, this strategy keeps the students' focus on a careful re-examination of language of the text and its core ideas. Plus, the performance only requires dramatic reading, so groups don't need to spend a lot of time worrying about theatrical effects. Students just have to keep rereading and honing their script interpretations.

Time Requirement

Typically, two class periods are needed. One for script writing and practice and one, though it may not take the whole period, for performance.

Standards Skills Students Will Practice

Reading	Writing	Speaking and Listening
■ Read with fluency ■ Pick out important details ■ Determine author's purpose ■ Recognize author's tone	■ Organize for structural clarity ■ Revise and edit for greatest meaning ■ Convey information via a variety of genres	■ Speaking clearly ■ Share ideas, collaborate successfully to complete a project ■ Rehearse effectively ■ Oral interpretation ■ Use body language to convey a message ■ Assess how language and delivery affect the mood and tone ■ Present orally original work supported by research

Starting with the End in Mind

As students begin work on their Readers Theatre piece, they need to first focus on including important content and then begin to discuss how to script and then interpret that content.

FIGURE 7.2 Readers Theatre Rubric

C	B	A
Content	**Content**	**Content**
■ Main details covered	■ Important points and details covered thoroughly	■ Information scripted in a way that creates emphasis so that audience will remember important info
Scripting	**Scripting**	**Scripting**
■ Few "ALL" lines ■ Everyone has a part ■ Predictable script divisions—parts are all in big clumps or show repetitious order	■ More "ALL" lines ■ Everyone has a part ■ Parts are more split up— not predictable/ repetitious	■ "ALL" lines are at the parts that need unity or emphasis ■ Line divisions play with words and emphasis
Interpretation	**Interpretation**	**Interpretation**
■ Some eye contact ■ Easily heard ■ Clear diction ■ Good posture	■ Good eye contact with audience ■ Enthusiastic, expressive ■ Good pace—not too fast, not too slow ■ Scripts are marked up	■ Emotion comes through on all lines ■ Facial expressions mirror interpretation ■ Vocal control: variation in volume and pitch ■ Advanced pacing: speed up, slow down, pause— for emphasis
Collective Performance	**Collective Performance**	**Collective Performance**
■ Well-practiced, few stumbles ■ Group stands so that members can see/cue each other ■ Nothing distracts from performance ■ Everyone knows where to stand	■ "ALLs" are spoken in unison ■ Individual parts read with emotion and confidence	■ "ALLs" are precise and convey feeling ■ Lines feed off each other—smooth transitions ■ Some movement and gestures

FIGURE 7.3 Readers Theatre Scoring Sheet

READERS THEATRE

Name _____

Source _____ **Date** _____ **Period** _____

Directions: Referring back to the rubric, rate your presentation in the following categories. Please jot down any notes about details you want me to notice about your script and performance before I assign the final grade. Do not repeat the rubric phrases. Remember to attach your script that has your interpretation notes. Turn in your group's score sheets together.

Category	Points	Weight	Score
Content	1 2 3 4 5	x 6	/30
Scripting	1 2 3 4 5	X 4	/20
Interpretation	1 2 3 4 5	X 4	/20
Collective Performance	1 2 3 4 5	X 4	/20
Script Interpretation Notes	1 2 3 4 5	X 2	/10
	Total Points		**/100**

May be photocopied for classroom use. © 2009 by Nancy Steineke from *Assessment Live!* Portsmouth, NH: Heinemann.

Getting Ready

The best way to introduce students to Readers Theatre is to have them perform an already prepared script. If you are looking for some instant scripts with which to begin, Google *Readers Theatre scripts*. You will discover page after page of Readers Theatre titles that are geared to specific grade levels and content areas. On the other hand, if you've got a bit more time, consider creating your own example from a text you *always* teach; that way, you'll have exactly the example you want your kids to emulate plus, once written, one you can reuse as long as that text remains in the curriculum.

See Figure 7.4 for an example—Sojourner Truth's famous speech is a piece of text that can be found in almost any American literature or U.S. history textbook. Speeches from history make great Readers Theatre!

FIGURE 7.4 Readers Theatre Script Example from Sojourner Truth's Speech, "Ain't I a Woman?"

READERS THEATRE FOR THREE VOICES

Sojourner Truth (1797–1883) "Ain't I a Woman?" (ABRIDGED)
Delivered 1851
Women's Convention, Akron, Ohio

Introduction: Sojourner Truth was born into slavery in 1797 and sold away from her family when she was nine. She suffered many hardships under her new owner, who raped and beat her frequently. During her life she was bought and sold repeatedly, saw the man she loved beaten to death, and was forced to marry an older slave from the same plantation. Though the slaves of New York state were emancipated on July 4, 1827, Truth managed to escape her owner in late 1826. In 1843 she began traveling and preaching about abolition, women's rights, and religious tolerance. In 1851 she delivered her most famous speech.

1	Well, children, where there is so much racket
2	There must be something out of kilter.
3	I think that 'twixt the negroes of the South and the women at the North, all talking about rights,
ALL	The white men will be in a fix pretty soon.
3	But what's all this here talking about?
1	That man over there says that women need to be helped into carriages,

continues

FIGURE 7.4 *continued*

2   And lifted over ditches,

3   And to have the best place everywhere.

1   Nobody ever helps me into carriages,

2   Or over mud-puddles,

3   Or gives me any best place!

ALL   And ain't I a woman? Look at me!

1   I could work as much and eat as much as a man

2   —When I could get it—

3   And bear the lash as well!

ALL   And ain't I a woman?

1   I have borne thirteen children,

2   And seen most all sold off to slavery,

3   And when I cried out with my mother's grief,

ALL   None but Jesus heard me! And ain't I a woman?

1   Then that little man in black there,

2   He says women can't have as much rights as men,

ALL   'Cause Christ wasn't a woman!

2   Where did your Christ come from?

3   Where did your Christ come from?

1   From God and a woman!

ALL   Man had nothing to do with Him.

1   If the first woman God ever made was strong enough to turn the world upside down all alone,

2   These women together ought to be able to turn it back, and get it right side up again!

ALL   And now they is asking to do it, the men better let them.

3   And now old Sojourner ain't got nothing more to say.

At the beginning of the class, pass out the example scripts, draft some student volunteers, and ask them to do a cold reading as the rest of the class follows along. After encouraging a round of thunderous applause (cold reading is difficult and risky), have students examine the script and make a list of the typical Readers Theatre conventions. Also, be sure to have the students compare the original text with the scripted version so that they can see which lines were used and how or if they were revised or rearranged. Students should notice the following conventions.

Readers Theatre Conventions

- An introduction is given if the audience is unfamiliar with the text. For example, most audience members would already know the story of The Three Little Pigs. On the other hand, it could not be assumed that everyone would know the story of Sojourner Truth.

- Each speaker is assigned a number, which corresponds to his or her speaking part in the script.

- There are choral parts where more than one person reads at the same time.

- The lines and paragraphs are broken up differently in the script when compared to the original text.

- Lines may be cut from the text when making the script.

- Words may be added to the script.

- Sometimes lines are repeated for emphasis.

Once students understand these conventions, it is time for you to assign the text. As I mentioned earlier, just about any piece of text can be turned into a piece of Readers Theatre. Our traditional textbooks are crammed with pieces that are often dry and difficult to read, particularly when the kids are left on their own as they try to make sense of the material. However, once students re-examine the text together for importance and drama, their understanding increases while the information takes on a life of its own.

Scripting the text begins with breaking paragraphs up and picking out which lines are important. Initial scripting is easiest if each member has a photocopy of the text. Together, all readers should go through it with pencil, marking parts and crossing out parts that need to be cut. As students work to find the most important material, monitor their progress. If you notice a group that is off target, don't be afraid to intervene. Ask some questions that will help re-direct their thinking and point out some text parts they might have missed. Remind them that the goal of the script is to offer an energetic end-of-unit review. The scripts should be no longer than 175–300 words in length, a concentrated, concise script that captures the highlights and cuts away the extras. Once these changes are marked, students often find it helpful to color code the photocopy: the choral parts are highlighted in one color and each individual part is highlighted in a different color. After the preliminary script is negotiated, each member needs to neatly write out (or retype) a final version of the script from the photocopy. Otherwise, when students go to present their Readers Theatre to the class, there will be a lot of stumbling and confusion because it's hard to read the lines with all of the scribbles, cross-outs, and changes. And actually rewriting the lines together offers groups one last chance to revise the script as well as review the material!

Besides the script, the group also needs to compose an introduction that explains a little bit about the text being performed. It's also important that the introduction explains what the group personally found significant and why it stood out to them.

When students have their final scripts written out, it's time to rehearse. Direct students to stand up in a slight semi-circle so that everyone can see the person in the center who've they've designated their leader. When the choral parts arise, everyone looks at the leader who uses a slight nod to make sure readers start at the same time. Without a leader, it's very difficult to synchronize the parts where everyone must read together as one voice.

Encourage them to make eye contact with the audience when speaking and to adjust their volume so they can be heard. During rehearsal, students should have their pencils in hand for making notes about how they should be interpreting the lines. When should they shout? When should they use a stage whisper? Where should they pause? What emotion should a word or line convey? If your kids still read as if they were sleepwalking, have them listen to an old radio show (something like *The Lone Ranger*). In radio theater, actors *had* to be expressive because there was no visual element for the audience. Those disembodied voices had to carry the listener into an imaginary world. Tell the kids that if they feel like their reading is super corny and hammy then it's probably about right!

Planning and Rehearsal Tips

Getting the kids to write their scripts is usually not too difficult. They enjoy the work of discussing, rearranging, and debating the content. Getting them to rehearse enough to refine their oral interpretation is the challenge. For some reason (and I know I've mentioned this before) kids do not immediately understand that practicing the script means practicing it *a lot*—as many times as possible in the time you've given them, not just once or twice. Unless you monitor the room and maybe even give points for how many times you witness a group going through their script from start to finish, your kids may think they are done after one or two read-throughs. Because they've seen so many movies but never seen all of the rehearsals and takes before the films are edited, they assume that acting just comes naturally and needs no practice. Of course, when they get up in front of the class and choke, it dawns on them that practice would have helped. But, then it's too late.

As students practice, they will need coaching. Help them with displaying emotion and giving an effective oral interpretation. Conducting a minilesson on script marking makes the interpretation more concrete. Mark pauses between words with a slash. Underline the words that need emphasis. Triple underline where to get louder and draw a dotted line under sections that are quieter. If a voice inflection goes up in pitch, mark an up-pointing arrow; if the pitch lowers, mark with a down-pointing arrow. Mark notes about emotion in the margin. Margin notes can also denote gestures, movement, or facial expressions needed for certain words or lines. After the minilesson, give the kids five minutes of silent time to reread and mark up their own lines. Then have the groups meet to practice their interpretation aloud and offer further suggestions to each other. Last, introduce the rubric (see Figure 7.2) and have them compare their notes against interpretation requirements for an A or B grade. Encourage them to discuss what they need to refine or add to their interpretation notes in order to give an A performance.

Once in a while, a student may balk at all this "acting." Just remind these reluctant learners that the goal of rehearsing the script is to help remember the important details from the unit just studied, and that there's a bonus, because these skills will help the students present themselves confidently and even make a good first impression on a job interview!

Now it's time for groups to pair up and practice together. While one group practices, the other group listens carefully and observes how well they've met the rubric requirements. After a run-through, the audience group notes what was present and what was missing. Audience group members do not have to fill the rubric out, just orally give feedback based on the rubric. In turn the performance group should write on their scripts how they will change their reading based on this feedback, and then try another run-through with the suggestions in mind. After that, it's time for the other group to take the stage. Be sure to remind everyone that the most common problem readers have is speaking too quickly. People tend to do this during a performance when they get nervous, so the more groups practice, the calmer and more confident they are likely to be.

Assessment Live!

On performance day, give students time to run through their scripts once or twice before the show begins. Remind them to practice their introductions as well.

Since the ultimate goal of this assessment is reviewing material in order to learn and remember it, ask audience members to jot down three key pieces of information emphasized in each performance. This heightens the audience's attention and keeps everyone focused on the content. After the performances conclude, conduct a large-group share during which the audience points out what information each group emphasized. Afterwards, the teacher can offer one last review of the material, hitting any bits the groups might have missed or asking probing questions whose answers require that students explore the text yet again.

On the day students perform, record the audio so that they can later listen to and self-assess their oral interpretation. Focusing on how their voices sound helps to improve future oral presentations because students have to evaluate the clarity and dramatic interpretation (or lack thereof) of their reading. This may surprise you, but don't be tempted to record a video. When the visual element is added, students ignore the quality of their oral interpretation and tend to refocus on how they looked. On the other hand, once students become more fluent in their interpretive skills, get the video camera out. Now it is time to start assessing for stage presence and communicating through body language as well.

As always, when students listen to or watch their own performances, they should have a copy of the rubric in hand. Since Readers Theatre has such a strong individual element given the assignment of lines, I encourage students to evaluate only their own performance. Afterwards, students need to get back in their groups to compare notes and discuss what they could do differently the next time in order to refine and polish their next performance (see Figure 7.3 for a sample scoring sheet).

Predictable Problems

Making the performances both thoughtful and entertaining is usually the biggest challenge. Students might be working with pieces taken from nonfiction or informative texts, which aren't always written with emotion. The key is to direct the debriefing to help groups understand how they can improve their scripts or how they would practice differently the next time. Also, if a lot of kids have the "monotone" problem, you probably need to offer some direct instruction on the facets of oral interpretation and have them practice with some short pieces of text. The activities using tongue twisters and group memorization in Chapter 2 offer some specific ideas on how to accomplish this.

Variations

Though this chapter focused on how to get kids to reread and reinvent content-area text, remember that Readers Theatre scripts can be created from *any* text. Once students know the basics, you can send them out to find their own text on a given topic and they might choose to transform poems, speeches, magazine articles, blogs, interviews, or scenes from a novel into scripts. Students may even choose to write their own original Readers Theatre scripts. As they search for the perfect text, remind students to look for pieces that have some action or excitement and a strong emotional hook. When using text from a short story or novel, a mix of dialogue and narration works best. Take a look at the Readers Theatre script shown in Figure 7.5, from *The Watsons Go to Birmingham—1963* (by Christopher Paul Curtis). The script highlights the beginning of the episode when Kenny believes that his little sister Joey has been killed in a church bombing. This dramatic moment is a turning point for Kenny as well as the rest of his family.

FIGURE 7.5 Readers Theatre Script from *The Watsons Go to Birmingham—1963*

(4 Speakers)

1	I know it was Sunday because I heard Joetta getting ready for Sunday school.
2	I don't know why, but I said,
3	"Joey . . .You look real pretty."
1	She had on a lacy white hat
2	and little lacy white socks
ALL	and her shiny, shiny black shoes.
1	The people that came to get her saw me and one of them said,
4	"How come you ain't coming to Sunday school, young man?"
2	I smiled and said,
3	"I forgot to get up in time."
1	It was too hot even this early in the morning,
2	so I went in the backyard and started going to sleep under the giant magnolia tree.
ALL	And thought I was dreaming when the noise came.
1	Dad came to the back door.
4	"What was that?"
2	He kept looking toward the sky.

continues

FIGURE 7.5 *continued*

4	"Hmm, must have been a sonic boom."
1	I leaned back and closed my eyes,
2	but Momma's scream made me jump.
1	I ran indoors, but Momma and Dad were gone.
2	Byron, my brother, was trying to wrestle on a pair of pants.
3	"By! What happened?"
4	"A guy just came by and said somebody dropped a bomb on Joey's church."
1	And he was gone, exploding out the front door.
ALL	It looked like someone had set off a people magnet.
1	Everyone in Birmingham was running down the street,
ALL	so I followed.
1	I looked into the church and saw smoke and dust flying around like a tornado.
ALL	I could see a shiny, shiny black shoe
2	lying halfway underneath some concrete.
1	I bent down to pull the shoe from under the concrete,
2	but it felt like something was pulling it back.
1	Oh, man. I gave the shoe one more hard tug
2	and it popped loose
3	from a frilly white sock.
ALL	I got real scared.

Quick Guide: Readers Theatre

1. Choose dramatic, interesting, and meaningful lines from a piece of text—or write your own original text. Remind students that the goal is to review and highlight the most important concepts, information, scenes, etc. as the class draws to the close of a unit of study. As they begin work on the scripts, they should first reread the source material several times.

2. Divide the text up into lines. Don't be afraid to break up sentences (think free-verse poetry) into several lines, cut lines, or change wording a bit to make it sound better.

3. Decide which lines are the most dramatic or important. These are the lines that are marked ALL and read chorally.

4. Assign numbers to the remaining lines—the number of parts is determined by the number of group members.

5. Once the script is completed, the group should practice reading it aloud, adjusting lines as needed so that the message is clear. Then the script should be neatly recopied so that each member has a final draft.

6. Continuing to practice aloud with the final scripts, students should stop to discuss possible interpretations and then make notes on the script.

7. In front of an audience group, students practice performing the script, using their interpretation notes and honing the choral parts, remembering to get the signal from the center person—the leader. After reading aloud, the audience group gives feedback based on the rubric.

8. Hold the performances and then debrief, discussing the importance of the information presented as well as the performances themselves. Later on, when students participate in other assessments that require reading aloud or memorization (Tableaux, Book Buddy, Performing a Scene, Talk Show, Story-telling) remind them that the scripting and interpretation skills used for Readers Theatre need to be applied to these performances as well.

Tableaux

What Is It?

The Tableaux strategy is a series of scenes presented by groups of four to eight students who are frozen in poses or positions that depict an historical event, famous speech, scientific concept, or scene from a novel. One student reads the Tableaux captions while the others create the scene being described (Wilhelm 2002). The Tableaux script can be based on existing text (textbook, novel, short story, magazine article) or original text written in response to something the students have read or studied. Fiction requires students to reexamine scenes and character while nonfiction requires students to imaginatively create characters that represent people, ideas, or symbols. The following script, and the photo in Figure 8.1, depict the series of Tableaux scenes that a fifth-grade literature circle group designed in order to convey the startling true story the readers could not forget once they finished the book *My Heart Is on the Ground: The Diary of Nannie Little Rose, a Sioux Girl* (Rinaldi 1999). This book portrays the life of a young Sioux girl, ripped away from her family and community and sent to live in a government-run boarding school in order to be assimilated into white culture.

Tableaux Script Based on *My Heart Is on the Ground*

1. If Indian parents did not agree to have their children taken to the school, they were taken by force.

2. Once the children arrived at the school, they immediately had to get their hair cut. For them, it meant taking away their Indian past.

3. The kids struggled to learn English and were forced not to talk or sign in their past language.

4. The children were given diaries to write about what they did each day.

5. Many kids died from various diseases at the school.

6. Many kids tried to escape because the school was not a great pleasure.

No matter the genre, Tableaux require that students be ruthless in their scripting since the narration must capture key points in a series of single sentences. Creating an effective Tableau requires solid comprehension of the material in order to take the text or information, write a succinct series of captions, and transform each caption into a three-dimensional living illustration. Students must think seriously about the accuracy of their blocking (visual composition, gestures, facial expressions) and frozen scene depictions, which requires careful rereading of the text.

When and Why to Use It

Tableaux are useful in any content area. This is an energizing, active way for students to return to the text and think about it more deeply. In addition, as students negotiate what information is vital for Tableaux representation, they must grapple with or discuss alternative reader responses. Listening in on these conversations as you monitor offers a unique way for the teacher to assess the students' internalization of key material. In addition, this assessment is intensely kinesthetic and spatial. Students are moving around as they compose living pieces of sculpture. While the movement and rehearsal enhance memory connections, the physical aspect is perfectly in tune with how boys want to respond in a physical way to their reading (Wilhelm and Smith 2002).

But Tableaux is also a great ongoing assessment tool. After some reading has been completed, student groups work with assigned pages to create and perform some frozen scenes that highlight the information or drama. While a quiz is individual and ends with either having the answers—or not—a Tableaux assessment requires students to revisit the text, explain significant aspects to each other in order to construct further meaning, and then reinvent the most important information in a new medium. Interestingly, even if you assign six different groups the exact same three pages of text, each group will script and block differently because every reader's visualization of the text is unique. Creating Tableaux forces students to make inferences when they combine textual clues and their imaginations in order to forge logical conclusions. Plus, each group's comprehension and creativity gets shared with the entire class.

Time Requirement

One to two class periods is needed. The time factor depends on how much text students are working with as well as how many scenes they need to create.

Starting with the End in Mind

As you explain the assignment and students study the rubric (see Figure 8.2), discourage them from immediately discussing costumes; their focus needs to be on creating a dramatic script and visually interesting and informative frozen scenes. Notice that costumes are also de-emphasized by point value on the scoring sheet (see Figure 8.3); the greatest values are awarded to the script and the blocking.

Getting Ready

Begin by showing some photos of actual statues. Ten minutes of searching Google images should yield some good results. Look for statues that depict groups of people in dramatic poses (grand gestures; vivid expression; multiple visual levels where subjects are simultaneously standing, sitting, crouching, kneeling, or reclining). As you search for images, start with the phrase "statues in [your state here]". That way you might find some images with which students are already familiar. Another dramatic statue that deserves study (and is easily found on the Internet) is the Flag Raising at Iwo Jima. Explain that when students

FIGURE 8.2 Tableaux Rubric

C	B	A
Script	**Script**	**Script**
■ Introduction gives audience necessary background ■ Caption for each scene clearly describes action ■ Neat final draft copy of introduction and Tableau narration turned in	■ Scene choices reflect important parts of text ■ Audience can easily follow from one scene to the next ■ Captions are correct length	■ Demonstrates insight into characters, ideas, and text ■ Scene reflects high drama, conflict, action ■ Helps audience remember key information
Narration	**Narration**	**Narration**
■ Easily heard ■ Correct pacing of speech	■ Good oral interpretation: emotion and energy present ■ No stumbles	■ Interesting, entertaining ■ High energy
Scenes/Blocking	**Scenes/Blocking**	**Scenes/Blocking**
■ Makes sense to those unfamiliar with text ■ All actors fully visible ■ Well practiced	■ Scenes are important to the text ■ Tight compositions—actors close together ■ Spacing shows relationships between characters	■ High drama, conflict, action depicted ■ Body heights staggered ■ Each frame is substantially different
Performance	**Performance**	**Performance**
■ Remains frozen entire time ■ No upstaging—"breaking up"—laughter ■ Hair does not hide face	■ Actors face the audience, "cheating out" when necessary ■ Identifiable gestures, fits context	■ Exaggerated expression and gestures portray accurate characterization ■ Audience thoroughly entertained ■ Very polished
Props/Costumes	**Props/Costumes**	**Props/Costumes**
■ Slight suggestion of character/scene ■ Contributes positively, enhances audience understanding	■ Costume/character connection is clearly obvious to audience (i.e., casual clothes does not make it clear you are a housekeeper)	■ Creativity and obvious outside effort reflected

FIGURE 8.3 Tableaux Scoring Sheet

TABLEAUX

Name _____

Source _____ **Date** _____ **Period** _____

Directions: Referring back to the rubric, rate your presentation in the following categories. Please jot down any notes about details you want me to notice about your writing and performance before I assign the final grade. Do not repeat the rubric phrases. Atttach a copy of your script, and turn in your group's score sheets together.

Category	Points	Weight	Score
Script	1 2 3 4 5	x 6	/30
Narration	1 2 3 4 5	x 3	/15
Scenes/Blocking	1 2 3 4 5	x 5	/25
Performance	1 2 3 4 5	x 4	/20
Props/Costumes	1 2 3 4 5	x 2	/10

Total Points   **/100**

Standards Skills Students Will Practice

Reading	Writing	Speaking and Listening
■ Interpret and evaluate the impact of ambiguities, subtleties, contradictions, ironies, and incongruities in a text	■ Synthesize information from multiple sources	■ Analyze historically significant speeches
■ Analyze interactions between main and subordinate characters in a literary text	■ Revise writing to improve the logic and coherence	■ Assess how language and delivery affect the mood and tone
■ Read, view, and interpret texts and performances in every medium	■ Draw comparisons between specific incidents and broader themes	■ Use appropriate rehearsal to achieve command of the text, and skillful artistic staging
■ Recognize unstated assumptions	■ Use tone and language appropriate to the audience and purpose	■ Recite poems, selections from speeches, or dramatic soliloquies with attention to performance details
■ Recognize and analyze the relevance of literature to contemporary and/or personal events and situations	■ Use prewriting activities	■ Listen respectfully and responsively
■ Explain and justify interpretation	■ Use the writing process	■ Apply delivery techniques such as voice projection and demonstrate physical poise
	■ Take notes from written and oral texts	■ Use nonverbal communication techniques to help disclose message
		■ Recognize the use and impact of effective language
		■ Respond to constructive criticism
		■ Determine points of view, clarify positions, make judgments, and form opinions

create a tableau, they are making a living statue. Together their groups will create frozen dramatic scenes. Instruct them to notice how the drama of the statue is composed: the posture and pose of the subjects vary, gestures and facial expressions are clear, faces can be seen by the audience unless a face is hidden to intensify dramatic impact.

Now distribute a handout of six to ten numbered captions from a piece of text with which the students are already familiar. When you create this sample set of captions, remember to keep them short, about ten to twenty words each. They are like the captions one would find underneath a newspaper or magazine photograph. Break the class into groups of four or five and have each group pick one or two captions to put into a scene. Remind students to use the statue photographs for inspiration as they create a freeze-frame that captures the characters, action, ideas, and emotion of their caption. Because each group is using the same script, all group members will be part of each scene; the teacher can serve as the narrator this first time. Remind students that the most interesting Tableaux scenes are created when they remember the following:

- Keep the composition tight—actors should be close together versus far apart.

- Consider the relationships between the characters or ideas. Characters or ideas who agree or are on good terms with one another will be physically closer to each other as opposed to conflicting forces who may stand apart or at an angle to others.

- Exaggerate your character's feelings through your expressions.

- Stagger positions and heights of the actors—it is visually boring when everyone is standing or sitting a the same level.

Give the groups about ten minutes to brainstorm and practice before performing the scenes. As they rehearse, pay particular attention to how they are orienting their poses in relation to where the audience would be. Students often will create a literal scene, a scene that depicts how people would stand in real life versus a staged scene for an audience. In real life, there is no audience, so all players are focused directly on the action being played out. When students create poses like this, often half of the actors are hidden from view because they are standing behind someone else or they have their backs turned to the audience. Try to catch these blocking faux pas as they occur and teach students how to "cheat out," which means angling one's body outward so that the audience can still see the actor's face. Actors in Tableaux should never turn their backs to the audience unless it is to make a strong visual, emotional statement.

Viewing the scenes is best appreciated when the audience members close their eyes until each group is frozen in position. Watching the actors set up their positions can take away from the effect. Getting the students to cover up their eyes can be challenging—you may want to take digital photos of each scene to capture the blocking and that "frozen moment." The kids love to look at the photos and they are a good start for studying visual composition and refining blocking in future Tableaux.

Patrick Henry's "Give Me Liberty or Give Me Death" speech offers some great Tableaux opportunities for American literature or U.S. history students. As the following example script illustrates, Tableaux is a very useful strategy in content areas. Though most students have heard of the famous slogan "Give me liberty or give me death," few know its author, its context, or that in terms of craft it's one of the greatest examples of a powerful closing statement ever written. Unfortunately, when the full text is revealed to kids via their American literature or U.S. history books, it comes off as a difficult-to-read snore selection. Putting Patrick Henry's great lines in the physical context of Tableaux makes his words come alive (see Figure 8.4) and helps students remember key points of his speech.

PATRICK HENRY—Speech to the Second Virginia Convention
St. John's Church, Richmond, Virginia, March 23, 1775

1. I have but one lamp by which my feet are guided; and that is the lamp of experience. I know of no way of judging of the future but by the past.

2. Are fleets and armies necessary to a work of love and reconciliation? . . . I ask, gentlemen, sir, what means this martial array, if its purpose be not to force us to submission?

3. We have petitioned; we have remonstrated; we have supplicated; we have prostrated ourselves before the throne . . .

4. Our petitions have been slighted; our remonstrances have produced additional violence and insult; our supplications have been disregarded . . .

5. Shall we acquire the means of effectual resistance, by lying supinely on our backs, and hugging the delusive phantom of hope, until our enemies shall have bound us hand and foot?

6. Three millions of people, armed in the holy cause of liberty, and in such a country as that which we possess, are invincible by any force which our enemy can send against us.

7. Besides, sir, we shall not fight our battles alone. There is a just God who presides over the destinies of nations; and who will raise up friends to fight our battles for us.

8. I know not what course others may take; but as for me, give me liberty or give me death!

FIGURE 8.4 Students depict Henry's words: "Besides, sir, we shall not fight our battles alone. There is a just God who presides over the destinies of nations; and who will raise up friends to fight our battles for us."

After watching the scenes, pass out photocopies of the original text from which the Tableaux were created and have the students compare it to the script. They should notice that specific lines are chosen for their power. Seldom are all the sentences in a paragraph used for one freeze-frame. One paragraph might actually contain two or three scenes. Also, lines can be combined from several different paragraphs in order to create a powerful scene caption.

Now it's time for students to create their own scenes from another piece of text they have read and studied. The only real requirements for the text selection are that the information is important for kids to remember, and that the passage have some action to it. But use your imagination! There is a ton of action going on during cell mitosis! Once students have their piece of text, it is their job to ferret out the key information and portray it in narrated

Tableaux. In this initial phase, monitor the groups closely and ask them to explain their text choices to you. If they have traveled down an obscure path, help them rediscover some key text elements they should be including. Then, as they compose their script, remind students that each scene should have action and emotion, and five or six scenes should tell a story. All group members should write a copy of the caption script as it is negotiated. Remind the groups to keep the freeze-frame captions short because, among other reasons, when a narrator reads a long paragraph, it gets hard to keep standing statue still. Once the script is finalized, the groups need to practice so that their blocking is memorized for each freeze-frame.

Planning and Rehearsal Tips

Just like all the other performance projects, you will need to remind the kids to keep practicing and refining their freeze-frames. Explain that their audience will suffer if they are still "dragging members into position" and finalizing their blocking when they are supposed to perform some polished scenes. Watch their blocking and don't be afraid to give suggestions.

Assessment Live!

In addition to enjoying the live performances, be sure to videorecord the Tableaux. The digital photos I mentioned earlier are for the Tableaux introduction, when the teacher is acting as the narrator. Now that students are the narrators, you'll need to capture sound as well as image. When you're taping, remember this key step: hit the pause button between each freeze-frame. That way, when you play back the tape all the "getting in position stuff" is eliminated and the viewers get to see the scenes the way they would have originally if they had shut their eyes between scenes.

While reviewing the class videorecording, students watch all of the performances carefully, taking notes on the content and performances. They might consider the following:

- What key information did the performances help you remember?

- What makes a good Tableaux performance?

- What would your group do differently the next time?

After the performances, talk about the content first and then use their ideas from the other two questions to make some lists. (See some examples in Figure 8.5.) Next time this live assessment comes around, review those lists in order to improve students' planning and rehearsal.

FIGURE 8.5

WHAT MAKES GOOD TABLEAUX?

NARRATION	SCENE ACTING
■ Lively, enthusiastic voice ■ Clear speaking ■ Speak slowly ■ Speak loudly ■ Show emotion ■ Pause between sentences ■ Practice lines ■ Emphasize certain words ■ Sound confident, decisive ■ Make character voices	■ Audience can see facial expressions from a distance ■ Don't laugh—stay in character ■ Stand still ■ Make each scene look different ■ Overexaggerate facial expressions and gestures ■ Blocking shows relationships between characters ■ Use staggered levels ■ Creates feeling of action or motion ■ Creative poses ■ Face the audience ■ Audience can see everyone (no one is behind someone else)

WHAT WE NEED TO WORK ON NEXT TIME

NARRATION	SCENE ACTING
■ Read narration enthusiastically ■ Talk loudly and clearly ■ Emphasize words ■ Speak with more confidence	■ Don't laugh and goof around ■ Practice more—know what we're doing ■ Overexaggerate gestures and facial expressions ■ Stand still ■ Make poses more dramatic ■ Poses use varied levels (standing, leaning, sitting, etc.) ■ Make each scene look different ■ Face the camera—don't turn back to the audience ■ Create a feeling of motion ■ Be dramatic/creative ■ Get/keep the audience's attention ■ Stand so audience can see all actors

Predictable Problems

The part of Tableaux that almost always needs the most teacher coaching is the narration. A group will spend a load of time on writing good captions and planning their blocking but never think twice about how the narrator should orally reflect the vivid action of the scenes. As you monitor, watch for this. When you view the videotape, if the groups' narrators often fail to match the energy of the acting, take some time out for the direct instruction of basic oral interpretation techniques mentioned in Chapter 2.

Quick Guide: Tableaux

1. Choose a dramatic, emotional, or active part of a text—or write your own original script.

2. Divide the text up into five or six scenes.

3. Find a line or two of text that will serve as a caption for each scene.

4. Block each scene. Think about tight composition and conveying emotion/action. Varying pose levels will make the visual composition more interesting.

5. Practice! The actors need to memorize their positions for each scene and rehearse moving seamlessly from one Tableau to the next. Also, standing stock-still while the narrator reads each caption takes practice. Remind actors to face the audience rather than facing away.

6. Pay particular attention to narrator's oral interpretation. The teacher needs to monitor, intervene, and coach the narrator and the group. Their discussion of the oral interpretation should have the same attention to detail as the physical interpretation. Encourage the narrator to mark the caption script. Underline words to emphasize, mark pauses by placing slashes between words, write down what emotions the voice should reflect as the caption is read.

7. Practice before another group and then together discuss how well the narration and Tableaux met the rubric requirements. Revise and practice again!

8. Public performance. Afterwards, debrief discussing the information presented as well as how successfully the groups portrayed that information. What worked and what would groups need to do differently the next time?

Talk Show

What Is It?

Oprah, Ellen, Dr. Phil, Letterman, Conan, Jerry Springer, Tyra Banks. Talk shows are a television staple and we teachers are well advised to adapt their popular formulas for live assessment. Invite your students to bring fictional characters, historical figures, and scientific theories to life through a Talk Show performance. You can even add a twist by putting together real people from history—Abraham Lincoln and John Brown—with famous people from fiction, say, the main characters from Harriet Beecher Stowe's *Uncle Tom's Cabin*. Encourage students to base their interview questions and characterizations on fact and accurate inference while imagining how the characters might interact. Aside from the heavy-duty synthesis this live assessment requires, it also provides you with the chance to see that kid with the baggy low-slung pants show up, at least for a day, in a suit and tie when it's his turn to impersonate Jerry Springer or Dr. Phil.

What might a Talk Show script look like? The following script was created by Jen, Amanda, and Michelle from my American literature class after reading *The Crucible* by Arthur Miller. The girls' "Oprah-style" Talk Show script features two of the more despicable characters in *The Crucible*: Ann Putnam, a woman motivated to accuse other people of practicing witchcraft because of personal grudges and the belief that midwife Rebecca Nurse purposely caused the deaths of her children; and Abigail Williams, the girl who started the witch hunt by hurling accusations at others in an attempt to deflect attention from the fact that she was caught dancing in the woods and rumored to have an affair with John Proctor.

Talk-Show Script

OPRAH: Hello and welcome to our special theme show on Dirty Deeds. We have two special guests from Salem, Massachusetts, where recently several community members have been accused of being witches. Our first guest is forty-five years old and has had seven babies that all died in infancy. She blames her midwife, Rebecca Nurse, for cursing her babies. Put your hands together for Ann Putnam!

(Ann comes out with a solemn look on her face.)

OPRAH: We're happy to have you here today. So tell me, what's your story?

ANN: It was such a tragedy. I remember it like it was just yesterday. My husband and I wanted children, but each time they died. Rebecca Nurse delivered all seven of them. I didn't understand how this could have happened because they were all healthy when they were born. But I knew, I knew, I knew all about Rebecca Nurse! She did it to them; she cursed them. That witch!! *(She is so angry her face becomes red as if steam would shoot out of her ears.)*

OPRAH: *(Slightly surprised by the loud outburst.)* Okay, so what did you do?

ANN: Whatever do you mean? I did nothing. *(Lays her hand on her chest as if swearing to God but has difficulty concealing a smirk.)*

OPRAH: Weren't you the one to drop Rebecca Nurse's name to the authorities, accusing her of being a witch? Aren't you jealous because she has all those beautiful children and grandchildren? What was the real reason you named Rebecca Nurse as a witch?

ANN: She's a murderer and people should know the truth!

OPRAH: Answer the question. What was the real reason you named Rebecca Nurse as a witch?

ANN: *(She shrugs.)* It was so obvious. She had so much land and a family. How else could someone have so much land and all those children? They all lived; they are all healthy. It just can't be!!

OPRAH: So you named Rebecca Nurse as a witch because you were jealous of her family and her estate, isn't that right?

ANN: Yes! Yes! I said she was a witch because I was jealous of her. I don't like her, I never did. She's bad! *(She starts to cry and covers her face with her hands.)*

OPRAH: *(Hands Ann a tissue, takes a deep breath, and smiles at the audience.)* Alright, we'll be right back with our next guest after we take a quick break.

BREAK

OPRAH: Welcome back to Dirty Deeds. Next we have an eighteen-year-old who claims to have seen many of her neighbors with the devil. Let's welcome Abigail Williams!

(Abigail comes out basking in her newly found fame and smiling at the audience.)

ABIGAIL: Hi Oprah, how are you?

OPRAH: So you have seen many of your neighbors with the devil?

ABIGAIL: Yes, I have seen plenty of people walking with the devil.

OPRAH: How many people would you say have walked with the devil?

ABIGAIL: Currently, I think the count is around six. *(She gives a grin.)* But that could change.

OPRAH: *(Cocks her head suspiciously.)* Have you really seen the devil?

ABIGAIL: Yes! And many people from Salem were with him!

OPRAH: Oh really? What does the devil look like?

ABIGAIL: Uh . . . uh . . . uh . . .

OPRAH: *(Completely unconvinced she's telling the truth.)* Right. You know all of these witches, right? You even worked for Elizabeth Proctor; is that how you know she's a witch? Or are you just naming her as one because she fired you?

ABIGAIL: Elizabeth fired me because I had an affair with her husband. . . . Oh, Oprah, you're right. I haven't seen the devil or anyone with him. There aren't any witches; I only said those things so none of us would get in trouble for dancing in the woods!! But I'm proud of it! I love to dance and married men are the best! *(She stands up, laughs, and twirls off stage.)*

OPRAH: Well, there you have it. People doing things for their own benefit with complete disregard for anyone else's well-being. Thanks for joining us today. Tune in next week for Secrets Behind the Curtain and Tricks for Getting Cheap Liposuction.

(Audience applauds.)

When and Where to Use It

This performance works best as a summative assessment when students must take everything they've studied and turn it into an entertaining script that reflects their learning and insight. Writing the script requires careful rereading of their sources (e.g., text and notes) as well as ample inference and imagination. For example, if a cell's nucleus is the talk-show host, what questions would it pose to its guest organelles? How would the cell's mitochondria act and behave compared with the Golgi apparatus or a ribosome? How would these organelles interact with each other and the host? Does the nucleus have favorites? Is there an organelle rivalry? Unless you're a science teacher, I bet your recollection of these concepts is somewhat foggy even though you took a year of biology in high school. That's exactly why the Talk Show assessment is so perfect for important content that can be difficult to retain. It forces students to get up close and personal with the material in memorable ways that a traditional test assessment cannot provide. Brain research strongly supports role playing because it creates strong emotional connections to the material and provides a real-life context (Sylwester 1995).

Whatever subject you teach, your curriculum is a nearly limitless cornucopia of possible Talk Show interview guests, but to get the idea wheel turning, here are a few suggestions.

U.S. History: Historical figures: Chief Seattle, Geronimo, Sitting Bull; famous events: Boston Tea Party, Signing of the Declaration of Independence; important vocabulary: *democracy, totalitarianism, dictatorship, fascism.*

Physical Science: Elements from the periodic table; the electromagnetic spectrum: radio waves, infrared rays, visible light, ultraviolet rays, x-rays, gamma rays; fossil fuels.

Psychology: Famous psychologists: Sigmund Freud, Carl Jung, Abraham Maslow, Carl Rogers; competing theories: behaviorism, cognitivisim, constructivism, nature versus nurture.

Government: The executive, judicial, and legislative branches of federal government; the Bill of Rights; the Electoral College.

Biology: Dangerous diseases and the vaccines that prevent them; cell structures; invasive species; climate change.

Geometry: Points, lines, line segments, midpoints, rays, planes, space.

Health: Calories; polyunsaturated, monounsaturated, and saturated fats; simple and complex carbohydrates; protein; fiber; aerobic exercise, resistance training.

Mathematics: Formulas, equations, vectors.

Time Requirement

Three to five class periods should be sufficient, depending on the depth of the research and how much of the work students will complete in class.

Standards Skills Students Will Practice

Reading	Writing	Speaking and Listening
■ Interpret and evaluate the impact of ambiguities, subtleties, contradictions, ironies, and incongruities in a text	■ Use precise language	■ Assess how language and delivery affect the mood and tone
■ Analyze interactions between main and subordinate characters in a literary text	■ Develop the main ideas through supporting evidence	■ Apply appropriate interviewing techniques
■ Evaluate the qualities of style	■ Synthesize information from multiple sources	■ Use appropriate rehearsal to achieve command of the text, and skillful artistic staging
■ Recognize unstated assumptions	■ Revise writing to improve the logic and coherence	■ Listen respectfully and responsively
■ Recognize and analyze the relevance of literature to contemporary and/or personal events and situations	■ Draw comparisons between specific incidents and broader themes	■ Apply delivery techniques such as voice projection, and demonstrate physical poise
■ Share reading experiences with a peer or adult	■ Use tone and language appropriate to the audience and purpose	■ Use nonverbal communication techniques to help disclose message
■ Engage in a variety of collaborative conversations	■ Use prewriting activities	■ Recognize the use and impact of effective language
■ Explain and justify interpretation	■ Use the writing process	■ Respond to constructive criticism
	■ Evaluate written work for its effectiveness and make recommendations for its improvement	■ Deliver impromptu and planned oral presentations
	■ Write for real situations	■ Present orally original work supported by research

Starting with the End in Mind

There are four main criteria students need to be focused on as they prepare their talk shows: script, characterization, performance, props/costumes. A group's first concern should be creating a high-quality script because the other assessment components are completely dependent on that. When groups practice for each other, feedback should be based on the rubric (see Figure 9.1). Later, students will self-assess their performance by checking off the specific criteria they met as they watch the video recording.

Though it is important that students understand how points for the various categories have been distributed, the scoring sheet for Talk Show (see Figure 9.2) is intended for student self-evaluation. All students receive a copy of the rubric and the grade sheet, followed by teacher grade finalization. The most heavily weighted component of the assessment is the script, since this document demonstrates depth of thinking and research.

Getting Ready

As students finish up a book or unit and are ready to synthesize the key ideas, that's the time to offer them the talk-show model as a way to show what they know. Ahead of time, I've recorded a few excerpts of talk shows to show to the class. My three favorite hosts are Dr. Phil, Oprah Winfrey, and Jerry Springer because they all have larger-than-life personalities and their shows each have a specific structure. Finding useful excerpts takes some patience because you'll be looking for segments that best illustrate the structure, have themes interesting to your students, and, of course, feature school-appropriate topics. Don't be surprised if you first run across Oprah's show on plastic surgery makeovers before you find the one on lying family members, and I can guarantee it will take several tries before you find a segment of a Jerry Springer show that you can show in school. However, once you've got those recordings, you might be set for life since neither Phil, Jerry, or Oprah show any signs of retiring soon. And even if they do, cable/satellite channels such as TV Land or Reality TV will be replaying the reruns for eternity!

What makes these three particular talk shows great models is that they all focus on a theme of the day and each host has a very specific interview style. Before we view the excerpts, I tell the students they will be creating and performing their own talk shows based on one of the shows excerpts, so they need to study how the segments are structured.

- What is the show's theme?

- How does the host introduce a guest?

- How does the host interview the guest?

FIGURE 9.1 Talk-Show Rubric

C	B	A
Script	**Script**	**Script**
■ Host introduces celebrity self and theme of show ■ Host asks questions ■ Typed final draft copy of script turned in	■ Host asks each guest at least five questions ■ Actors have equal speaking parts ■ Dialogue is entertaining and informative ■ Research evident	■ Reflects designated talk-show style ■ Lots of textual information imbedded in dialogue ■ Imaginative yet faithful to original text
Characterization	**Characterization**	**Characterization**
■ No distracting accents or gestures ■ Reflects specific text details ■ Face and body can be seen clearly ■ Well practiced	■ Good eye contact with audience, guests, and host ■ Character's personality and physical traits easily recognized by audience ■ Playing character not self	■ Emotion shown in face and voice matches lines ■ Characters interact appropriately with each other ■ Lines memorized
Performance	**Performance**	**Performance**
■ Loud, clear diction ■ Correct pacing (no fast talk) ■ Everyone knows his/her part ■ No upstaging—"breaking up"—laughter	■ Well practiced ■ Good eye contact with audience ■ Emotion, gestures, facial expressions match spoken lines	■ Audience thoroughly entertained ■ High-energy performance ■ Very polished
Props/Costumes	**Props/Costumes**	**Props/Costumes**
■ Slight suggestion of character/scene ■ Enhances audience understanding	■ Costume/character connection is clearly obvious to audience (e.g., casual clothes do not make it clear you are a houskeeper) ■ Props enhance performance	■ Creativity and obvious outside effort reflected

FIGURE 9.2 Talk-Show Scoring Sheet

TALK-SHOW PERFORMANCE

Name _____ **Character Played** _____

Talk Show Theme _____

Talk-Show Model (circle)   Oprah   Dr. Phil   Jerry Springer

Directions: As you watch the video, rate yourself in the following categories based on the rubric. Please jot down any notes about performance details you want me to notice before I assign the final grade. Do not repeat the rubric phrases. Turn in all of your group's sheets together as well as one copy of the script.

Category	Points	Weight	Score
Script	1 2 3 4 5	x 6	/30
Characterization	1 2 3 4 5	x 5	/25
Performance	1 2 3 4 5	x 5	/25
Props and Costumes	1 2 3 4 5	x 2	/10
Good Use of Planning/Rehearsal Time	1 2 3 4 5	x 2	/10

Total Points   **/100**

May be photocopied for classroom use. © 2009 by Nancy Steineke from *Assessment Live!* Portsmouth, NH: Heinemann.

- If several guests are interviewed simultaneously, how does the host maintain order and do the guests interact with each other?

- At the end of an interview, how does the host wrap it up?

- Throughout the entire interview, what role does the audience play? Are they quiet or are they cued to respond at key moments?

As students watch with an eye towards interview analysis, they see these shows in a brand-new way and delight at their discoveries. While Oprah makes eye contact and nods sympathetically, she lets her victim, oh I mean guest, tell her sad regret-tinged story. After a pause and one more sympathetic nod, Oprah pounces, asking the "gotcha" question that totally stuns the guest and completely proves that "sticky fingered" mother of three isn't sorry enough for making her toddler a shoplifting accomplice. For increased stun power, Oprah typically interviews her guests one at a time. On the other hand, Jerry Springer doesn't ask too many questions. His job is to introduce the theme and then introduce each of the inmates, oh I mean guests, as they're released to inflict the details of their sordid infidelities upon one another. Jerry stays out of chair tossing range while the bouncers make a show of keeping guests from seriously injuring themselves and each other. In the end when the coast is clear, Jerry comes back to sum it all up. Unlike Jerry, Dr. Phil wants all his patients, I mean guests, together for a group therapy session. His routine allows them to accuse and blame each other nonstop, usually with one particularly obnoxious relative dominating the "session" while the others cower in their chairs. Finally, bored by the repetition of accusations, Dr. Phil bluntly tells them all to shut up, points his finger at the real culprit, and analyzes their family dysfunction with some quick pop psychology. Then with thirty seconds left before the commercial break, Dr. Phil looks his guests straight in the eye and confidently prescribes the solution to the festering problem that has been making their lives a living hell for the past twenty years.

After viewing, the students discuss what they noticed about the various interview structures. Then I allow students to choose groups of four to six. Previewing the project, I tell them: Your group will be putting on a seven minute talk-show segment. All members of your group will play a part. One member will be the host and the rest will be interview guests that you choose based on the unit of study we just finished. In order to get started, you will need to do some preliminary brainstorming:

- Which talk-show style (based on the excerpts viewed) best fits the content we've been studying? Why?

- Who will play the host? Who will be the guests? What do they have in common? How are they in conflict?

- What will be the theme of the show?

- How would the members of your group portray these characters? How would you talk? What would you say? How would you move and gesture? How would you dress? How would you react to the other characters? What kind of personality would you reveal?

- What questions will the host ask so that the interview is entertaining and revealing to the audience?

Once the initial brainstorming is completed, all members of the group need to complete an individual review of the academic material, searching for information, quotes, or character details that will inform the script—so the content is accurate—and will provide rich information along with entertainment. Members should take notes and mark important text passages with sticky notes. They should search for characterization details that will drive their portrayal as well as direct pieces of dialogue that they might be able to insert into the script.

Focused on the genre and their notes, groups get to work on the scripts. If you think your students are unfamiliar with the conventions of a script, all you need to do is photocopy a couple of pages from a play as an example so that they can see how dialogue and stage directions are indicated. But if your curriculum does include plays, take the time to have the students read specific scenes aloud in front of the room and always assign someone to read the stage directions. Like the graphics in our textbooks, students ignore stage directions unless they are pointed out. In writing their own scripts, it is the inclusion of the stage directions that forces the students to bring action and life to their characters.

I tell my students the script needs to be written like a play. *Every* line is spelled out; there is *no* improvisation. And yes, they must include detailed stage directions. During each interview, the host must ask each guest at least five questions. Also, I tell students to talk about how they want the audience to react to their talk show's guests. Typically, audiences are prompted to respond appropriately by a stage manager holding up cue cards. For Oprah the audience needs to know when to applaud. For Dr. Phil, the audience needs to know when to applaud and when to go "Ohhhhh" as they react to a particularly offensive guest comment. For Jerry Springer, the audience is almost another character. Groups choosing that format will use a collection of cue cards, so students will need to inventory all of the different audience reactions that are part of a typical Springer show. Monitor the groups closely to be sure they are on track, giving them one or two class periods in which to write the script. As I circulate, I consistently emphasize that as they write the script and later perform in their own talk show, they need to focus on the content of their script and the portrayal of their characters, but not get too hung up on trying to impersonate the actual celebrity interviewer. In the earlier example interview, the girl playing Oprah did not try to be Oprah (I mean, get real—who could?). However, she did lend a sympathetic ear to Anne Putnam's story about her dead babies before she asked her "gotcha" question. We watched those excerpts in order to capture the structure, not the nuances of the celebrity host.

The Head Writer

Once all group members have had ample input, it's often easier if one student takes the script home and finishes up the final fine-tuning on the writing. Though this sounds unfair, I often find there is one student in each group who turns out to be a natural at script writing, and who will jump at the chance to become the "head writer," taking control and giving the script those final dramatic or humorous tweaks that the larger group just doesn't have time for. Be sure to give the "head writer" a couple of days between each script meeting.

Two days later, the "head writer" brings in a copy of the script for each group member to read and revise. Once again, remind students to focus on the goal of providing both content information and entertainment. They should return to the original source text and notes as they work to strengthen the interpretation and add further details to the script. After the in-class revision is completed, give the "head writer" a couple more days to enter the changes and print out final drafts for everyone.

Writing as a Group

As you have already inferred, using the "head writer" approach requires that these students be reliable in regards to getting the work done as well as attendance. It also requires that the other group members take serious responsibility for the initial script writing as well as the revisions. But a "head writer" is not necessary. All of the script writing can take place in class, as long as you are willing to devote a few more class periods to this step. And to prevent any members from slacking off, require that every group member writes down every word of the script so that they each have their own working copy. This solves two problems. First, engaged writers stay busy and focused. Second, if a member is absent during one of the writing days, the rest of the group can continue the work without her. Once groups have finished their scripts, each member is responsible converting his handwritten version into a typed final draft script copy.

Planning and Rehearsal Tips

Once the groups have their finished scripts in hand, give them ten minutes a day for two or three days to practice reading through them. Monitor the practice and insist that the kids stand up and follow the stage directions as well as reading their lines. They'll also need to figure out how they want to arrange the furniture and props. Remind the groups that on the day of the performances they will have only seven minutes to complete their talk shows, starting from the time their group is called. Letting the kids know that up front keeps them much more organized. Otherwise, groups will waste precious minutes on performance day figuring out where people are going to sit, how to arrange the chairs, and so on.

Students generally have few problems coming up with their Talk Show idea and writing the script, but they tend to run into trouble when it comes to their portrayal of the characters or concepts, so it's important that you coach them on this crucial aspect. As you visit each group, ask the members to explain their characters to you. How will they enter? What clothing will convey that character? How will they portray that character's personality rather than their own? Remind them that the answers to all of those questions should be written into the stage directions. As rehearsals progress, pair up groups and have them act as audiences for one another. Review the rubric with the class before this rehearsal and instruct the audiences to view the performances with an eye on the rubric, helping the other group recognize where they've hit the mark and where they need more work.

Also, as kids move from writing to rehearsal, it's best to discourage them from attempting to use dialects other than their own. Though I don't think they intend it, these amateur attempts at accents sometimes contribute to ethnically insensitive, stereotypical portrayals. Besides, accents are hard to do even for professional actors. Put *Titanic* on your Netflix list and when you watch it, play this game: do a shot (assuming you are of age) or eat some junk food every time Leonardo DiCaprio drops his Irish brogue. By the end of the movie you will be flat on your face or begging for antacid. But then, once you've sufficiently recovered, take a look at Leonardo DiCaprio in *Blood Diamond*, made approximately ten years later. In this film he manages to sustain a flawless South African accent. Bottom line: it takes years to master accents other than your own.

Assessment Live!

There is some real excitement on Talk Show Day, almost like the opening night of a play. The kids are in their costumes and the audience is in for some great surprises. None of us will ever forget Michelle's Tony award–caliber performance as Ann Putnam (you saw the script at the beginning of this chapter). In class, Michelle quietly participated in her small-group discussions, but no one ever heard her speak in a whole-class setting. She was not one to raise her hand and command everyone's attention, yet when she performed, that's exactly what she did. The story of her dead babies was heart rending, her voice filled with anger as she accused Rebecca Nurse of their murders, and her sobbing seemed real when "Oprah" handed her a tissue and broke for a commercial. That's what is so cool about assessments that shift modality. I see a whole different cohort of kids succeeding. It's not that they don't know the material; it's just that we often don't give these kids the best way for them to show what they know.

Depending on the size of your class and the number of groups, you might be able to fit all of your Talk Show performances into a single period. Don't worry about it getting boring. While you can definitely watch too many PowerPoint presentations in one period, you can never watch too many talk shows. On the day of the performances, videorecord each Talk Show. The students will need the recording for self-evaluation and you can harvest good examples to use as future models. After seeing one good student video, everyone understands the project and will work to make their performance as good as the one they reviewed.

The day after the performances, replay the video of all the projects, so students can self-evaluate, take notes on the content, and note what makes a good performance.

Content

- What key character traits came out in the performances?

- How did the shows portray conflicts between the characters?

- What actual lines from the source material did groups incorporate into their scripts?

- In what ways did departures from the source make sense and offer insight into the characters?

Performance

- What makes a good talk show?

- What techniques, bits, or character interactions worked well?

- What problems did a lot of the groups seem to have in common?

- How could groups plan and rehearse differently to eliminate these problems?

After viewing the video, discuss the content and performance notes as a large group. While the content discussion offers students yet another opportunity to rehearse important information, the observations and reflections put forth during the performance discussion will offer future guidance. These points can be used as a reminder for students when they embark on their next drama-oriented live assessment or the chart can serve as great advice for next year's students when they are practicing their Talk Shows. Figure 9.3 shows what my students noted as they watched the repeat performance of their Talk Shows based on *The Crucible*.

Self-Assessment

In addition to the content and performance note taking, students need to sit up and pay extra special attention to their own performances. When the video rolls to their Talk Show, each student should score themselves on the rubric for each criterion, checking off the specific descriptors they met. I tell students that I will be collecting their self-assessments and comparing them with my own observations. Since I sometimes miss details and nuances of their individual performances, it's important that they also include notes about the details they want me to notice. For example, if a student checks off "holds audience's attention," it would benefit them to include some notes on the scoring sheet about how they attempted to do that in their acting. Of course, as the students observe, reflect, and assess, I jot down grading notes too. Combining the student self-evaluation with my own observations gives me plenty of data in order to render a grade, so I seldom need to take the video home for a second viewing.

Predictable Problems

The first time the kids try this, expect varied results. Some shows may be amateurish yet entertaining but others will astound you. That quiet guy at the corner desk will suddenly come alive playing Stanley Kowalski (*A Streetcar Named Desire*) on the Jerry Springer Show. However, as with all Assessment Live! activities, the main goal is for kids to review the content and take it to the next level. Not everyone is going to be a great actor; it's the thinking behind each script that is truly important.

FIGURE 9.3

STUDENT THOUGHTS ON WHAT MAKES A GOOD TALK SHOW

Script and Speaking

- Speak slowly and clearly
- Host should give good description when introducing each guest
- Write script so that people who haven't read the book understand what's going on—give enough background info
- Audience can follow script easily
- Write script so that it covers the important parts of the book
- Speak loudly
- Rehearse lines—don't say *um, like, you know*
- Make sure host gives enough details so that audience understands what's going on
- Stress some words over others
- Characters should give their opinions, make a specific point
- Talk with enthusiasm
- Give a good summary of the book to get the audience interested
- Put emotion in voice; don't talk monotone
- End by giving the audience something to think about—don't just trail off

Acting

- Don't look bored—look excited, like you're having fun, give it some spunk
- Memorize your lines—don't stare down at your paper
- Talk and dress like the characters in the book—shows characters' personalities—distinguish the characters so that the audience can tell them apart easily
- Get into character; don't play yourself
- Make the conversation sound casual, real
- Use lots of props
- Interact with the other characters—look interested in them—react to what they are saying
- Know when you are supposed to speak—act like you know what's going on
- Use humor when appropriate
- Look at the audience
- Sit up straight, don't fidget
- Act confident
- Use gestures and facial expressions
- Show some action—don't just sit there
- Use cue cards for audience

Quick Guide: Talk-Show

1. Introduce the Talk Show project. Show recorded Talk Show examples and analyze them for structure and interview style. Explain that the kids will be creating their own Talk Show based on one of these formats.

2. Present students with a play excerpt and study the conventions of script writing: how character dialogue is written, what is included in stage directions.

3. Students create groups of four to six and meet to negotiate show style, which characters will be portrayed, and basic storylines for interview segments. All students must have an acting role.

4. Groups begin their script writing in class. If the entire script is to written in class, each student keeps his own handwritten copy of the script as they work. Or groups may begin their work in class and then allow a "head writer" to finish the writing. The "head writer" takes the rough script and other ideas home, adds final touches, and prints copies for the group.

5. Each group reconvenes to read through the script and apply revisions.

6. The "head writer" makes revisions; prints out new copies. Or each member takes home his handwritten copy and types up a final draft version of the script.

7. The groups rehearse their talk shows, incorporating their stage directions. Ten-minute rehearsal sessions are conducted over three to five consecutive days.

8. Performance! A copy of the final script is turned in to the teacher on performance day.

9. On a later day, students view the performance video recording. They evaluate their own performances against the rubric, adding notes of explanation when necessary. Students also take notes on other performances, noting how information was conveyed as well as what worked well in regards to script, line delivery, and acting.

CHAPTER

10

Storytelling

What Is It?

Storytelling is exactly that: A story that is told out loud (from memory) with the purpose of entertaining and informing an audience.

Now it's pretty obvious that Storytelling could be a great assessment for language arts or English classes. But it also works in the world of facts and concepts that make up the curriculum in science, social studies, or mathematics. One of the acclaimed nonfiction trade books of recent years has been David Bodanis' $E=mc^2$ (2005). In this book, Bodanis explains Einstein's theory of relativity (now there are some hard core facts!) completely through storytelling. He writes accounts of the discoveries of all the previous scientists on whose shoulders Einstein finally stood, and through pure narrative gives the reader a deep understanding of this tremendously challenging concept. So Storytelling can work across the curriculum.

A great way to jump into studying storytelling with your students is to research urban legends, those bare bones stories that spread on the Internet as if they were truth (but are in reality fictitious though cautionary tales). These stories cry out for personalization, additional imagery details, and then a good oral telling. Once kids get the idea of how to tell a good story, the possibilities are endless since all subject areas have lots of great stories that need telling (see the list, which just scratches the surface of story possibilities, in the Why and When to Use It section). Plus, telling a story requires creativity, an important skill necessary for success in a career in any of our content areas. There is no such thing as unimaginative scientists, historians, or mathematicians (Norton 2008). And, don't feel as if your content-area storytelling is limited to previously existing stories—*any* original stories your kids make up can help them think more deeply about the material as long as their storytelling remains faithful to the important facts. Also, as I've mentioned earlier, telling a good story requires lots of practice and requires the kind of rehearsal that is essential for long-term memory retention.

Why and When to Use It

When kids tell stories, they internalize the information and make it their own in a very personalized way. The Storytelling assessment capitalizes on the power of emotional connections made between the person and the message. If you want your kids to remember something long after your class is over, have them create and tell stories about it. When students complete research assignments, make the final assessment a story they've created based on the information they studied rather a formal paper, a PowerPoint with bullets, or an oral report accompanied by a poster. Furthermore, crafting a good story means persistent revision, which is something that is often absent from other research project assessments. And the revision and oral practice required to tell a good story is the kind of rehearsal that builds memory as well (Sylwester 1995).

Though the study of urban legends is a great springboard for introducing Storytelling, every content area has lots of great tales that need retelling:

- *History:* It's full of stories! And lots of times we teachers are the ones telling them. Now wouldn't it be great if the kids told some of those stories instead of us?

- *Geography:* Legends of different countries and cultures are great to revisit and retell.

- *Psychology:* Find stories that changed psychology. Who wouldn't want to tell the story of Phineas Gage, a railroad worker who had a misfortunate accident when a large iron rod pierced his head, destroying both frontal lobes? The result: His personality completely changed!

- *Science:* Research famous scientists and their discoveries.

- *Math:* Learn about famous mathematicians and their discoveries.

These are the stories of people who shaped our fields of study. These stories give our content areas a human dimension. Why ignore the stories that might pull kids into those subjects in a new and richer way?

In addition, the skills students need to effectively practice and value the art of conversation itself are worth strengthening. Going beyond our own content areas, I believe there is an increasing need for teachers to promote performance and oral tradition, to ensure students can be articulate speakers in later life. Thanks to email and text messaging, Facebook and Twitter, people are talking to each other less and less.

However, even in this new era of communication technology, many business dealings still need to be conducted face to face. At a recent party, I talked with a friend who works at large Chicago law firm. She complained that "the youngsters" just didn't know how to

Standards Skills Students Will Practice

Reading	Writing	Speaking/Listening
■ Analyze interactions between main and subordinate characters in a literary text	■ Use precise language	■ Assess how language and delivery affect the mood and tone
■ Analyze characteristics of subgenres (e.g., satire, parody) that are used in poetry, prose, plays, novels, short stories, essays, and other basic genres	■ Synthesize information from multiple sources	■ Use appropriate rehearsal to achieve command of the text and skillful artistic staging
■ Read, view, and interpret texts and performances in every medium	■ Revise writing to improve the logic and coherence	■ Recite poems, selections from speeches, or dramatic soliloquies with attention to performance details
■ Recognize unstated assumptions	■ Write historical investigation reports	■ Listen respectfully and responsively
■ Recognize and analyze the relevance of literature to contemporary and/or personal events and situations	■ Use tone and language appropriate to the audience and purpose	■ Apply delivery techniques, such as voice projection, and demonstrate physical poise
■ Share reading experiences with a peer or adult	■ Use prewriting activities	■ Use nonverbal communication techniques to help convey message
■ Engage in a variety of collaborative conversations	■ Use the writing process	■ Recognize the use and impact of effective language
	■ Take notes from written and oral texts	■ Respond to constructive criticism
	■ Evaluate written work for its effectiveness and make recommendations for its improvement	■ Deliver impromptu and planned oral presentations
	■ Evaluate research information, present in logical manner	■ Present orally original work supported by research

interact with their coworkers effectively. When a real face-to-face conversation needed to take place, they still chose to email. And when they did talk with the "adults," they lacked the poise and basic social skills required to come across as competent and focused; instead they came off as distant and unmotivated. Don't forget; these are twenty-somethings with law degrees, so on some level we know that they are smart! Being able to confidently converse with a coworker and convey your message with a story is an important skill. According to *The Leader's Guide to Storytelling* by Stephen Denning, someone who can tell the right story at the right time is generally a more effective manager (2005).

Time Requirement

Five class periods spread out between two weeks is needed.

Starting with the End in Mind

The rubric provided in Figure 10.1 focuses on three main criteria: the story, the delivery, and the overall performance. As students develop their stories, the focus is on adding details and word choices in order to create imaginative yet believable and entertaining tales. Later in the process of telling, students turn their focus to the delivery and performance aspects.

Figure 10.2 shows a scoring sheet used for student self-evaluation and teacher grading. Notice that several aspects of the story are scored separately and given extra weight, while delivery and performance are scored holistically.

Getting Ready

Choosing the Stories

Classic urban legends, textbook story sidebars, Aesop's fables, or American folktales all work well as story starters because they are already written yet yearn for a storyteller to embellish them with his own unique details. Look for pieces that are short, dramatic, and, when told well, seem completely believable despite their hyperbole. And the kids enjoy the stories, so the work of writing, revising, practicing, and performing does not seem quite so onerous.

Urban legends are easy to find. A quick Internet search using the keywords "classic urban legends" will reveal pages of potential material. Probably the most famous site

FIGURE 10.1 Storytelling Rubric

C	B	A
Story	**Story**	**Story**
■ Basic plot is clear and easy to understand ■ Story contains three acts (clear beginning, middle, and end)	■ Characters fleshed out with interesting details ■ Clear, believable setting ■ Definite elements of hyperbole ■ Seems as if it really happened ■ Story reveals significant information/research (if applicable)	■ Creative, imaginative ■ Uses concrete nouns and vivid verbs ■ Point of view clear—story told by character, bystander, someone who heard it secondhand, etc. ■ Story weaves significant information/research with imaginative details (if applicable)
Delivery	**Delivery**	**Delivery**
■ Clear diction ■ Confident stance ■ Easily heard ■ Correct pacing (no fast talk)	■ Good eye contact with audience ■ Voice connects emotion with story details ■ Facial expressions match words	■ Integrated use of vocal interpretation, gestures, and movement
Performance	**Performance**	**Performance**
■ Memorized—few stumbles ■ Less than 3 minutes	■ Holds attention of audience ■ Knows story well, no stumbles ■ 3–5 minutes long	■ Audience thoroughly entertained ■ Very polished ■ Tells story confidently and naturally ■ 5 minutes long

FIGURE 10.2 *Storytelling Scoring Sheet*

STORYTELLING PERFORMANCE

Name _____

Original source story title _____

Title of your story _____

Directions: As you watch the video, rate yourself in the following categories based on the rubric. Please jot down any notes about performance details you want me to notice before I assign the final grade. Do not simply repeat the rubric phrases. Attach the final draft of your story to the scoring sheet.

Category	Points	Weight	Score
Story: Details	1 2 3 4 5	x 6	/30
Story: Concrete nouns and vivid verbs	1 2 3 4 5	x 2	/10
Story: Believability	1 2 3 4 5	x 2	/10
Delivery	1 2 3 4 5	x 5	/25
Performance	1 2 3 4 5	x 5	/25

Total Points /100

related to this category is Snopes.com because their mission is to debunk urban legends. Plus, there are tons of urban legend books. *Urban Legends: 666 Absolutely True Stories That Happened to a Friend…of a Friend…of a Friend* by Thomas Craughwell (2005) is a complete collection, but my favorite is *The Big Book of Urban Legends* by Jan H. Brunvand (1994). What makes this book different from the others is that the stories are told in graphic novel style and each story is told completely and concisely in one page. When students use these stories as the foundation for their own, they automatically have to fill in the gaps and provide the embellishment. Also, studying the drawings closely will give them ideas for the story details. Unfortunately, *The Big Book* is out of print, but a quick trip to Amazon.com shows used copies for sale.

Rather than sending your kids straight to these books or websites, I recommend you peruse the legends yourself and make up your own collection. Pick the ones with a dramatic story as well as those that are school appropriate. The problem with having the kids search for their own tale is that so many urban legends are pretty lurid, revolving around sex, violence, or perversion, topics for which you probably don't want to create a classroom audience. Nor do you want parents complaining about your corrupt influence upon their child when another student tells the story of how he accidentally microwaved his pet. When preparing your legend collection, work to find a different story for every student in class. That way there will be no repetition or competition in the telling. Though it may sound overwhelming, you'll be surprised at how quickly you'll find twenty or thirty different suitable stories. When your collection is complete, create a classroom set. Give each story a separate number and put each story on a separate page. Finally, make up a set of slips for each class, each with a different story number. Then you can assign the stories using a "grab bag" approach. Everyone randomly draws a number and then each slip is exchanged for the corresponding story.

Introducing the Art of Storytelling

Rather than announcing a Storytelling project, I like to creep up on my unsuspecting audience with my own personalized urban legend.

Beehive Story Example

Last night I happened to be visiting my parents; they still live in the house I grew up in. As I was leaving, I glanced at the house across the street and remembered something that happened to my neighbor, an accident I hadn't thought of in years.

When I was growing up in the early sixties, I remember three things that were popular: beatniks, The Beatles, and beehive hairdos. There was a girl who lived across the street from me named Linda. She was in high school and I was in second grade. From my seven-year-old perspective, she seemed to have it all. Boys were always dropping by her house and most of them drove Mustangs or Camaros. Even though Linda was attractive, I think what really made her cool was her beehive hairdo. Nowadays when we think of beehive hairdos we think of Marge Simpson, but back in the early sixties beehives were high fashion and the bigger the better. It seemed like every week Linda's hair grew taller. When I mentioned this to my mother, she said it wasn't my imagination. Every time Linda saw another girl at Riverside-Brookfield with a beehive almost as tall as hers, Linda canceled her dates and marched straight to the beauty parlor, demanding that her hair be ratted higher and higher. My mother also told me that I should never ever think about getting a beehive because once the hair is set you can't wash it or brush it or even touch it if you want it to keep its shape. Plus, you have to sleep sitting up. Even though I knew Linda must have been uncomfortable and sleep deprived, she still looked like the coolest teenager I had ever seen and I would have traded places with her in a second...that is until that one fateful day.

Summer vacation had just started and June was turning out to be a pretty hot month. Since this was way before air conditioning was commonplace, everyone in the neighborhood had their windows open. That's why we all heard these blood-curdling shrieks coming from Linda's house. An ambulance arrived, and all the neighbors flew out of their houses to see what had happened. Being first on the scene, I saw the emergency workers carry Linda out the front door on a stretcher. She looked like she was in a coma and her face was covered in blood. I was pretty close and I tried to get closer for a better look. Just then my mother yanked me by the arm, dragged me back into our house, and told me to quit being so nosy. My mother had a knack for ruining my fun.

From that day on, I spent a lot of my time sneaking peeks out the front window when my mother's back was turned. I never did find out exactly when Linda got out of the hospital, but one day I saw her mother pushing her down the sidewalk in a wheel chair. I was shocked! Her beehive was gone, replaced by what looked like a crew cut. To top it off, she looked totally out of it. Her head lolled to one side and a string of drool hung from her mouth. Her eyes were open yet unseeing. Even though I was only in second grade, I could tell that the Linda I had known didn't live at that address anymore. I kept asking my mother what happened to Linda, but all she ever said was that it was none of my business, so I asked my nosy next-door neighbor, Mary, instead.

Mary was retired and spent part of every day combing the neighborhood for juicy bits of gossip and she knew all about Linda. She told me Linda was the victim of a spider! Apparently, the top of her beehive had brushed against a spider web. When the spider got in her hair, it found a pretty safe place since Linda never ever touched her hair. So, the spider laid its eggs. A few days later, the baby spiders hatched, and some of them crawled into her ear. By the time she went to get her beehive redone at the beauty parlor, all of the spiders had disappeared so her beautician never noticed anything unusual even though the spiders were already crawling down her ear canal and eating up her brain. When she passed out a few days later, her brain was half gone and nothing could be done to help her. No boys ever visited Linda again.

After the telling, the kids automatically ask rather uncertainly, "That isn't true, is it?" If my timing is right, that's when the bell rings. And if my timing is off, I suggest that they try to find out for themselves. After checking with other teachers, their parents, or Snopes.com, the kids return to class the following day and announce the story wasn't true. Of course, I admit it's an urban legend but also point out that I told it in a convincing manner that made them picture the story and believe it (at least partially). Now the students are hooked and are ready to try out Storytelling for themselves.

Writing the Story

The day following my own oral Storytelling performance, I pass out a written version of my story, which was based on "The Spider in the Beehive" story found in *The Big Book of Urban Legends.* I want them to understand how much of what I wrote I totally made up. As I read through the written story, I point out how I personalized it by adding pieces from my own life, which are what make it believable. I also point out the importance of having the teller of an urban legend be in some way connected to the victim (yes, every urban legend needs a victim) as either a participant, a witness, or a relative or friend.

Now it's time for the urban legend grab bag mentioned earlier using those numbered slips. Put the slips in a fish bowl and have the students each choose one. Then have the students trade in their numbers for the corresponding story. After reading it a couple of times, everyone jots down ideas and details from their own lives they could use to embellish the story and make it sound true. As the final step, for homework or the following day in class, have the students write their stories. With ample details, the drafts should be between 500 and 700 words, far longer than the original stories which typically run 200 words or less.

Revision

Read Around

For the first day spent on revision, students should bring in a typed copy of their completed story, double-spaced, and without their names. Ask the kids to come up with a combination of six characters that combine numbers and capital letters in order to create an identifying code for them. Here's a good example: THX777. Here's a not so good example: ASSS69. Since the codes become part of the sharing, insist that they not spell out swear words or allude to other gross-out content. Then have the class form groups of four. The following are steps for a read-around, a useful strategy adapted from Kelly Gallagher's book *Teaching Adolescent Writers* (2006).

1. Each four-member group needs one sheet of paper on which to record their reader responses. Passing the paper around to each member, everyone prints their first and last name at the top. Then the group assigns one member to be the Recorder (the person who will keep the response sheet).

2. The group gathers up their own four stories and passes them on to another group. (By the time the read-around is completed, each set of papers should have reached each group in turn, so depending on your room setup, plan for an orderly and consistent way for this passing to occur.)

3. Now the groups pass out the new stories to their members so that each student has one to read.

4. Members read that story for one minute until the teacher says, "Pass." Of course, students will not be able to read the whole story in a minute, probably only the first page. For timing this, you can use a computer, clock, or stopwatch. The most fun way is if you have your computer hooked up to an LCD projector. Go to www.online-stopwatch.com. There are all sorts of different displays, but I like to just set it to count down from four minutes.

5. After each member has read one minute's worth of all four stories, the groups stop and discuss which one they thought was the most effective and why. The recorder writes down that story's code and the group's reasons for picking it. For urban legends, and actually most stories, students should be looking for the following:

   ■ Believability

   ■ Specific imagery details

- Dialogue

- Complete story

- Build-up to some sort of surprise or ending "twist."

Write the criteria on the board so that they are a constant reminder. When the groups jot down their reasons, tell them to explain, for example, what they liked about the ending. They should not just write down "ending."

6. After groups record their votes, the stories are gathered and passed on to the next group. This continues until all groups have read all the papers.

7. Once the reading is completed, the stories stay with the last group. They are not immediately returned to their owners.

8. One at a time or together if your board is big enough, the recorders go up to the board and write down the codes of the stories their group chose.

9. When the votes are in, the class looks for the codes that have multiple endorsements and then search for them in their current pile of stories.

10. Once found, volunteers from the groups, not the author, read a minute's worth of the "winning" stories to the class. The stories' authors are always kept secret. The point of the read-around is to provide a checkpoint for feedback, not a competition or humiliation.

11. After the read-alouds, the groups' reader response papers with the votes are turned in and the stories are returned to the owners.

After the read-around, I instruct the students to make their stories better. They've seen how entertaining (or not) some of the other stories are. They need to take those good ideas from others and transform their own papers, remembering the criteria listed in step 5. The read-around is a great wake-up call. The kids who, up to this point, haven't put in much effort, now realize their drafts *do* need some work. And seeing what other students have done effectively can help those who are struggling to better envision the assignment. Also, even those whose papers were read aloud in the end can still pick up some technique and craft from the others in order to already enhance a good story.

Peer Conferencing

The next draft is due a couple of days after the read-around. In pairs or groups of three, students take turns reading their revised stories aloud. Since this story will be published orally, members need to hear the story rather than see it. They need to listen carefully and think about the following:

- What would help grab the audience in beginning?

- Where does the story lose direction or make it hard to follow?

- What details or story parts need to be cut?

- Which lines or details really work?

- What needs to be added?

- How can the ending be changed to increase the surprise element?

After each student reads her paper, group members give their suggestions, which the author writes down. The final drafts are due two days later. Notice that editing for grammar, spelling, and conventions has been eliminated since the stories will be heard not read. Nevertheless, if you collect the drafts, you'll notice that a substantial amount of editing has taken place just because of the conferencing.

Rehearsal

On the day the final drafts of the stories are due, students return to their original groups. First, they read their final drafts to their group. Then they pass the paper to another member and tell the story from memory. Each student takes a turn reading their tale aloud and then retelling it without the written text. Explain to the students that during this practice, the storyteller should stand in front of the group in a confident stance (feet shoulder-width apart, back straight, maintaining eye contact with the listeners). As the teller performs, the member holding the story can give cues if the teller forgets something.

After a telling, the group should look over the paper and underline all of the really good lines, the lines with great phrasing and description that should be used just as they are when the story is told orally. Good storytelling is not pure invention but is actually a combination of carefully honed great lines and improvisation. For homework, ask students to make sure that they internalize their final draft. Rather than memorize the story word for word, students should visualize it, trying to see each scene clearly and in as much detail as possible. As they tell the story, the scenes should be playing in their heads. However, students should try to commit their most descriptive, well-phrased lines to memory because they really work in the story.

As they practice for homework, students should also begin to time themselves; each story should take between three to five minutes. If the story is under three minutes, there probably isn't enough detail. If the story is over five minutes, it needs cutting or the teller needs to become more organized since the present performance is probably cluttered with unnecessary pauses and stalls. After the first official practice, develop a practice chart that specifically defines what good practicing looks like. This keeps students focused on what to work on as well as makes it clear what you are monitoring for. Figure 10.3 shows an example.

On the subsequent days of practice, students hone their delivery and performance. Each student should stand and practice as if she were actually performing before the class. As the group members continue to coach the teller, remind them to time the delivery as well. If the teller goes longer than five minutes, members need to figure out what the teller has to change so that the story comes in at five minutes or less. (If necessary,

FIGURE 10.3 Sample Practice Chart

WHAT DOES GOOD REHEARSAL LOOK AND SOUND LIKE?

Looks Like	Sounds Like
■ One person is telling	■ One person talking at a time
■ Teller is using confident stance	■ Discussing performance and story—on task
■ Listeners focus on the teller and ignore other groups	■ Recognizing the good parts of a telling—compliments
■ Listeners look interested	■ Asking teller questions that help him or her think about the performance:
■ Enthusiastic storytelling	• "Where should you pause?"
■ Eye contact	• "What kind of gesture should go with that line?"
■ Teller uses gestures and facial expressions	• "Will you talk loudly or softly in this part?"
■ Listeners give teller suggestions	• "Which part of your story do you like the best? How can you use that idea in the rest of your story?"
■ Speaker jots down suggestions on story	• "What do you want us to help you with?"
■ Timekeeper is keeping track of time	• "What could you exaggerate just a little bit more?"

have groups assign a member to take on the role of timekeeper and either use a stopwatch or face the classroom clock.)

Observe the practicing carefully. Use the Practice Chart as you make short interventions, noting what they are doing well or what a group might need to attend to. Give students only enough time for each member to run through their performance once or twice on any given day. Insist that tellers stand when it is their turn to perform. This makes it very easy for you to verify whether groups are on- or off-task. Also, the tellers will be standing when performing for the class, so they might as well get used to it now!

Assessment Live!

The final performances are the main assessment, but do not hesitate to assess the process as well. Though I do not read the rough drafts, I do check them in and I develop a good feel for content as I peer over shoulders during the read-around and listen in on the practicing. And while I eavesdrop, I also offer short impromptu performance coaching and writing conferences aimed at one important revision, the missing element that when added will take the story to the next level. Students do receive points for participating in the read-around and in their work groups. I assign points for practice, using the "What Does Good Rehearsal Look and Sound Like?" chart as an assessment checklist. If students want all the points, they had better be exhibiting the defined behaviors!

Depending on the size of your class, presentation of all the stories could take several days. Though you might think groups would be bored by the stories they've heard repeatedly during practice, they are not. Groups are invested in each other's stories and want to see their members enthrall the crowd. Therefore, they are great supportive audience members even though they totally know how the story will end. Remind students as often as necessary that the stories should be three to five minutes in length, and, if you want to go all Tough Love on this, tell them that after five minutes they'll have to leave the stage whether or not they've finished.

Once the stories are completed, give students the opportunity to talk about the content they learned. Even in the case of urban legends, there's a chance to talk about the embedded cautionary lessons as well as why urban legends persist and multiply even now.

As I'm always saying, videorecord the presentations if you can. It is unlikely that you'll have class time to watch all the performances a second time, but it's not hard to roll a television/VCR out into the hall and have each student step outside the room for five minutes to watch his or her own performance in order to complete a self-assessment. Plus, if you have any outstanding storytellers, you'll be able to show that model to your students next year.

Predictable Problems

As I mention time and again, it's important that you continually monitor the room as the kids practice, intervening whenever you notice group work that is not matching up with the chart. Don't be afraid to pull up a chair and join a group. Listen to part of a telling, give a suggestion or two, and move on. This listening in is important because you want to catch problems early. Lots of times I find that the students' written stories are pretty good, but then they fall apart in the telling. If this is the case, take a timeout and return to the activities in Chapter 2 to review performance skills. You could try warming up with Applause Pass, practice emotions with the tongue twisters, and then make gestures with the game Who Are You and What Are You Doing? Then have students go back to their groups and try some re-energized storytelling. When kids grasp the importance of stage presence and delivery, their stories will totally capture their audience because the personalized details are ones taken from everyday teen life, as Katie's tanning bed story reveals.

Urban Legend Example, Katie's Tanning Bed Story

Last week my best friend Julie invited me to the salon where her aunt works and she told us this totally bizarre story that she had heard from one of her customers. Believe me, by the time I finish, you are NEVER going to want to get into a tanning bed ever again!

Susan, the customer's niece, was invited to be the maid of honor at her best friend's wedding. Knowing that she had to look perfect for Alisha's wedding photos, Susan practically had a stroke the day before the wedding when she had a curling iron accident. Trying to talk on her cell phone while also curling her hair, she wasn't paying attention and ended up burning herself on the neck and shoulders. Now the burns weren't that bad and would eventually heal, but the wedding was the following day and the bridesmaids' dresses were strapless! First she experimented with makeup, but the foundations and concealers only made the burns look redder and uglier. Alisha was going to be so mad at her! What was she going to do?

That's when she thought of the tanning salon. Maybe if she got a tan, the burns would fade or maybe blend in better. So Susan rushed out of the house, jumped in her car, and stopped at the first tanning spa she saw.

Up front, the attendant told Susan that since this was her first time using a tanning bed she could only tan for fifteen minutes.

"But that's not enough time!" Susan wailed. "How am I going to have a good tan by tomorrow if I can only tan for fifteen minutes?"

Clearly annoyed, the attendant sighed, "You can't. Even if you weren't new to tanning, it would still take a few weeks to get a good tan. Tanning bed tanning can be really dangerous in large amounts. Believe it or not, too much time in a tanning bed could actually cook you."

"Yeah, right, I am *so* certain," Susan thought to herself as she entered room five, stripped to her undies, laid down on the bed, and donned the protective goggles. "I just won't set the timer. Maybe the attendant will forget and let me tan longer."

Exactly fifteen minutes later, the attendant was pounding on the door, demanding she get up and get dressed. Checking herself out in the mirror, Susan's burns looked just as mean and the rest of her skin didn't look tanned at all. What was she going to do?

Then she had it. She could just keep going to different spas all day, fifteen minutes here, fifteen minutes there. Those minutes would add up and by the end of the day she'd have a great tan just in time for Alisha's wedding. Fifteen tanning beds later, Susan looked like she had spent a week on the beach in Jamaica. Plus, her burn was blending in with the tan! Everything was going to turn out fine after all. Susan was so happy she called her boyfriend, Tony, and he suggested they go out for dinner.

At the restaurant, Susan couldn't help noticing that other parties seated next to them kept requesting different tables after just a few minutes. It was so weird. Finally, Susan asked Tony if he could explain it.

Uncomfortably, Tony replied, "Honey, I didn't want to say anything, but you do smell kind of bad, sort of like charred meat or something—like a steak some-one forgot on the grill."

Just before she fainted, Susan told Tony she had been to fifteen different tan-ning beds earlier that day. Tony picked her up, lugged her to the car, and drove like a maniac to the emergency room. The doctor ran some tests and came back with the results. All that tanning had microwaved her organs; her insides were completely cooked and shriveled! She probably wouldn't live another twenty-four hours! Susan never made it to Alisha's wedding.

Variations

Reducing Presentation Time

For classes with twenty-five or thirty students, individual presentations could fill a week or more of class periods. If that is a concern, have students work with a partner. Together they will write the story and determine how they will tell it as a team. On the day of the read-around, have students work in groups of six, partners reading each paper together simultaneously. For practice, put two pairs together. While one pair performs, the other listens and makes suggestions.

Folktales, Fairy Tales, and Myths

Though this project is demonstrated with urban legends, fairy tales, myths, or folklore are all highly adaptable. Social studies students might research folklore, either American or world. Americanfolklore.net offers loads of half-page American folklore stories while the University of North Carolina at Chapel Hill's site "Stories, Legends, and Folktales Around the World" is a great resource for international folktales. It would be easy to create a class collection of folktales from one of these sites and then follow the process previously outlined.

The Storytelling project could be extended with an historical figure research project. After students read and take notes, they write an original story based on their historical research (possibly throwing in a bit of hyperbole, an element that is a key ingredient of many tales).

Quick Guide: Storytelling

1. Develop a source collection so that each student will have a different story and no storytelling is duplicated.

2. Start the project by telling your own story, which is based on the genre your students will use.

3. Pass out copies of the original story source as well as your embellished personalized version that you wrote.

4. Start with the story number grab bag and then have students trade in the number for the story it corresponds to. Students read their original story and then write their own personalized story based on the source. Set the due date for first draft.

5. Conduct a read-around. Allow time for content revisions.

6. Students meet in revision/practice groups. Stories are read aloud and suggestions are made. Allow time for content revisions. Set the due date for final draft.

7. Students continue practicing performance by reading their final drafts aloud to group and then telling the story from memory, members cueing the teller as needed.

8. Students practice the story at home, memorizing key lines word for word, but mostly working to visually memorize the scenes. As they tell the story, the scenes should be playing in their heads.

9. Give students a few days (fifteen to twenty minutes per period) to practice their telling. Use the practice chart for assessing the quality of practice and the rubric for making specific improvement suggestions. The teacher monitors consistently. Remind tellers to stand whenever it is their turn to practice.

10. Perform stories and complete self-evaluations. Discuss the content as well as the embedded messages revealed in urban legends or cultural folklore.

CHAPTER

11

Songs That Make Ideas Stick

What Is It?

Have you ever heard anyone say, "Oh, I can't memorize anything"? It might have been a student or an adult. It might even be something you've said yourself. Now think about this: Have you ever caught yourself singing along to a tune while driving? Really, who hasn't? But wait a minute, if someone *can't memorize anything*, why can he remember the words to a song without even trying? Gotcha. It turns out that music uses a different part of the brain than spoken language. Pairing language with melody enables the brain to flex its mental muscles, add some weight to the barbell, and dead lift with ease because the brain loves rhyme and rhythm (Wolfe 2001b). Want the kids to remember something forever? Have them write a song about it and sing it. The song doesn't have to complicated; familiar nursery rhyme tunes can take on a whole new meaning.

Check out the new lyrics written to the tune of "Twinkle, Twinkle, Little Star." This song is no longer about stars; it's about the Supreme Court decision of 1857 concerning *Dred Scott v. Sanford*. The Court determined that slaves were not citizens and therefore had no rights afforded U.S. citizens, which meant a slave could not file a lawsuit. This opinion expanded slave owner's rights and even questioned the legality of free state laws that prohibited people from bringing slaves in or selling them in free states. The decision heightened tensions between the North and the South, galvanized the resolve of the abolitionist movement, and probably hastened the Civil War. Seems like a pretty important moment in our country's history, yet I'm willing to bet that if you stood on a busy street corner and asked passersby about the Dred Scott decision, most would just give you a shrug. But the chances are good that your kids would remember that decision if they learned it in connection with a song.

Original Lyrics	New Lyrics
Twinkle, twinkle, little star,	Dred Scott lived in Missouri,
How I wonder what you are!	Then moved to a state's that free.
Up above the world so high,	Claimed that freedom was his right.
Like a diamond in the sky.	Filed suit, prepared to fight.
Twinkle, twinkle, little star,	High court ruled slaves not citizens.
How I wonder what you are!	Existing laws didn't apply to him.

Of course, this song, created quickly during the last few minutes of a class, does not capture every detail of the *Dred Scott* decision, but it's still a great quick summary of the prose explanation and one that is far more likely to be remembered in the future.

So if this is such a great learning strategy, why don't more teachers, other than early primary, use it in their classrooms? Simple—we are afraid! People might sing in the shower or in their cars, but they *don't* sing in public. I was chicken too until a student from another English class told me about the great songs they were writing for Ms. Fear-Petrakis. The student's enthusiasm for the project combined with her teacher's inspired me to try it out and I've been a believer ever since. As long as the classroom environment is friendly and supportive, the kids will be willing to take a risk and sing, writing new lyrics to old songs or possibly even writing original songs.

Why and When to Use It

Taking the time to write a song is time well spent if you are teaching something that you want the kids to recall years later:

- The Bill of Rights

- Three branches of U.S. government

- How a bill becomes a law

- Details surrounding the founding of the thirteen original colonies

- The Missouri compromise

- The process of photosynthesis

- Deciphering the periodic table of the elements

- Stages of cell mitosis

- Cell organelle functions

- The Sun-Earth-Moon system (why we have day/night, seasons, tides, etc.)

This effective activity can be quick and easy to do, yet yield lasting results. When using simple tunes like "Twinkle, Twinkle, Little Star," kids can put their heads together for ten minutes to review the material and hammer out the verse. And later on, those same songs can help them review for an upcoming test.

As a matter of fact, writing a song together as a class is a great way to review a unit you've just finished. Written to the tune of "Lola" by The Kinks, my American literature class collaborated on these lyrics after they finished their unit on Henry David Thoreau:

Thoreau
Met him in the square down in old Concord
Where he talked so long and I thought, man, this is a
Bore B-O-R-E Bore

He caught my snore and he picked me right out
I asked his name and in a brisk sharp voice he said
Thoreau T-H-O-R-E-A-U Thoreau
Thor-Thor-Thor-Thor-Thoreau

Well I'm not the world's most romantic guy
But that "different drummer" sure philosophized
Yeah that's Thoreau Thor-Thor-Thor-Thor Thoreau

At Walden Pond we rowed out on the lake
And we chased some loons but they all got away
Oh my Thoreau Thor-Thor-Thor-Thor Thoreau

Well we huckleberried and we fed the mice
Listened to rain—it was very nice
He whispered, "Simplify," said, "Get rid of your stuff."
That's when I knew I had more than enough

Well I'm not the world's most political guy
But when he bashed the war, the government he'd defy

Thoreau
Thor-Thor-Thor-Thor-Thoreau
Thor-Thor-Thor-Thor-Thoreau

Said John Brown saw
That slavery's wrong
John Brown was strong
He's no crazy fool
Then I realized that Thoreau was no tool

That's when he said, "Go to jail with me."
Skip those evil taxes, show the world what you think
Thor-Thor-Thor-Thor-Thoreau

Self-reliance is the way we should live
Check out Emerson—he's a dude you can dig besides
Thoreau
Thor-Thor-Thor-Thor-Thoreau

Well I left home just a week before
And I'd never ever had transcended before
But Thoreau smiled and took me by the throat
He warned me, "Buddy, you're beginning to gloat."

Well I'm not the world's most political man
But my eyes are open and I see the whole plan
So does Thoreau
Thor-Thor-Thor-Thor-Thoreau
Thor-Thor-Thor-Thor-Thoreau
Thoreau-Thor-Thor-Thor-Thor-Thoreau
Thor-Thor-Thor-Thor-Thoreau

My students had to review their notes as well as several different readings in order to work key details into their lyrics:

- Excerpts from *Walden* and *Civil Disobedience*

- A speech defending abolitionist John Brown after his attack on the Harpers Ferry arsenal

- The play "The Night Thoreau Spent in Jail"
- Biographical pieces on Henry David Thoreau and Ralph Waldo Emerson
- Informational pieces on romanticism and transcendentalism

Time Requirement

One class period is needed for writing and performing short tunes. Plan for three class periods when individual groups write longer songs and then perform them for the rest of the class.

Standards Skills Students Will Practiced

Reading	Writing	Speaking and Listening
■ Interpret and evaluate the impact of ambiguities, subtleties, contradictions, ironies, and incongruities in a text ■ Analyze interactions between main and subordinate characters in a literary text ■ Read, view, and interpret texts and performances in every medium ■ Recognize unstated assumptions ■ Share reading experiences with a peer or adult ■ Engage in a variety of collaborative conversations ■ Explain and justify interpretation	■ Use precise language ■ Synthesize information from multiple sources ■ Revise writing to improve the logic and coherence ■ Use tone and language appropriate to the audience and purpose ■ Use prewriting activities ■ Use the writing process ■ Write for real situations ■ Use electronic formats	■ Use appropriate rehearsal to achieve command of the text and skillful artistic staging ■ Listen respectfully and responsively ■ Apply delivery techniques such as voice projection and demonstrate physical poise ■ Recognize the use and impact of effective language ■ Respond to constructive criticism ■ Determine points of view, clarify positions, make judgments, and form opinions ■ Deliver impromptu and planned oral presentations

Starting with the End in Mind

The song (see Figure 11.1) focuses on the length, originality, and detail of the lyrics as well as the different components of the song performance.

The scoring sheet (Figure 11.2) refers to the various categories defined on the rubric. Notice that category point values vary, with lyrics being the the most heavily weighted category. After all, it is the informational quality of the lyrics that speaks to the degree of student study and review of the content.

Getting Ready

Before starting this project with a class, give them a chance to dip into the art of song parody. Start with a tune everyone knows and get everyone to sing it together: "Twinkle Twinkle, Little Star" (see the example described on p. 176) is a good choice. Students will be timid at first, but run through it a few times and then have some fun with it. Have opposite sides of the room sing alternate lines, standing up when they sing their lines. Or, add a little competition. See which side of the room can sing louder. Each side takes a turn and sings to the other. Once the tune is stuck in their heads, pass out a handout with the original lyrics printed in the left-hand column (see Figure 11.3). Be sure to have an overhead of the handout as well.

First, have students point out the rhyming scheme (AA, BB) and mark it on the overhead as they mark it on their handout. Next, tell them to count the syllables in each line and mark it down. Conveniently, they'll find that each line has seven syllables. Finally, have each pair or trio write new lyrics to the "Twinkle Twinkle" melody based on the short story they've just read, the chapter they've just finished, or the lecture you've just concluded. Students will find it easier to match up rhyming and syllabication by writing their new lyrics in the right-hand column of the handout. Once done, hand out transparencies so that each group can write down their final lyrics. Then, one at a time, each group can get up, present their lyrics, and lead the class in song. It is always interesting to see how different the lyrics are even though both the song and source of inspiration (whatever they've recently studied) are the same. The diverse lyrics are an active demonstration of reader response: there can be many ways to be insightful and be "correct."

Once students understand the steps in writing a song parody, I introduce the assignment directions (Figure 11.4) as well as the rubric (Figure 11.1) and scoring sheet (Figure 11.2).

Even though students have worked through the "Twinkle, Twinkle" example, they still often want another example after they've received the assignment instructions. I've found the kids enjoy singing some songs that previous classes have written. My high

FIGURE 11.1 Song Rubric

C	B	A
Lyrics	**Lyrics**	**Lyrics**
■ Cover basic information ■ Mostly new lyrics ■ Two verses and a chorus	■ Expanded details ■ Totally original lyrics	■ Incorporates text quotes and very specific text details ■ Covers information thoroughly ■ More than two verses
Musical Accompaniment	**Musical Accompaniment**	**Musical Accompaniment**
■ A few stumbles	■ Sings song well with vocal version	■ Displays poise/stage presence during instrumental sections
Rhythm	**Rhythm**	**Rhythm**
■ Stays with beat of song	■ Stays with beat of song and moves to music	■ Stays with beat of song and includes simple choreography
Diction	**Diction**	**Diction**
■ Most words understood	■ All words can be understood	■ Lyrics are crisp, easily understood
Musical Mastery	**Musical Mastery**	**Musical Mastery**
■ Tune is recognizable	■ All members are really singing	■ All members singing confidently
Outside Voice	**Outside Voice**	**Outside Voice**
■ Most of song can be heard	■ All of song can be heard	■ Loud enough to overcome original vocals
Entertainment Value	**Entertainment Value**	**Entertainment Value**
■ Some members have energy	■ All members have energy	■ Singing is lively and energetic

May be photocopied for classroom use. © 2009 by Nancy Steineke from *Assessment Live!* Portsmouth, NH: Heinemann.

FIGURE 11.2 Song Performance Scoring Sheet

SONG PERFORMANCE

Name_____

Original song title and artist _____

Title of your song_____

Directions: As you watch the video, rate yourself in the following categories based on the rubric. Please jot down any notes about performance details you want me to notice before I assign the final grade. Do not simply repeat the rubric phrases. Be sure to turn in all of your group's sheets together, as well as a copy of the original song lyrics and your new lyrics.

Category	Points	Weight	Score
Song Introduction	1 2 3 4 5	X 1	/5
Lyrics Details	1 2 3 4 5	x 6	/30
Lyrics Originality	1 2 3 4 5	X 4	/20
Chorus and Verses	1 2 3 4 5	X 2	/10
Musical Accompaniment	1 2 3 4 5	X 1	/5
Diction and Rythm	1 2 3 4 5	X 2	/10
Outside Voice	1 2 3 4 5	X 2	/10
Musical Mastery	1 2 3 4 5	X 1	/5
Entertainment Value	1 2 3 4 5	X 1	/5

Total Points   **/100**

FIGURE 11.3 Song Lyrics Practice Assignment

Original Lyrics	New Lyrics
Twinkle, twinkle, little star,	
How I wonder what you are!	
Up above the world so high,	
Like a diamond in the sky.	
Twinkle, twinkle, little star,	
How I wonder what you are!	

FIGURE 11.4 Song Assignment

SONG ASSIGNMENT

Working with your current group (book club, discussion group, lab table, etc.) take an existing song, write new lyrics based on what you've read or studied, and perform it for the class.

Why are we doing this?

- It's easier for the brain to remember information when it's in the form of a song.

- Review important information.

- Get other people interested in your book or topic.

Do we have to use an existing song or can we compose an entirely new one?

- Either way—It's your choice.

What do we need to turn in on the due date?

- A typed copy of the new lyrics.

- A copy of the original song lyrics including the title and who originally performed it/wrote it.

Do we need accompaniment?

- Yes. You can sing along with the original CD, bring in a karaoke machine or just the disc and sing along to the background accompaniment, or you can provide your own instrumental accompaniment. (If you bring your own instruments, though, be sure to arrange for storing them safely during the school day.) Also if you're burning a CD, bring it in ahead of time so that we can see if it plays on the room's CD player. And if you plan to use your iPod, remember to bring a docking station with speakers.

How will we be graded?

- Your grade will be a combination of points earned from your planning, practicing, lyric writing, and performing. Review the rubric and scoring sheet handout for more specific details.

school juniors love singing the new lyrics about *To Kill a Mockingbird* to the oldie tune "Build Me Up Buttercup." Though some of them probably grumbled when they were forced to read the novel as sophomores, by the time they're juniors they fondly remember the novel and appreciate the new lyrics.

ORIGINAL LYRICS TO "BUILD ME UP BUTTERCUP"
Originally performed by The Foundations
The song hit # 3 on the Top 40 charts in 1969

CHORUS
Why do you build me up (build me up) Buttercup, baby
Just to let me down (let me down) and mess me around
And then worst of all (worst of all) you never call, baby
When you say you will (say you will) but I love you still
I need you (I need you) more than anyone, darlin'
You know that I have from the start
So build me up (build me up) Buttercup, don't break my heart

VERSE 1
"I'll be over at ten," you told me time and again
But you're late, I wait around and then
I went to the door, I can't take any more
It's not you, you let me down again

(Hey, hey, hey!) Baby, baby, try to find
(Hey, hey, hey!) A little time and I'll make you mine
(Hey, hey, hey!) I'll be home
I'll be beside the phone waiting for you
Ooo-oo-ooo, ooo-oo-ooo

CHORUS

VERSE 2
You were my toy but I could be the boy you adore
If you'd just let me know
Although you're untrue, I'm attracted to you all the more
Why do I need you so

(Hey, hey, hey!) Baby, baby, try to find
(Hey, hey, hey!) A little time and I'll make you mine
(Hey, hey, hey!) I'll be home
I'll be beside the phone waiting for you
Ooo-oo-ooo, ooo-oo-ooo

CHORUS

Student Song Lyrics for *To Kill a Mockingbird*
"Why Don't You Come Outside? (to the tune of "Build Me Up Buttercup")

CHORUS
Why don't you come outside? (come outside)
Come on Boo Radley
Just to talk with us, don't make a fuss
So we can learn (we can learn)
Why you're in there and
What you do inside (do inside)
And why do you hide?
To meet you (to meet you)
Would be great Mr. Arthur
You'd make our dreams come true
So come outside (come outside)
Come on
Talk to us now

VERSE 1
On my way home from school
I found some gum in the tree
I thought it was a gift for me (bah-dah-dah)
I run to the tree, and find a statue of me
It's just you, leaving gifts again

(Hey, hey, hey) Me and Jem, we found some more
(Hey, hey, hey) An arrowhead, a watch, and a penny
(Hey, hey, hey) We went home
Put them in the trunk, and thought of you
Ooo-ooo-ooo, ooo-ooo-ooo

CHORUS

VERSE 2
Walking on home in the dark all alone
Heard a noise, so froze in our tracks (bah-dah-dah)
So unaware of all the dangers that lurked in the night
Why was I scared so bad?
(Hey, hey, hey) I heard Jem cry for help
(Hey, hey, hey) It's too dark to see what's the matter
(Hey, hey, hey) Then you came
And Jem's okay, thanks to you
Ooo-ooo-ooo, ooo-ooo-ooo

CHORUS

If this is your first time trying this performance, you won't have any class examples, but don't despair—there are plenty of sources out there! For example, Weird Al Yankovic has an "Ultimate Video Collection" DVD. Not only does he parody songs from the '80s and '90s, but he also parodies the original music videos. (As usual, be sure you view the disc ahead of time to select which videos you want your class to watch.)

Or that old standby, YouTube, can always be mined for song parodies; try searching songs by the kooky Chicago-area TV movie host, Svengoolie. The great thing about Svengoolie (a.k.a. Rich Koz) is that he is not a great singer, just someone who has fun with music and a talent for wrenching a rhyme from almost any line.

Once you've decided on the source song, the strategy is the same: List the original lyrics on the left-hand side of the paper and the song-parody lyrics (if available) on the right. After viewing, examine the original lyrics for syllabication and rhyming and then compare to the parody lyrics.

Planning and Rehearsal Tips

Once students understand the concept of song parody and the requirements of the project, their first job is to individually search for songs and lyrics that their group might use. Give students a week to conduct their individual research on their own time since many school search engines automatically block most of the websites that post song lyrics. The biggest point to emphasize during this phase is that students should pick songs that are familiar and easy to sing. If you can't easily hum it, you sure won't be able to sing it! Also, songs with vulgar or profane lyrics are off limits!

On the first meeting, students need to bring in their lyrics and music on a CD or an iPod. It's helpful to have an extra CD player or two as playing options, though most of the kids will opt to play their iPods and willingly share their earbuds (yick!). Once again, reinforce the concept of picking an easy-to-sing song with a recognizable melody. Encourage groups to start writing the new lyrics as soon as they've picked the song. Remind them to determine the rhyming scheme and count line syllables before they begin. The following day, give students one more class period to work on the lyrics and then tell them someone needs to take them home, finish them up, type them, and print out copies for everyone. Encourage group members to communicate with each other about the lyrics outside of class so that they can continue to give input as the "chief lyricist" finishes up.

Three or four days later, students will need to have their accompaniment (original song, karaoke version, musical instruments) and copies of the lyrics ready. Now the singing practice starts! Tell students to sing the parody through a couple of times, revising lyrics that don't quite fit. Once the lyrics seem to be working pretty well, ask students to sing the song over and over. As I have said repeatedly, rehearsal is when kids so often balk. For some reason, they think that if they've practiced something twice it's all done. Do not hesitate to give grade points for both the quality and quantity of practice. And yes, during those minutes of practice it's going to be pretty noisy and chaotic, so if you have the option of spreading the groups out into some unused spaces, by all means do. However, rest assured that all the kids can practice in the same room if they have to. Also, for this performance, costumes can be a distraction, so you may want to mention to students that no extra credit will be given for this.

Assessment Live!

Though this project focuses on singing, the assessment focus should be on how well the lyrics capture the information and how practiced the performance is. Being a good singer is not part of the equation; knowing the song is! The final performances will be better if you require the groups to get the rubrics out every time they practice. As you monitor and coach, pick up the rubric sheets and confer with the group on what's strong and what needs work. Or pair groups up and have them practice together, in which case one group acts as the audience while the other group sings. After a run-through, the audience group discusses the rubric with the performing group. In addition to providing an audience, pairing up groups is also an excellent way to share CD players.

On performance day, capture the performances on video so that students can watch themselves and complete self-evaluations after all the groups have sung. Usually, each song lasts about three minutes, so within a typical-length class period of 45 minutes there is enough time for five minutes of practice, the show, and then a viewing of the "music videos" and accompanying self-evaluation using the rubric.

Predictable Problems

Surprisingly, I've found that much more can go right with this assessment than wrong. I've often seen students who haven't demonstrated their content mastery to me on tests and papers become truly engaged in song performance and show what they know with talent and enthusiasm. One of my students who seldom could remember to bring a pen to English class had absolutely no problem remembering to bring his electric keyboard to class two days in a row (see Figure 11.5). He also willingly took on the positions of the group's chief lyricist and musical director, roles that were not assigned but ones he spon-

FIGURE 11.5 Griffin, seated at keyboard, acts as musical director for his song-parody group.

taneously created and volunteered for. Another student who had previously completed very few assignments blossomed during the song project—not only did he contribute to the lyrics, but it turned out he had a great voice and even did a dance solo.

But of course minor things *can* go wrong. The biggest mistake the kids make is picking songs that are too difficult to sing or not practicing enough, problems that can be identified and turned around in the project's earliest stages. And for the most part, the students won't be great singers. Years devoted to sports practice versus taking piano lessons, combined with the testing movement's elimination of "extras" like music instruction have taken its toll. But that doesn't mean music can't be rediscovered! And the kids' untrained voices won't interfere if the lyrics are well written and energetically performed.

Immediately after the performances, ask students to give examples of what important information was included in the songs. It's also interesting to ask each group how they decided what information to include. Then, as always, watch the video recording so that students can rate their final performance against the rubric criteria. And if there's time after viewing, have students get back in their groups and make an advice list for future performers. Figure 11.6 shows what one class came up with.

Variation—The Blues

I am indebted to Ted DeMille for introducing me to this song variation: writing new lyrics in the style of the blues. Why blues in particular? It's because many blues songs have melodies that are simple and easy to sing, most use a slow rhythm, and blues verses use a predictable rhyming and rhythm pattern. Guy Davis' "Writing Paper Blues" works well as a model and that song is available on iTunes. Another great recording to use is available from Ted's own CD (available by emailing him at rahlee@suscom-maine.net), which features a couple of blues tunes with and without the lyrics. Whatever blues song you choose to use, begin by projecting the lyrics or passing out copies and then listening to the song and noticing the conventions of this song genre (see Figure 11.7).

After familiarizing students with the genre, play the song again and this time have everyone sing along so that they get a feel for the melody, rhyme, and rhythm. Then start brainstorming reasons why a character, historical figure, or human cell component might have the blues.

1. What would give this character the blues?

2. What is specific to this character's life or existence that would challenge them, make them feel sad, scared, oppressed, or upset?

FIGURE 11.6 Writing and Performing a Song—Student Advice

Pick a song that . . .

- Everyone is comfortable singing.

- Is slow and easy to sing.

- Is simple, not something complicated like Pink Floyd.

- Has an easy beat and clear rhymes.

When writing the new lyrics . . .

- Read it out loud to see if it sounds good.

- Include a lot of information in your song.

- Get everyone involved—don't leave anyone out.

- Make sure the lyrics fit the rhythm.

- Listen to the original version of the song.

- Trade phone numbers/email addresses and work on the song outside of school.

- Don't goof around when you have a chance in class to work on it.

- Don't make the song too funny—you'll start laughing uncontrollably when you're trying to sing it.

When practicing . . .

- Be sure to sing the song a lot!

- Make sure everyone knows the melody of the song and the timing.

- Play the accompaniment or background music every time you sing the lyrics.

- Memorize the lyrics.

When performing . . .

- Turn down the volume on the accompaniment.

- Have fun with it, but don't start laughing.

- Don't be afraid to sing just because you don't have a good voice—lots of people don't have good voices.

- Get into it—don't just stand there.

- Sing the song for real—don't chant the words.

FIGURE 11.7 Conventions of Blues Songs

- Blues songs have four-line verses.

- The two lines are generally the same—each line has between ten to fourteen syllables.

- The third line is often ironic and has seven to nine syllables.

- The last line has nine to ten syllables.

- Syllable count is also flexible—it is clear to the ear when you have too many or too few in a line.

When my sophomores brainstormed reasons why the characters in *Othello* have the blues, they came up with the list shown in Figure 11.8. After the class has a list of ideas, set them to work in groups of two or four to write a verse or two that could be sung along to the blues number the class just analyzed and sang.

As the groups finish writing their verses, have them come up to the boom box and try it out. Go ahead and sing along with them and if there's a line that doesn't fit rhythmically, don't be afraid to make a suggestion on how to fix it. Once the group knows the lyrics work, have them recopy the verses onto transparencies. In this quick song-writing structure, most groups will be reluctant to get up on their own and sing, but it will be a different story if you put the verses on the overhead and everyone sings along with the recording of the song you've been using as a model. Of course, if you or a student can play the guitar, go ahead and offer some live accompaniment.

Once students are familiar with the blues, it becomes another genre option for the song project. See the example of The Othello Blues shown in Figures 11.9 and 11.10: Lauren, Val, and Dan wrote a blues number that featured the viewpoints of both Othello and Iago. Though not encouraged to wear costumes, they chose get-ups in the style of The Blues Brothers. Dan accompanied Guy Davis' "Writing Paper Blues" recording on his drums while the girls sang. Lauren sang the first two verses as Othello and then Val sang the next two as Iago. The last verse they sang together. Part of the song-writing assignment required students to incorporate at least one direct line reference that came straight from the play. The line in verse three does this, incorporating reference to a line in Iago's soliloquy that concludes Act 2, Scene 1: "For I fear Cassio with my night-cap too."

FIGURE 11.8 Sophomore Brainstorm

OTHELLO BLUES LIST

Question: What would give these characters the blues?

Othello

- He hasn't had his honeymoon.
- His father-in-law doesn't like him.
- He knows people talk about him behind his back.
- He feels used; he's always the one who gets sent to battle.
- He doesn't have a place he can call home.
- His only friend is Iago.
- He thinks Desdemona is cheating on him.

Iago

- He got passed over for a promotion.
- He thinks Emilia cheated on him with Othello.
- He thinks Emilia might have cheated on him with Cassio.
- He thinks Othello favors Cassio.
- He's jealous of Othello for marrying Desdemona.
- People underestimate him.

Desdemona

- Her father disowned her.
- She's lonely in Cypress.
- She wishes she had been born a man.
- Every time she's alone with Othello he gets called away.
- Othello speaks meanly to her and slaps her.
- Othello thinks she is cheating on him.
- She lost the magical handkerchief that Othello gave her as a wedding present.
- She fears that Othello will kill her.

FIGURE 11.9 Student Example, Othello Blues

The Othello Blues
Oh Desdemona, I trusted you baby
Oh Desdemona, I trusted you baby
But you've been sneakin' around
And now I think we're through

Oh cheatin' Cassio, you've been getting too near
Oh cheatin' Cassio, you've been getting too near
Now I've got something to say
And I think you'd better hear

That job was so mine, but Cassio took it away
That job was so mine, but Cassio took it away
He made my wife his nightcap
And now there's hell to pay

That poor sap Othello, he believes everything
That poor sap Othello, he believes everything
The bit about the handkerchief
I've got him on a string

They've all got it comin', yeah they all do
They've all got it comin', yeah they all do
We've been through some troubles
And now I'm comin' for you

FIGURE 11.10 Val, Lauren, and Dan strike a "Blues Brothers" pose for Othello Blues.

Quick Guide: Songs That Make Ideas Stick

1. Pick a song that everyone likes and is easy to sing.

2. Find the song online and print out the original lyrics.

3. Practice singing the original song.

4. Using the original lyrics as a guide, write new lyrics. Pay close attention to rhythm and rhyming scheme.

5. Practice singing the new lyrics with the accompaniment you plan to use.

6. Perform! Discuss the information presented. Watch the video and self-assess. Groups reconvene and make an advice list for future song writers/performers.

Quick Guide: Blues

1. Find a recorded blues song that everyone can sing. Study the lyrics as the song plays, having students make note of blues verse conventions. Discuss how a verse is structured using these conventions.

2. Make a list of reasons why a character, person, or object might have the blues.

3. Develop four-line verses that follow the blues conventions.

4. Practice singing new lyrics with standard blues song melody.

5. For extra credit, encourage budding guitar players to learn how to play standard blues progression.

6. Practice with final accompaniment: recorded or live.

7. Perform! Discuss the information presented. Watch the video and self-assess. Groups reconvene and make an advice list for future song writers/performers.

Performing a Scene: The Ultimate Assessment

What Is It?

In this assessment, pairs, trios or groups of four work to memorize and perform carefully edited scenes from a play under study. As the groups present their scenes in order, a mini-production of the whole play is created for the class to enjoy and reflect upon.

Performing a scene from a play means more than memorizing lines and reciting them before an audience. Performing a scene requires:

- Determining character motivation.

- Imagining the hidden thoughts behind the words.

- Understanding the character's relationship with other characters.

- Building a physical sense of that character.

- Reacting to dialogue and events.

- Creating a realistic world/context in which the character resides.

- Inventing a background for the character, a life that existed well beyond the first pages of the play.

If you want your students to think deeply about a play, then they should be acting out scenes rather than taking a test. While the latter only requires momentary attention, the former requires students to take on an alternative perspective and create a character only after careful and deep examination of the text.

Why and When to Use It

If we want kids to really think about a play they are studying together, have the students memorize and perform a scene because it requires far more analysis and deconstruction than any other kind of homework, class discussion, or test. Memorization requires that the student read over the lines again and again until finally those lines are part of the person. Don't we always wish our students were more willing to reread? Memorization makes this a reality. In addition, when students perform a scene, they must examine every word their character says as well as the lines of the other characters, noting inferences, implications, and subtle subtext. They need to be fully cognizant of what happens before and after the scene they're performing because it is all connected. Finally, memorization itself is a lost skill. Few kids have ever been offered this challenge unless they audition for a play at school. Memorization is something anyone can do, but it takes time and lots of rehearsal. So if plays are a part of your curriculum, give this next live assessment some serious consideration.

The best time to begin scene work is just when you are beginning the study of an entire play. Put together a series of scenes that offer the play's highlights, scenes that when performed sequentially will create an abbreviated version of the play. Pass the scenes out to assigned groups (more on that in just a minute) and have them begin meeting daily in order to start memorizing their lines. Though this might sound confusing, it actually piques student interest because they begin to make predictions about how the play will unfold and then pay closer attention to each scene since they want to see how their part fits into the whole play.

Most students are glad they have plenty of time to work on the memorization, but a few might complain that you are "ruining it" by revealing plot developments prematurely. I just ask the kids if they've ever watched a rerun, seen a movie more than once, or gone to see a movie that was based on a video game they've played, book they've read, or previous television or movie they've seen. When surveyed, just about every hand goes up. In reality, audiences often prefer some familiarity with plot before they see a performance.

By the time the class begins to study the final act, the scenes are memorized and the groups can begin to work on their acting. The final production is a miniversion of the play!

Of course, most students will never become actors, but we do hope that they will all someday be gainfully employed. Participating in scene work can actually help our students reach that goal. Memorization and acting techniques come in handy in real-life situations. Recently, I ran across an online article titled "10 Acting Techniques That Work on the Job" (Lorenz 2005). The following are some acting skills from the article that improve performance in a job interview or business presentation:

1. "Become" the audience: Rather than focusing on your nervousness, imagine how the audience will enjoy your performance.

2. Carry yourself with "presence": Look confident even if you don't feel it. Balance your weight evenly on both feet. Sit tall and lean in slightly. Look interested in your audience!

3. Voice control and inflection: Speak in a friendly low tone. Allow pauses. Don't speak over another person's lines.

4. Have enthusiasm: Enter the room with energy and purpose.

5. Make graceful exits: Leave on a high note; make them want more!

Time Requirement

Plan two to five periods over the course of three to four weeks because, except for the performances that will take one period, the rehearsal sessions within a period should be no more than ten to twenty minutes on any given day, depending on the length of the scenes. Also, there needs to be a three- to four-week gap between the scene assignments and the final rehearsals and performances so that there is sufficient time for students to memorize their lines.

Starting with the End in Mind

The student rubric (see Figure 12.1) defines the quality expected in the memorization, performance components, and the script notes. You'll notice that one category, Off-Stage Demeanor, has no descriptors for the C and B categories. That's because either you are respectful to fellow actors or you aren't. Anything that distracts or prevents an actor from doing his/her best job means that "off-stage" the student has not comported herself properly.

Figure 12.2 is the scoring sheet. Students use this sheet along with the rubric for their own self-assessment, which is turned into the teacher after completion. Notice that students are encouraged to offer explanation and evidence that corroborate their point assignment.

Getting Ready

First, if students are to memorize a script, they need to have some successful prior experience, so make sure that you have completed some of the memorization activities that were outlined in Chapter 2. Once students feel confident in their memorization skills, you are ready to begin.

FIGURE 12.1 Scene Performance Rubric

C	B	A
Memorization	**Memorization**	**Memorization**
■ No more than 2 to 3 stumbles	■ No stumbles	■ Speaks as if words were his/her own
Blocking	**Blocking**	**Blocking**
■ Orientation toward audience	■ Some meaningful movement	■ Truly engaged with and reacting to other characters
■ Hair does not hide face	■ Face shows appropriate emotion	
Line Delivery	**Line Delivery**	**Line Delivery**
■ Clear, loud, and slow	■ Some appropriate expression	■ Truly sounds like a conversation
Staying in Character	**Staying in Character**	**Staying in Character**
■ Stays in character	■ Avoids upstaging others	■ Becomes the character—student's personality is invisible
Costumes and Props	**Costumes and Props**	**Costumes and Props**
■ Slight suggestion of character/setting	■ Costume is clearly different from typical classroom attire	■ Creativity and obvious outside effort reflected in choices
Off-Stage Demeanor	**Off-Stage Demeanor**	**Off-Stage Demeanor**
■ X	■ X	■ Silent and respectful
Performance Energy	**Performance Energy**	**Performance Energy**
■ Moments of performance come alive	■ Actors consistently engaged	■ Holds audience's attention
Script Notes	**Script Notes**	**Script Notes**
■ Notes found throughout scene	■ Specific notes on motivation, interpretation, and blocking	■ Notes reflect thorough scene dissection

FIGURE 12.2 Performance Scoring Sheet

SCENE PERFORMANCE

Name _____

Scene and Role _____ **Date** _____ **Period** _____

Directions: As you watch the video, rate yourself in the following categories based on the rubric. Please jot down any notes about performance details you want me to notice before I assign the final grade. Do not repeat the rubric phrases. Attach your script to the grade sheet and turn in all of your group's sheets together.

Category	Points	Weight	Score
Memorization	1 2 3 4 5	x 4	/20
Blocking	1 2 3 4 5	x 2	/10
Line Delivery	1 2 3 4 5	x 4	/20
Staying in Character	1 2 3 4 5	x 1	/5
Costumes and Props What did you wear? What did you bring in?	1 2 3 4 5	x 2	/10
Off-Stage Demeanor	5	all or nothing	/5
Performance Energy	1 2 3 4 5	x 1	/5
Script Notes	1 2 3 4 5	x 5	/25

Total Points   **/100**

Standards Skills Students Will Practice

Reading	Writing	Speaking/Listening
■ Interpret and evaluate the impact of ambiguities, subtleties, contradictions, ironies, and incongruities in a text	■ Take notes from written and oral texts ■ Write for real situations	■ Assess how language and delivery affect the mood and tone
■ Analyze interactions between main and subordinate characters in a literary text		■ Use appropriate rehearsal to achieve command of the text, and skillful artistic staging
■ Analyze characteristics of subgenres (e.g., satire, parody) that are used in poetry, prose, plays, novels, short stories, essays, and other basic genres		■ Recite poems, selections from speeches, or dramatic soliloquies with attention to performance details
■ Read, view, and interpret texts and performances in every medium		■ Listen respectfully and responsively
■ Recognize unstated assumptions		■ Apply delivery techniques such as voice projection and demonstrate physical poise
■ Share reading experiences with a peer or adult and engage in a variety of collaborative conversations		■ Use nonverbal communication techniques to help convey message
■ Explain and justify interpretation		■ Respond to constructive criticism

Preparing the Script

If your curriculum includes plays, this assessment will enhance your drama unit and increase your students' engagement in the study. But be forewarned: for Performing a Scene to work well and be meaningful, preparing the performance scripts is something you'll have to spend some time on. It's best to start with a play that you teach from year to year, ideally one you've already taught several times—your intimate familiarity with the play will make the script preparation a lot easier. And if you're like me, by the third or fourth reading you would love to get your hands on that text and edit the darn thing right once and for all!

Yes, creating this edited scene collection requires an investment of time for the teacher. But if you still have doubts about the work involved with creating these scripts, try to remember the last "from scratch" multiple-choice test you made up. That also took hours if you were trying to come up with really probing higher-order thinking questions. But all that work probably provided very little enjoyment for you or the kids in the long run. In contrast, these scenes are going to be great! The kids are going to have to work their little butts off and come performance time, they're finally going to entertain you for a change! And the really good news is that if this is a play you teach every year, once those scripts are done, you'll have them forever.

Though any play in the curriculum can be used, I find that the easiest scripts to create are from the plays of William Shakespeare. Shakespeare's works are in the public domain so there's no copyright infringement problem, and almost all of the plays exist online, so the cutting and pasting is a breeze.

Editing down plays to their core is the secret to having kids memorize and perform key scenes. For typical students, no scene should go beyond about three or four pages. No one group will be performing an entire scene as it is marked in the original text. All of the scenes you create will be parts of the big play scene, subscenes if you will. Remember, we want this assignment to be challenging, not overwhelming. Therefore, you've got to be an unsentimental editor. Does the character need to say all those lines to get his point across? If not, then cut them!

Your scenes will create an abbreviated version of the play, the most important scenes, the highlights. Aim for creating a set of scenes that your class can perform in one period. Scenes with only two characters work best. Try to avoid scenes with more than four characters because larger groups tend to be less accountable to one another. Also, even with the best editing, most of these multiperson scenes will have uneven line distribution as well, so it's almost guaranteed that some kids will be left with time on their hands. If a scene has too many characters, see if you can cut the minor characters, or at least combine the lines of two or three characters into one. Once you've lost your strict adherence

Daring to Edit the Bard

Do you feel guilty editing the Immortal? Don't be! Cut to the bone! Hack away. Do not worry about insulting Shakespeare; he is dead and really should be flattered that we've figured out a way to liven things up in spite of those five acts that go on forever and that 400-year-old language that barely uses a single word our students even recognize. Okay, my attitude might seem sacrilegious but stop and consider your ultimate goal. No matter how much you personally adore Shakespeare and would love to luxuriate upon every single one of his words, you're teaching Shakespeare in order to give kids a sample, an immersion, a shot of "cultural literacy," as E. D. Hirsch would call it. Most of the time the way we handle Shakespeare in school provides an inoculation against our students ever reading him again. But by the time the unit is completed, your students will remember Shakespeare fondly and maybe a couple of them will even major in British Literature!

to the original script, you'll be surprised at what you can do. And remember, you're not changing the spirit of the play; just making it accessible for your students to perform.

The following is an example of a scene I've edited down for my class. This is the last part of Act 2, Scene 3 from *Othello*. Cassio has lost his position as Othello's lieutenant after participating in a drunken brawl that ended with his stabbing the governor of Cypress, Montano. Demoralized, Cassio solicits advice from Iago. While the original Scene 3 excerpt contains thirty-six lines for Iago and thirty for Cassio, the streamlined version cuts each character's lines by about a third. Also notice the heading on the abridged script: 2.3B, Pages 120–124, Lines 259–335 ("2.3" indicates it is Act 2, Scene 3; "B" indicates I have split the original scene into subscenes; "Pages 120–124" refer to the pages on which the original uncut text can be found in their textbook; and "Lines 259–335" refers to the original line numbers within that text).

Abridged Scene, Othello, Act 2, Scene 3

2.3B, Pages 120–124, Lines 259–335
Iago, 23 lines
Cassio, 18 lines

IAGO: What, are you hurt, lieutenant?

CASSIO: Ay, past all surgery.
Reputation, reputation, reputation! O, I have lost
my reputation! I have lost the immortal part of

myself, and what remains is bestial. My reputation,
Iago, my reputation!

IAGO: As I am an honest man, I thought you had received
some bodily wound; there is more sense in that than
in reputation. Reputation is an idle and most false
imposition: oft got without merit, and lost without
deserving: What, man! there are ways to recover the general again: you
are but now cast in his mood, a punishment more in
policy than in malice.

CASSIO: O thou invisible
spirit of wine, if thou hast no name to be known by,
let us call thee devil!

IAGO: What was he that you followed with your sword? What
had he done to you?

CASSIO: I know not.
I remember a mass of things, but nothing distinctly;
a quarrel, but nothing wherefore. O God, that men
should put an enemy in their mouths to steal away
their brains!

IAGO: Come, you are too severe a moraler:
I could heartily wish this had not befallen;
but, since it is as it is, mend it for your own good.

CASSIO: I will ask him for my place again; he shall tell me
I am a drunkard!

IAGO: I'll tell you what you shall do. Our general's wife
is now the general: confess yourself freely to her; importune
her help to put you in your place again: she is of
so free, so kind, so apt, so blessed a disposition,
she holds it a vice in her goodness not to do more
than she is requested: this broken joint between
you and her husband entreat her to splinter; this
crack of your love shall grow stronger than it was before.

CASSIO: You advise me well.
I will beseech the virtuous Desdemona to undertake for me:

IAGO: You are in the right. Good night, lieutenant; I
    must to the watch.

CASSIO: Good night, honest Iago.

When using scripts still under copyright, there's a good chance you won't find them online. In order not to infringe on the author's rights, you'll need to start with a clean original script and work through it in pencil, marking where the subscenes begin and end as well as crossing out unnecessary lines. Then you can use one of two options. You could project the pages using an Elmo and let students lightly pencil in your edits into their own books. Or, if you feel your students could handle it, assign scenes to the groups and workshop the editing, letting them make the decisions as you coach and give suggestions since you've already figured out how the scenes could be edited.

Finally, if you are intrigued by the interpretive memorization aspect of this project, but don't teach the same play consistently from year to year or just don't have the energy or time for creating these script cuttings, there are other accessible genres for kids to practice memorization and performance. So read through the rest of the chapter to get a handle on the process but use the ideas in the Variations section instead.

Casting and Memorization

I do not have students attempt scene memorization until I am well into the school year, when they already memorized some poems (Chapter 2) or participated in the Talk Show assessment. They also need to know their classmates and consistently treat each other with respect, since getting up in front of the room and taking on a different character is a big, big risk. That said, I start by telling students that they will be memorizing a scene and they need to find a partner with whom they want to work and can depend on. The pairs write their names on an index card. I collect and then use these cards to create the acting groups and cast the scenes. While some pairs remain only pairs, I match others up to form groups of four. Though the foursomes did not all request that they work together, every student has at least one partner that they chose, so no one ever seems distraught over my group decisions. After organizing the groups, I match them to scenes. I consider the number of lines and difficulty of the acting in a scene. As the casting director, I use the knowledge I have of my students, and try to assign each group to a scene at which they will excel.

I prepare and (if copyright allows) photocopy the scripts well in advance of assigning the scenes. Each script is labeled with the act, scene, and original text pages it came from as well as a coding number that helps me keep the scenes straight and in order. For example, if I've divided the first scene of act 2 into three subscenes, I would label them 2.1A, 2.1B, 2.1C. I also photocopy each scene on different color paper. When I pass the scripts out, I make a huge deal about each person only getting one script since their acting notes will be used for part of their grade. And, for the most part, the kids take this seriously. Of course I make sure I have a few extra copies for the kids who destroy their scripts through use. I've had several boys trade in scripts tattered from pocket wear (they carry them around all the time in the hopes that they'll remember to pull them out and work on their lines). When an actor needs a script replacement, it's easier for me to just match up the script color to his partner's script than look up the scene, number, and so on. This also helps me stay organized; all the extra scripts can just sit in a pile in your cabinet versus a separate folder for each scene.

As I mentioned earlier, I pass out the scripts early, maybe even a day or two before we start the play. Students begin to memorize their lines well before we study that particular scene in class. At this stage in the process, they only have to have the lines memorized; they do not have to have them interpreted. That will come later. I just want them to get a jump on getting those lines in their heads! Also, the day before I pass out the scripts, I have everyone stand up and recite the Witches Chant from *Macbeth* (this was one of the memorization activities described in Chapter 2). The kids are absolutely astounded that they remember almost all the lines after not rehearsing it at all for about four or five months; the last time they recited the poem was October 31 and typically we start *Othello* at the end of March. Then I say, "Remember how we rehearsed that poem every day for a month? Well, look how well you remember it after all that time. That's exactly what has to happen with your lines."

Once the groups and scripts are assigned, the members meet and decide who will play each part. Then each actor highlights all his lines and the teams read through their scripts a couple of times. From then on, I try to give the groups five minutes every day to rehearse their lines. For the first week, I just let them keep reading from the script. By the second week I encourage them to start trying to look away from the script and say lines from memory. I also tell them to take the scripts home every night to continue their memorization and I give them these instructions:

1. Start with your longest, hardest speech. Study the first line; cover it with your hand or an index card and see if you can say it out loud or in your head. If you can, move on to the second line. If not, study the first line and try again. Keep repeating the process for each long passage that needs to be memorized.

2. Once you have the hardest parts memorized, start from the beginning of the scene and learn the rest of your lines. Read through the lines from the beginning

but then cover up your lines as you come to them and try to say your part aloud or in your head. Take a peek if you get stuck, but then cover the lines back up and try again.

3. Keep rehearsing every day and always be sure to read what the other characters are saying in between your speeches because these lines are your cues that tell you what to say next.

4. Continue rehearsing every day even when you think you have all of your lines memorized. Remember that part of the memorization process is forgetting. Just when you think you have all your lines memorized, you'll blank out on one. That's just part of the process and if you keep rehearsing the lines they'll be there whenever you want them.

By the third week, students are saying more and more of their lines from memory. You'll see them gazing up and to the side as they try to retrieve their lines. I tell them that's good because that shows the lines are starting to sink in. Now their job is to learn the lines so well that they can actually make eye contact with the other actors when they deliver them.

When I pass out the scripts, I also give them a memorization performance deadline. On this date, usually about four weeks in the future, acting teams will have to perform their lines before the class from memory. This is not the final performance. This is only a memorization performance. I originally did not do this and found that some groups would procrastinate and then try to memorize their lines the night before the big show. Line memorization takes time and must be rehearsed every day. Setting the memorization deadline well before the final performance forces the kids to learn their lines in advance of the blocking (see the following discussion). In turn, as they rehearse their scenes for the final performance, the focus can move from "What was my line?" to "How am I going to say that line?"

On the day of the memorization performances, each acting team gets up and recites their lines from memory while the rest of the class rehearses being a good audience (see the chart "Being a Good Audience Member" in Chapter 2). I grade each student individually on a scale of 1 to 10, with a 10 signifying "You've got it all memorized!" Building in daily rehearsal time as well as offering students concrete memorization strategies results in a celebratory day since very few students fail to know their lines by the deadline. The kids are relieved that they "passed the test" but also very proud of themselves since many came to this project thinking they were never going to be able to memorize their parts.

Line Interpretation

The next step after memorization is to begin work on the actual acting. I introduce the concept by telling the class that all human interactions have a reason for occurring. It is because both people want something. They might want love, respect, or money. It might be something obvious or it might be something subtle, but people always have a motive for their interactions with others. Depending on the playwright, a script may have ample stage directions or virtually none, as in Shakespeare. Sometimes the stage directions may help with character motivation, but actors almost always have to examine their lines closely in order to find some depth for their interpretation.

Ask students to take a look at their lines and think about their character's motivations. Next to each of their speeches, write down what the character wants. Why are they saying this? What do they want from the other character? As students study their lines carefully, they'll begin to notice that many times the character wants more than one thing: something obvious and something hidden, something only that character knows about. Make sure kids jot down these observations. Also, as a scene progresses, a character's motivations can change. Tell students not to assume that your character will want the same thing at the beginning and end of the scene. Ask them to note these changes as well. Remind them to be thorough since the quality and quantity of their notes will be part of their final project grade.

When students are finished with their character motivation notes, I direct them to reread their lines. Now that they know *why* their character says each line, they need to determine *how* the character would say it in order to get what they want. For each speech, ask students to write on their scripts (or on a separate piece of paper if they are using books they do not own) how they would say it. Ask students to consider how honest and truthful their character is with the others. If their character is not forthcoming, how will this be shown through the performance? As students work, remind them to underline the words they think are especially important and powerful—words they think their character should emphasize. Finally, have them consider where pauses could be used for emphasis. It might be after a word. It might be before they respond to another character. Have the students mark their pauses with a slash between words or before the beginning of a line (see the example shown in Figure 12.3).

I make a big deal out of these interpretation notes because this is the evidence that the kids have really thought deeply about their characters. Consistently, I've discovered that the more notes they have for each line, the better the performance. After the final curtain calls and video viewing, groups must clip their scripts to their scoring sheets and turn them in to me. Take another look at the scoring sheet (Figure 12.2), and you'll notice

FIGURE 12.3 Script Notes for Emilia *(Othello)*

TALKING TO
HERSELF

2 Actors
3.3D. pp 158-162, 290-330

EMILIA (20), IAGO (12)

EMILIA
I am glad I have found this napkin: EXCITED – GOOD FORTUNE MAY
This was her first remembrance from the Moor: COME OF THIS!
My wayward husband hath a <u>hundred</u> times   THINKS FONDLY OF DESDEMONA
Woo'd me to steal it;   Sick of nagging – wonders why
I'll have the work ta'en out,   he WANTS IT
And give't Iago: what he will do with it
Heaven knows, not I;   Obedient   LIKES THE PATTERN – WANTS HER
I nothing but to please his fantasy.   Sighing   OWN COPY

Re-enter Iago   Resigned KNOWS NOT TO QUESTION
HUSBAND — A little hopeful too
IAGO   Since she has Something he WANTS
How now! what do you here alone?

EMILIA   Hopes she'll get Something in
Do not you chide; What will you <u>give</u> me now   reTURN FOR HER TROUBLES
For the handkerchief?   TEASING – KEEPS
HANDKERCHIEF BEHIND BACK

IAGO
What handkerchief?

EMILIA   CAN'T believe it – he's been nagging her
What handkerchief?   for it. Rolls her eyes
Why, that the Moor first gave to Desdemona;
<u>That</u> which so often <u>you</u> did bid me <u>steal</u>.   WANTS Iago to value her, See
that she's clever

IAGO
Hast stol'n it from her?

EMILIA   Proud of her craftiness
No, 'faith; she let it drop by negligence.   (still surprised Desdemona was so
And, to the advantage, I, being here, took't up.   careless)
Look, here it is.   Buts wANTS to make it clear
Shaking it   She just found it, didn't steal IT
IAGO   in front of him
Give it me.

EMILIA   Curious, And concerned – Iago grabbed
What will you do with it?   it from her roughly — NoT like a husband
getting his wife a gift (the work taken
IAGO   out)
[Snatching it] Why, what's that to you?

1

continues

FIGURE 12.3 Script Notes for Emilia *(Othello), continued*

2 Actors
3.3D. pp 158-162, 290-330

EMILIA ~Attempts defiance~

Rushed

If it be not for some purpose of import,
Give't me again: poor lady, she'll run mad
When she shall lack it.

Anxious

~Realizes how upset Desdemona will be when she finds its gone. Knows SHE MADE A mistake and doesn't trust Iago.~

IAGO
I have use for it.
Go, leave me.

~Demands it back – Powerful stance, Reaches out to TAKE IT BACK~

Exit EMILIA

I will in Cassio's lodging lose this napkin,
And let him find it. Trifles light as air
Are to the jealous confirmations strong
The Moor already changes with my poison:
Look, where he comes!

that those script notes are weighted more heavily than any other aspect of the performance; they're that important!

Once students are finished with these notes, they get together with their acting teams and read through their scripts, seeing whether their combined motivations and interpretations make sense, discussing and modifying as needed. Then they need to continue running through the script several times, working to memorize the interpretation that goes with the lines. They need to rehearse outside of class as well.

Blocking

Students should just work on memorizing the interpretation and honing their line delivery for a few days before moving on to last stage: blocking, which is the planning of how the actors will move through a scene and physically interact with one another. In order for students to understand the basics of blocking, you'll need to do a quick demonstration. First, indicate what part of your classroom will be the "stage." Mine is from the whiteboard to the front of my desk and sideways between my desk and the podium.

Ask for a couple of volunteers, and purposely choose someone with long loose hair (see "Hidden-Face Syndrome" on page 213). Demonstrate basic blocking as you direct your volunteers to various stage positions (adapting the directions, of course, on the lay-

Hidden-Face Syndrome

Have you noticed that lots of teenagers have the same hairstyle, long and hanging loose? That long hair hides their faces if they lean forward even slightly or stand in profile. In acting this is a huge problem because hiding one's face monumentally diminishes the actor's ability to portray any character. You'll notice throughout this blocking demonstration, I've used a student with this type of hairstyle because I want the class to see how it affects the acting. After this demonstration, require that the students pull their long hair back whenever the groups rehearse. And after you offer them one school-issue hair-tearing rubber band, most will remember to bring their own hair constraining devices for the remainder of the project. Once their faces are consistently revealed, they'll do a better job honing their facial expressions and the rest of the group will have a better handle on coaching them.

out of your classroom and depending on whether your students have any previous theater experience). See Figure 12.4 for a basic blocking diagram.

1. Both students stand against the whiteboard. This is upstage. It's okay to start a scene upstage, but you do not want to stay there because it's too far away from the audience.

2. Both students line up with the front edge of the desk between the desk and podium. This is downstage, the front of the stage. Most of a scene should take place from the middle to the front of the stage.

3. One student steps back against the whiteboard (upstage) while the other remains downstage. Then the downstage person looks toward the upstage person. This forces the downstage person to turn their back to the audience. (Avoid actually using this blocking in performances whenever possible; the audience does not want to see your back; they can't see your emotions that way!)

4. Both students return to center downstage and face each other as if engaged in conversation. (Here's where loose hair hanging over a student's face reveals itself.)

5. Both students stand in profile to the audience, almost nose to nose. Remind students that how you position characters indicates their relationship to each other. What might blocking like this indicate about their relationship? Are they about to tell a secret? Have an argument? What else?

FIGURE 12.4 **Stage Diagram**

Back (whiteboard)

Upstage Right	Upstage Center	Upstage Left
Stage Right	Centerstage	Stage Left
Downstage Right	Downstage Center	Downstage Left

Front

6. Both students stand next to each other, facing the audience. Remind students to play their scenes close. Student actors tend to stand too far away from each other. They should be able to reach out and easily touch the other person's shoulder unless greater distance is needed for a specific reason.

7. Both students face each other in profile but then angle themselves toward the audience so that the audience can see their faces versus just their profiles. This is called cheating out. Though blocking might briefly feature actors in profile, they should move to "cheating out" quickly.

8. Both students stand on the actor's (versus the audience's) left-hand side of the stage, about the middle of the stage. This is stage left. They move up to the front of the stage. This is downstage left. They move against the whiteboard on the same side and this is upstage left. Repeat demonstration for stage right.

9. Both students move to stage left (actors' left). Tell the student on the outside to cross in front of the other and end at downstage right (actors' right). Then tell the partner to walk over next to him. Crossing in front of a person is a more powerful move than crossing behind. Also, since the other person had to "chase" him across the stage, it puts the character that crossed first in control.

10. Now have the person who crossed first stay in position while the other walks to center and turn his back to the audience. If a scene has only two characters, it is clear to the audience that they are speaking to each other, so it is not nec-

essary for them to face each other all the time. Not having two characters consistently face each other can create some interesting blocking.

11. Pull two chairs onto the "stage" and push them next to one another. Have one student sit while the other stands. Have both sit next to each other. Have one student turn sideways, facing away. Have one person sitting on a chair, the other kneeling on the floor looking toward the partner but cheating out. The acting teams should think about how they might use classroom furniture to create some interesting blocking by using levels (one person standing, one person sitting; one person sitting, one person kneeling, etc.). The use of levels and proximity can all be used to indicate the shifting relationships between characters within a scene as well as create blocking that is more visually compelling.

This demonstration seems like it would take forever but it actually takes less than ten minutes. Afterward, have the students individually review the motivation and interpretation notes on their scripts. Then ask them this question: For each of your speeches, what physical gesture or movement might help your character get what he or she wants from the other character? How close should you be standing to him or her? Who has the most power in the relationship? How can you show that through your gestures and stage position? Students should take a few minutes to jot down ideas and then join their acting teams to compare notes. Have them discuss this question: What is the location of your scene? Sometimes stage directions are very specific about location. Other times—Shakespeare once again—they are not. If the location is ambiguous, think about using a location that makes logical sense but also offers greater blocking potential. For example, if the setting is an empty street, the characters are fairly limited to just standing and talking to each other. On the other hand, if the setting is in the room of a house, a character might sit, stand, recline on a couch, look out a window, lean on a table, and so on.

Rehearsal Tips

As you see the students' blocking discussions winding down, encourage the teams to find a spot in the room and rehearse their moves. This is the hardest part. Though acting is as much physical as it is mental, the kids would rather just sit in their seats rehearsing their lines. If you need to, make the physical rehearsal part of their grade or assign points to it. You might even stop and brainstorm a chart of what effective rehearsal looks like (see Figure 12.5).

Another way to get the students to loosen up and become more attuned to movement and blocking is to return to the Improving Physical Interpretation section in

FIGURE 12.5

REHEARSING A SCENE

Looks Like	Sounds Like
Everyone standing	Saying lines from memory.
Moving through scene	Remembering to say the lines so that the character gets what he or she wants.
Using classroom furniture for scene	
Using gestures	"Try standing over here."
Showing character relationships through blocking	"Move closer to him/her."
	"How can we make this scene more interesting?"
Experimenting with different blocking	
Rehearsing scene over and over until blocking is memorized	"We need to move the scene downstage; we're too far to the back."
Getting into character	

Chapter 2. The Emotion Walk, Character Sculptures, and Who Are You and What Are You Doing? activities all work well in getting student actors to think more about gestures and facial expressions. You can also develop a rehearsal ritual. Before every rehearsal opportunity, pick one of the activities from Chapter 2 as a warm-up and keep using it so that it becomes the signal to get everyone in a rehearsal frame of mind. Allow only ten minutes a period for scene rehearsal unless the students really use the time well. It's better to have lots of little, short rehearsals rather than a couple of big, long ones.

About a week or two before the big performance, try to schedule two periods back to back for a dress rehearsal and critique. On the first day, have all the student teams perform their scenes and video-record them. Beforehand, mark the outline of the stage on the floor with masking tape so that the students always stay within the range of the camera. On the second day, have the class watch all the scenes and give blocking suggestions for each. Then have the teams meet and incorporate the suggestions into their remaining rehearsals. When kids actually see that they are standing miles apart and playing the entire scene upstage, they are much more likely to work harder at creating more engaging blocking.

Assessment Live!

There is lots of excitement on the day of the big show. While some groups will have minimal costumes and props, other groups will be far more elaborate. Though they could get a few extra points for costumes, the bulk of the grading focuses on character interpretation and the detail of the script notes. Depending on the length of the scenes, your performances may flow over two days, but this assessment will have greater momentum if it can be completed in a single day because, when you put all the scenes together in order, the students get to see an abbreviated version of the play.

Be sure to videorecord the final performances. No matter how much the kids complain about being filmed, they love watching the class' performances as they complete their self-evaluations. Finally, viewing these scenes twice gives the entire class an opportunity to review the most important scenes from a significant piece of drama (Figure 12.6).

FIGURE 12.6A **Students in Character** *(Othello)*: Iago *(right)* advises Othello: "Do it not with poison, strangle her." (Though Steve [Iago] had shoulder-length hair, his blocking kept him facing forward so that his hair did not obstruct his face.)

FIGURE 12.6B **Students in Character** *(Othello)*: Lodovico *(left)* delivers news from Venice to Othello.

Predictable Problems

Since performing a scene is complicated, there are a lot of places where things can go wrong. But they can all be avoided with proper guidance and planning. The following chart will help you review the details and head off trouble before it arises.

Memorization	■ Provide experience and successful memorization opportunities earlier in the semester. ■ Keep the script length manageable. ■ Structure the setup: highlighting lines, strategies for individual rehearsal, daily team rehearsals. ■ Provide short, frequent opportunities to rehearse. ■ Make the completed memorization due well before the final performance.
Interpretation	■ Insist on detailed notes on character's motivation and student's interpretation. ■ Short, frequent rehearsals to incorporate interpretation into memorized lines.
Blocking	■ Start with demonstration. ■ Relate blocking to motivation and interpretation. ■ Return to movement activities in Chapter 2.
Final Rehearsals	■ Make a "Rehearsing a Scene" T-chart. ■ Use the chart to assess quality of rehearsal; assign points. ■ Remind students to refer to grade sheet and rubric during rehearsal sessions ■ Have groups rehearse for each other. One group watches, one group performs. Critique using the rubric. Switch. ■ Videorecord a rehearsal, give suggestions, and rehearse some more.

Variations

If plays are not part of your curriculum, you can complete a similar project using poetry. Pick poems that tell stories and are fairly long: "Casey at the Bat" by Ernest Thayer or "The Highwayman" by Alfred Noyes are good examples. The poems can be divided up among several pairs of students. After reading through the entire poem, partners get their stanza assignments. As with the play scenes, students first complete the memorization. Then, instead of examining their lines for motivation, they'll need to ask these questions:

- Why is this line important?

- What idea or feeling is it trying to get across?

- How do I need to say that line in order to get that idea or feeling across?

- What words do I need to emphasize?

Once these questions are answered, partners rehearse their memorized lines until they've effectively developed their interpretation.

And because these poems tell a story, blocking can be used to convey the drama of it. Conduct a demonstration of blocking and let partners brainstorm and jot down notes about how they will perform their poem. Rehearse as you would the play scenes and modify the grade sheet and rubric as needed.

QUICK GUIDE: Performing a Scene

1. Earlier in the year, students should have had the experience memorizing a class poem through call and response. This is an activity described in Chapter 2. Then, before passing out the scripts, have students say the poem again, which proves that time and daily practice are required for memorization that lasts.

2. Using a play you will study in class, prepare abridged scripts of two to four pages in length.

3. At the beginning of the drama unit, have students pick a partner. Create acting teams based on these pairs and assign different scenes. Pass out prepared scripts and assign the completed memorization due date.

4. Show students how to memorize a script covering up the lines with an index card. Remind them that they need to recognize their line cues as well.

5. Give students five or ten minutes to work on lines daily. Memorization takes time!

6. Perform lines from memory on due date.

7. Begin script note taking. Determine character's motivation line by line. The motivation will inform the character's gestures and movement (blocking).

8. Provide five or ten minutes most days for groups to rehearse their scenes from memory, incorporating interpretation and blocking.

9. If possible, videorecord a run-through about a week before the final scene performances. Watch as a class and give suggestions to each group.

10. Video-record final scene performances. Afterward, watch video as students self-assess. The performance and video follow-up offer students two more opportunities to review the most important scenes from the play they have studied.

Study Guide

On this book's website page, www.heinemann.com, are step-by-step plans for a multi-meeting teacher study group. This experiential, interactive process helps you to try out live assessments both with colleagues and with kids, fine-tuning them for use in your own classroom. Please have a look at this resource. Meanwhile, following are listed some more traditional discussion questions (also included on the website), just to get you started. Enjoy.

Chapter 1 Study Questions
The Lively Art of Assessment

1. When you think back to the assessments you experienced in elementary, middle, and high school, which ones stand out for you? Do you remember them positively or negatively? Why? How would your classmates remember them? Would their memories be similar to yours? Why or why not?

2. What assessments have you used in the past that truly fired kids up? Which assessments did they seem ambivalent about? What made them boo out loud? When you compare these assessments, what is similar and different about them?

3. What are some skills or knowledge you personally possess that are a result of multiple rehearsals?

4. How do students benefit from collaborating with their classmates?

5. What problems have you encountered when structuring lessons or assessments that require students to work together? Brainstorm ways these problems could be solved.

6. How can students be a better audience for one another?

7. Review the research on test preparation done by the Consortium on Chicago School Research. What surprises you about it? How might the findings inform or reform your own classroom practices with regard to test preparation?

8. Review your own state's standards skills for your grade level and content area. What kinds of assessments, other than multiple-choice tests or written essays, might enable students to show their mastery of these standards? Brainstorm a list.

9. What rubrics do you use with your students? Which ones help students achieve better-quality work? What components do effective rubrics reflect that are missing from less useful rubrics?

10. Imagine that an administrator observes your students as they complete a live assessment. Using all of the information available in this chapter as well as additional support your study group has collected, develop a strong rationale for using performance assessments in addition to or instead of traditional assessment formats such as objective tests and essays.

Chapter 2 Study Questions
Getting Kids Ready to Go Live

1. What are your favorite icebreaking activities? How can you work to incorporate them in the classroom on a more frequent basis?

2. Review the interview activity and try it out with a partner. When teaching this questioning strategy to the students, how will you model it so that they understand the concept of follow-up questions?

3. Review the section called "Making Positive, Supportive Behavior the Norm." With your colleagues, brainstorm some additional positive skills that your students need to practice and then create a T-chart for one of those skills. (What does the skill look like and sound like?). Skills you might consider: using quiet voices, staying on task, recognizing members' contributions, disagreeing with someone's idea respectfully, careful listening, asking questions that further discussion, adding to each other's ideas. After you've completed the chart, discuss how you will guide your students in the creation of their own chart for this skill.

4. Much of this chapter focuses on getting kids up from their desks and on their feet. With your colleagues, brainstorm ways that you can help students learn the content in more physical ways.

5. Looking back at your own career as a student, what were some text pieces you were required to memorize? Was it a pleasant or unpleasant experience? Why? With the goal of creating positive feelings as well as increasing your students' ability to memorize, what are some potential memorization pieces that might be suitable for your grade and content area?

6. Review the section called "Co-Creating Rubrics with Students." With your study group, brainstorm a list of favorite foods. Pick one and, using the Pizza Rubric as a model, see if you can come up with appropriate descriptors that would separate that food into A, B, and C categories.

Chapter 3 Study Questions
Academic Controversy

1. Consider the curriculum and mandated testing for your grade level or content area. For which assessments and assignments do students need to present well-supported arguments or write persuasively?

2. What are some topics in your curriculum or content area that offer an opportunity for academic controversy? These topics need not be polarizing but should have two sides to an issue that require further investigation.

3. Pick one of the topics you've brainstormed and work with your support group to move through the Academic Controversy model. Be sure to designate preparation partners and argument partners.

4. Brainstorm ways Academic Controversy could be used in your classroom. When an oral controversy is completed, what follow-up activities or assignments might you connect to the controversy?

5. Review the "Controversy Skills Checklist." Pick a skill students might be uncertain of and develop a T-chart for it. (What would the skill look like and sound like?) Skills you might consider: careful listening and note taking, arguing with enthusiasm, emphasizing support facts and examples, questioning the opposition, criticizing ideas rather than people, combining the ideas for the best solution. After you've completed the chart, discuss how you will guide your students in the creation of their own chart for this skill.

6. Review the section "Predictable Problems." With your study group, discuss what problems you might run into when implementing this live assessment. Be sure to brainstorm practical and positive solutions for each problem.

7. With your study group, review the scoring and rubric sheets for Academic Controversy. How might you revise these documents to better fit your needs?

8. After your students have completed an Academic Controversy, bring your observations back to the group. What went well? What would you do differently the next time you use this assessment?

9. How will completing an Academic Controversy help students think more deeply about the material they've studied? How will it help them in using supportive details in their writing?

10. Develop a strong rationale using Academic Controversy based on the information available in this chapter as well as in Chapter 1. Include the action research you have gathered as your students participated in Academic Controversy.

Chapter 4 Study Questions
Book Buddy PowerPoint

1. During PowerPoint presentations, students often turn their backs to the audience as they read their slides aloud. What tips and ideas can you share that help make these presentations lively and engaging for the audience?

2. How do you provide time for your students to read books of their choice? Share your Sustained Silent Reading (SSR) strategies and how you assess them.

3. What are some of your students' favorite choice books? With your study group, brainstorm a list of high-interest titles.

4. With a partner, choose a high-interest student title to read together and discuss. What do you notice about your reading and how it changes when you know you'll be talking about it with someone else? After your postreading discussion with your partner, what ideas/noticings did your partner present that were different from your own?

5. Photocopy a two- or three-page section from a novel you would like to share with students. Work with your study group to edit and dramatically interpret the text. Then perform it with your students in class and discuss how it went back in your study group.

6. How could the Book Buddy PowerPoint presentation format be adapted to projects other than book reports?

7. Review the section "Predictable Problems." With your study group, discuss what problems you might run into when implementing this live assessment. Be sure to brainstorm practical and positive solutions for each problem.

8. Review the scoring and rubric sheets. How would you adjust them to fit your own curricular goals and your students' needs?

9. After your students have completed their Book Buddy PowerPoint presentations, bring your observations back to the group. What went well? What would you do differently the next time you use this assessment?

10. How will completing a Book Buddy PowerPoint help students think more deeply about the book they've read? How will the presentations energize student interest in reading choice books?

11. Develop a strong rationale using Book Buddy PowerPoint presentations based on the information available in this chapter as well as in Chapter 1. Include the action research you have gathered as your students participated in this assessment.

Chapter 5 Study Questions
Found Poetry

1. What are some of your favorite free-verse poems? Bring in a couple to share with your study group.

2. Read aloud the example poem adapted from a science textbook, "The Scientific Method." How could free-verse poems be created using existing text from your textbooks? Bring content-area texts in and experiment with writing some free-verse poems.

3. Where in your curriculum might you introduce alternative perspective writing to your students? Brainstorm topics and possible prompts.

4. Discuss how original student alternative-perspective writing pieces might be transformed into free-verse poetry. Review the section "Creating Found Poetry: Finding Powerful Lines." Discuss how you would model the steps and then lead students through the process.

5. Review the found-poetry examples from Incan and Spanish perspectives. How did the students incorporate content details into their fictional poetic narratives?

6. Review the section "Predictable Problems." With your study group, discuss what problems you might run into when implementing this live assessment. Be sure to brainstorm practical and positive solutions for each problem.

7. Review the scoring and rubric sheets. How would you adjust them to fit your curricular goals and your students' needs?

8. After your students have completed this assessment, bring your observations back to the group. What went well? What would you do differently the next time you use alternative perspective writing and found poetry?

9. How will writing from an alternative perspective and then using that original text to create found poetry help students think more deeply about the material they've studied?

10. Develop a strong rationale using Alternative Perspective Writing and Found Poetry based on the information available in this chapter as well as in Chapter 1. Include the action research you have gathered as your students participated in this assessment.

Chapter 6 Study Questions
PostSecret Project

1. Review the "What Is It?" section and the student example. What full-length novels and nonfiction are parts of your curriculum? Consider the main characters or real people these books depict. What plausible personal experiences or feelings might these figures possess yet keep hidden from others? Discuss the secrets and the textual support to back them up.

2. Visit the website postsecret.com with your study group. Peruse the online gallery and pick some school-appropriate examples you could use with your students. The gallery changes weekly, so your group might want to repeat this activity.

3. Review the sections "Getting Ready," "Assessment Live!," and "Predictable Problems." Which parts of this assessment might pose challenges for your students? Which parts do you think your students will readily embrace?

4. Brainstorm alternative ways for students to interact with each other's PostSecret presentations.

5. Review the section "Predictable Problems." With your study group, discuss what problems you might run into when implementing this live assessment. Be sure to brainstorm practical and positive solutions for each problem.

6. Review the scoring and rubric sheets. How would you adjust them to fit your curricular goals and your students' needs?

7. After your students have completed their PostSecret presentations, bring your observations back to the group. What went well? What would you do differently the next time you use this assessment?

8. How will completing a PostSecret assessment help students think more deeply about the material they've studied?

9. Develop a strong rationale using the PostSecret Project based on the information available in this chapter as well as in Chapter 1. Include the action research you have gathered as your students participated in this assessment.

Chapter 7 Study Questions
Readers Theatre

1. Read aloud the Readers Theatre example (see Figure 7.1) adapted from a math textbook, "From the Mud to the Stars—The Reach of Geometry." What Readers Theatre scripts might you or your students create using existing text from your textbooks or other class books you regularly use? Bring them in and, with your study group, experiment with an example Readers Theatre script based on text used within your curriculum.

2. For a successful Readers Theatre, students must read their pieces dramatically. What oral interpretation skills might your students need some help with? Return to Chapter 2 and discuss which activities you might try to help students better develop their oral interpretation skills.

3. Brainstorm a timetable or agenda so that students use their time efficiently as they write and practice their Readers Theatre pieces.

4. What reflection questions might be useful for students to consider after they've created and performed their Readers Theatre pieces?

5. Review the section "Predictable Problems." With your study group, discuss what problems you might run into when implementing this live assessment. Be sure to brainstorm practical and positive solutions for each problem.

6. Review the scoring and rubric sheets. How would you adjust them to fit your curricular goals and your students' needs?

7. After your students have completed their Readers Theatre presentations, bring your observations back to the group. What went well? What would you do differently the next time you use this assessment?

8. How will creating a Readers Theatre piece help students think more deeply about the material they've studied?

9. Develop a strong rationale using Readers Theatre based on the information available in this chapter as well as in Chapter 1. Include the action research you have gathered as your students participated in this assessment.

Chapter 8 Study Questions
Tableaux

1. Review the "What Is It?" section as well as the photograph and accompanying student script for *My Heart Is on the Ground*. How might students better understand and remember what they have read when they must visualize it and then create a physical representation based on it?

2. Brainstorm ways that Tableaux might be used to study specific pieces of text or units of study.

3. Look for photographs that reflect a dramatic "tableau style" to share with your group and your classes. Your photographs might be the result of an Internet search, visiting the online sculpture collections of art museums, and/or photographs you take yourself of dramatic statues in your own community.

4. What physical interpretation skills do students need in order to make their scenes dynamic and dramatic? Review the activities from Chapter 2 and determine which ones you might use in order to hone your students' skills for Tableaux.

5. What collaborative skills will students need to use as they negotiate a script and stage their Tableaux? Develop a T-chart for a skill with which students might have trouble. (What would the skill look like and sound like?)

6. What are the benefits of being skilled at oral and physical interpretation? How might these skills serve students in their lives beyond your classroom?

7. What reflection questions might be useful for students to consider after they've created and performed their Tableaux?

8. Review the section "Predictable Problems." With your study group, discuss what problems you might run into when implementing this live assessment. Be sure to brainstorm practical and positive solutions for each problem.

9. Review the scoring and rubric sheets. How would you adjust them to fit your curricular goals and your students' needs?

10. After your students have performed their Tableaux, bring your observations back to the group. What went well? What would you do differently the next time you use this assessment?

11. How will performing Tableaux help students think more deeply about the material they've studied?

12. Develop a strong rationale using Tableaux based on the information available in this chapter as well as in Chapter 1. Include the action research you have gathered as your students participated in this assessment.

Chapter 9 Study Questions
Talk Show

1. In this chapter, several talk shows are mentioned as possible models for script writing, including Oprah, Dr. Phil, and Jerry Springer. What talk shows are popular with your students? Divide and conquer the list you develop with the help of your study group. Record clips of the shows you listed and bring them in to the next meeting to watch. Discuss how students could use these shows as models for creating their own talk shows.

2. Brainstorm ways that the Talk Show might be used as a culminating assessment when completing a unit of study.

3. Take a look at the standards skills this project addresses. Which skills would you want to emphasize with your students?

4. What physical interpretation skills do students need in order to make their Talk Shows dynamic and dramatic? Review the activities from Chapter 2 and determine which ones you might use in order to hone your students' skills for their Talk Shows.

5. What collaborative skills will students need to use as they negotiate a script and stage their Talk Show? Develop a T-chart for a skill with which students might have trouble.

6. What specific content or text details will you expect students to include in their scripts? How will you encourage them to return to their notes and the text for that information?

7. Once students have completed their scripts, how might you make use of student conferencing groups in order to check for specific content details, clarity and completeness, and stage notes?

8. What reflection questions might be useful for students to consider as they practice their Talk Show? How will you make sure they set specific goals they want to achieve in their practice?

9. Review the section "Predictable Problems." With your study group, discuss what problems you might run into when implementing this live assessment. Be sure to brainstorm practical and positive solutions for each problem.

10. Review the scoring and rubric sheets. How would you adjust them to fit your curricular goals and your students' needs?

11. After your student performances, watch some of the videos with your study group. What went well? What would you do differently the next time you use this assessment?

12. In what ways will creating and performing Talk Shows help students think more deeply about the material they've studied?

13. Based on the information available in this chapter as well as in Chapter 1, develop a strong rationale using the Talk Show as an assessment. Include the action research you have gathered as your students participated in this assessment.

Chapter 10 Study Questions
Storytelling

1. Name people you know who are good storytellers. They can be professional entertainers or storytellers, but they also might be friends, colleagues, or family members. What makes their storytelling engaging?

2. What are some examples of storytelling you use in your own teaching? How could you transfer some of this storytelling responsibility to the students? Remember, the more we tell a story or talk about information, the better we remember it. What stories and information do you really want your students to remember long after they leave your classroom?

3. This chapter uses urban legends as a basis for teaching Storytelling. What other types of stories might you use to reflect and reinforce areas of your own content? With your study group, work together to develop a collection of example stories with which students can work.

4. From the stories your study group has collected, have each member pick one that they want to use as an example with their students. Write your own version of the story and practice telling it. Perform it for your study group and then compare notes on how you moved through the process. Then use your own experiences to discuss how you will lead students through the Storytelling process.

5. Take a look at the standards skills for Storytelling. Which skills would you want to emphasize with your students?

6. What oral interpretation skills do students need in order to make their storytelling dynamic and dramatic? Review the activities from Chapter 2 and determine which ones you might use in order to hone your students' oral interpretation skills.

7. What collaborative skills will students need as they peer conference and rehearse with their groups? Develop a T-chart for a skill with which students might have trouble. (What would the skill look like and sound like?)

8. After a rehearsal, what reflective questions might you use so that students can analyze how effectively they used their time and set achievable goals for the next rehearsal?

9. If time is unavailable for each student to tell stories individually, what are ways that you can have students tell stories working in pairs or trios?

10. Review the section "Predictable Problems." With your study group, discuss what problems you might run into when implementing this live assessment. Be sure to brainstorm practical and positive solutions for each problem.

11. Review the scoring and rubric sheets. How would you adjust them to fit your curricular goals and your students' needs?

12. After your student performances, bring your observations back to the group. What went well? What would you do differently the next time you use this assessment?

13. In what ways will storytelling help students think more deeply about the material they've studied?

14. Based on the information available in this chapter as well as in Chapter 1, develop a strong rationale using Storytelling. Include the action research you have gathered as your students participated in this assessment.

Chapter 11 Study Questions
Songs That Make Ideas Stick

1. Brainstorm some simple songs that your students would know. Next, brainstorm content-area information you want your students to remember. With your study group, pick one of the songs and write some new lyrics that reflect content information. Take a look at the *Dred Scott* decision lyrics written to the tune of "Twinkle, Twinkle, Little Star."

2. Discuss how you will introduce Songwriting and singing to your students. Students will probably not be expecting to show what they've learned using this modality.

3. Take a look at the standards skills for Songwriting. Which skills would you want to emphasize with your students?

4. Since students often pick songs that are difficult to sing, brainstorm a list of ten recorded songs that are easy to sing and that have a verse and a chorus. Make sure the songs and lyrics are available for download. Talk about how you will introduce these songs to your students and whether you want them to pick a song from the list or choose one on their own.

5. What collaborative skills will students need as they work with their groups to write and rehearse their songs? Develop a T-chart for a skill with which students might have trouble. (What would the skill look like and sound like?)

6. What specific content or text details will you expect students to include in their song lyrics? How will you encourage them to return to their notes and the text for that information?

7. After a rehearsal, what reflective questions might you ask so that students can analyze how effectively they used their time and set achievable goals for the next rehearsal?

8. Review the section "Predictable Problems." With your study group, discuss what problems you might run into when implementing this live assessment. Be sure to brainstorm practical and positive solutions for each problem.

9. Review the scoring and rubric sheets. How would you adjust them to fit your curricular goals and your students' needs?

10. After your student performances, bring your observations back to the group. What went well? What would you do differently the next time you use this assessment?

11. In what ways will Songwriting help students think more deeply about the material they've studied?

12. Based on the information available in this chapter as well as in Chapter 1, develop a strong rationale using Songwriting. Include the action research you have gathered as your students participated in this assessment.

Chapter 12 Study Questions
Performing a Scene

1. Discuss the importance of memorization and how it can enhance your students' cognitive skills, aesthetic appreciation, and study of your content. Now talk about why memorization is typically avoided in many classrooms. How can you recapture this potentially valuable form of learning and assessment?

2. Review the memorization activities outlined in Chapter 2 and discuss how you might use these activities with your students.

3. Brainstorm a list of poems in your content area that have memorization potential. As a group, pick one and work together to memorize it. Now, take that poem back to the classroom and teach your students how to memorize it. Discuss the lesson with your study group.

4. Take a look at the standards skills for performing a scene. Which skills would you want to emphasize with your students?

5. Discuss how the skills necessary for acting can be useful elsewhere in life.

6. If the members of your study group all use the same play, brainstorm which parts of which scenes would be the best for students to act out. Try to create a series of scenes that when performed together form a "mini" version of the play. Once you have your scene list, divvy up the scenes so that each study-group member has one or two. For your next meeting, each member should prepare edited, shortened scripts to share.

7. In Chapter 2, review the following activities: Applause Pass, Rainstorm, Hand Jive, Dancing, Emotion Walk, Character Sculptures, and Who Are You and What Are You Doing? Which of these might be useful as acting warm-ups? Which ones might be used to improve your students' dramatic interpretation and physicality?

8. Review the sections on memorization and interpretation. Share ideas about how you might guide your students through these two phases of creating a performance.

9. With your study group, review the information on blocking and physically move through the activities listed. Talk about how you will teach these techniques to your students.

10. After a rehearsal, what reflective questions might you ask so that students can analyze how effectively they used their time and set achievable goals for the next rehearsal?

11. Review the section "Predictable Problems." With your study group, discuss what problems you might run into when implementing this live assessment. Be sure to brainstorm practical and positive solutions for each problem.

12. Review the scoring and rubric sheets. How would you adjust them to fit your curricular goals and your students' needs?

13. After your student performances, watch some of the recorded scenes with your study group. What went well? What would you do differently the next time you use this assessment?

14. In what ways will performing a scene from a play they've studied help students think more deeply about the play?

15. Based on the information available in this chapter as well as in Chapter 1, develop a strong rationale for performing a memorized scene. Include the action research you have gathered as your students participated in this assessment.

Bibliography

"100 Ways to Energize Groups." 2008. Sudan Capacity Building Forum. (16 Sept.). http://sudancapacity.org.

Allensworth, Elaine, Macarena Correa, and Steve Ponisciak. 2008. Consortium on Chicago School Research at the University of Chicago. *From High School to the Future: ACT Preparation—Too Much, Too Late.*

Archer, Jeff. 2005. "R.I. Downplays Tests as Route to Diplomas: Students Must Demonstrate Their Knowledge, Skills." *Education Week* 24 (13 April). www.edweek.org.

Armstrong, Thomas. 1994. *Multiple Intelligences in the Classroom.* Alexandria, VA: Association for Supervision & Curriculum Development.

Ataiyero, Kayce T. 2007. "Getting Socializing Down to a Science: Too Shy at Parties? Schmoozing Class Might Stir Things Up." *The Chicago Tribune* (23 July).

Bennett, Samantha. 2007. "The New Workshop." Reading, Writing, and Thinking—Best Practice Meets Standards and Accountability. Crowne Plaza Resort, Lake Placid, New York. 9 July.

Bolton, Natalie, Donna Shouse, Orville Blackman, and Julie Kuhnhein. 2008. "Nurturing Democratic Thinkers." *ASCD Express.* Association of Supervision & Curriculum Development. (4 Oct.)

Bond, Lloyd. 2006. "Carnegie Perspectives: My Child Doesn't Test Well." The Carnegie Foundation for the Advancement of Teaching. (28 Dec.) www.carnegiefoundation.org.

Brunvand, Jan H. 1994. *The Big Book of Urban Legends.* New York: Paradox.

Buehl, Doug. 2001. *Classroom Strategies for Interactive Learning.* 4th ed. Newark, DE: International Reading Association.

Burke, Kathleen B. 2005. *How to Assess Authentic Learning.* 4th ed. Thousand Oaks, CA: Corwin.

Campbell, Linda, and Bruce Campbell. 1999. *Multiple Intelligences and Student Achievement: Success Stories from 6 Schools.* Alexandria, VA: Association for Supervision & Curriculum Development.

Cech, Scott. 2008. "Showing What They Know: In Rhode Island, Performance-Based Assessments Are Now Required for High School Graduation." *Education Week* (18 June). www.edweek.org.

Chaplik, Robin. 2008. "Hopper on Stage." (Workshop) The Art Institute of Chicago, Chicago, IL. 23 Feb.

Cohen, Lewis, Raymond Pecheone, and Robert Littlefield. 2008. "Performance-Based Assessment." *Education Week* (1 July). www.edweek.org.

Craughwell, Thomas J. 2005. *Urban Legends: 666 Absolutely True Stories That Happened to a Friend . . . of a Friend . . . of a Friend.* New York: Black Dog & Leventhal.

Curtis, Christopher Paul. 2000. *The Watsons Go to Birmingham—1963.* New York: Laurel Leaf.

Daniels, Harvey, and Steven Zemelman. 2004. "Toward a Balanced Diet of Reading: Great Books for Middle and High School." In *Subjects Matter: Every Teacher's Guide to Content-Area Reading,* 68–97. Portsmouth, NH: Heinemann.

Daniels, Harvey, Steven Zemelman, and Nancy Steineke. 2007. *Content-Area Writing: Every Teacher's Guide.* Portsmouth, NH: Heinemann.

Darling-Hammond, Linda, Brigid Barron, and P. David Pearson. 2008. *Powerful Learning: What We Know About Teaching for Understanding.* San Francisco: Jossey-Bass.

Davidson, Jill. 2008. "Exhibiting Authentic Achievement." *Principal Leadership* (Sept.): 36–40.

DeMille, Ted. 2007. "Elements of the Blues." Email interview.

Denning, Stephen. 2005. *A Leader's Guide to Storytelling: Mastering the Art and Discipline of Business Narrative.* San Francisco: Jossey-Bass.

Frey, Nancy, and Douglas Fisher. 2007. *Checking for Understanding: Formative Assessment Techniques for Your Classroom.* Alexandria, VA: Association for Supervision & Curriculum Development.

Gallagher, Kelly. 2006. *Teaching Adolescent Writers.* Portland, ME: Stenhouse.

Graduation by Portfolio and Capstone Handbook: A Guide for Students, Parents, and Teachers. 2006. Coventry, RI: Coventry High School.

Green, John. 2008. *Looking for Alaska.* New York: Puffin.

Goff, Karen G. 2005. "Schools Learning About Boys." *The Washington Times* (10 Oct.)

Goleman, Daniel. 2005. *Emotional Intelligence.* New York: Bantam.

Gottlieb, Lori. 2001. *Stick Figure: A Diary of My Former Self.* New York: Berkley Trade.

Hirsch, E. D. 1988. *Cultural Literacy: What Every American Needs to Know.* Ed. Pat Mulcahy. New York: Vintage.

Hyett, Barbara Helfgott. 1986. *In Evidence: Poems of the Liberation of Nazi Concentration Camps.* Pittsburgh: University of Pittsburgh Press.

Jensen, Eric. 1998. *Teaching with the Brain in Mind.* Alexandria, VA: Association for Supervision & Curriculum Development.

Johnson, David W., and Roger T. Johnson. 1992. *Creative Controversy: Intellectual Challenge in the Classroom.* Edina, MN: Interaction Book Company.

Johnson, David W., Roger T. Johnson, and Edythe J. Holubec. 1993. *Cooperation in the Classroom.* Boston: Interaction Book Company.

Kagan, Spencer. 1994. *Cooperative Learning.* San Clemente, CA: Kagan Cooperative Learning.

Kagan, Spencer, and Miguel Kagan. 1998. *Multiple Intelligences: The Complete MI Book.* San Clemente, CA: Kagan Cooperative Learning.

Latrobe, Kathy. 1993. "Readers Theatre as a Way of Learning." *The ALAN Review.* Vol. 20, #2 (Winter).

Lazear, David G. 1991. *Seven Ways of Teaching: The Artistry of Teaching with Multiple Intelligences.* Upper Saddle River, NJ: Pearson Professional Development.

Lazear, David G., and Grant Wiggins. 1999. *Multiple Intelligence Approaches to Assessment: Solving the Assessment Conundrum.* New York: Zephyr.

Levy, Steven. 2008. "The Power of Audience." *Educational Leadership* 66: 75–79.

Lewin, Kurt. 1997. *Resolving Social Conflicts and Field Theory in Social Science.* Washington, DC: American Psychological Association.

Lorenz, Kate. 2005. "10 Acting Techniques That Work on the Job." CareerBuilder.com Jobs—The Largest Job Search, Employment & Careers Site. (23 Dec.) http://msn.careerbuilder.com.

Marcotte, Madeline. 2006. "Building a Better Mousetrap: The Rubric Debate." *Viewpoints: A Journal of Developmental and Collegiate Teaching, Learning, and Assessment.* Community College of Philadelphia. http://faculty.ccp.edu.

Marzano, Robert J. 2007. *The Art and Science of Teaching: A Comprehensive Framework for Effective Instruction.* Alexandria, VA: Association for Supervision & Curriculum Development.

Marzano, Robert J., Debra Pickering, and Jay McTighe. 1993. *Assessing Student Outcomes: Performance Assessment Using the Dimensions of Learning Model.* Alexandria, VA: Association for Supervision & Curriculum Development.

McCarthy, Mary. 2008. "Determining Character Motivation." Personal interview.

Milauskas, George, and Robert Whipple. 1991. *Geometry for Enjoyment & Challenge.* Boston: Houghton Mifflin Company.

Noddings, Nel. 2008. "All Our Students Thinking." *Educational Leadership* 65: 8–13.

Norton, John, ed. 2008. "The Power of the Imaginative Mind." *Teacher Magazine* (June 25). http://www.teachermagazine.org.

Nunley, Kathie F. 2003. *A Student's Brain: The Parent/Teacher Manual.* Amherst, NH: Brains.Org.

"Our View on Private Sector Soldiers: Bar the Mercenaries." 2008. *USA Today* (12 Dec.) http://blogs.usatoday.com.

Overbaugh, Richard C., and Lynn Schultz. 2008. "Bloom's Taxonomy." Old Dominion University. (28 Dec.) www.odu.edu.

Peterson, Lenka, and Robert Coles. 2006. *Kids Take the Stage: Helping Young People Discover the Creative Outlet of Theater.* New York: Back Stage Books.

Ratliff, Gerald L. 1999. *Introduction to Readers Theatre: A Guide to Classroom Performance.* Colorado Springs, CO: Meriwether Ltd.

Rinaldi, Ann. 1999. *My Heart Is on the Ground: The Diary of Nannie Little Rose, a Sioux Girl, Carlisle Indian School, Pennsylvania, 1880.* New York: Scholastic.

Rodgers, James W., and Wanda C. Rodgers. 1995. *Play Director's Survival Kit.* San Francisco: Jossey-Bass.

Schlosser, S. E. 2008. *American Folklore: Famous American Folktales, Tall Tales, Myths and Legends, Ghost Stories, and More.* (22 Dec.) http://americanfolklore.net.

Schmuck, Richard A., and Patricia A. Schmuck. 2000. *Group Processes in the Classroom.* New York: McGraw-Hill Higher Education.

Scruggs, Mary, and Katherine S. McKnight. 2008. *The Second City Guide to Improv in the Classroom: Using Improvisation to Teach Skills and Boost Learning in the Content Areas (Grades K–12).* San Francisco: Jossey-Bass.

Shakespeare, William. 1623. "Witches Chant Act 4, Scene 1." *Macbeth.*

———. 1623. *Othello.* 1623.

Snopes.com. 2008. Urban Legends Reference Pages.

Sprenger, Marilee. 1999. *Learning and Memory: The Brain in Action.* Alexandria, VA: Association for Supervision & Curriculum Development.

Steineke, Nancy. 2002. *Reading and Writing Together: Collaborative Literacy in Action.* Portsmouth, NH: Heinemann.

"Stories, Legends, and Folktales Around the World." The University of North Carolina at Chapel Hill. (22 Dec.) www.unc.edu.

Sylwester, Robert. 1995. *A Celebration of Neurons: An Educator's Guide to the Human Brain.* Alexandria, VA: Association for Supervision & Curriculum Development.

Warren, Frank. 2006. *My Secret: A PostSecret Book.* New York: ReganBooks.

———. 2007. *A Lifetime of Secrets: A PostSecret Book.* Scranton, PA: HarperCollins.

West, Julia. 2002. "CALLIHOO Writing Helps—Feelings Table." *SFF Net.* (16 June.) www.sff.net.

Wheelock, Anne, Damian J. Bebell, and Walt Haney. 2000. "Teachers College Record: What Can Student Drawings Tell Us About High-Stakes Testing in Massachusetts?" *Teachers College Record.* (27 Dec.) www.tcrecord.org.

Wilhelm, Jeffrey D. 1997. *You Gotta Be the Book: Teaching Engaged and Reflective Reading with Adolescents.* New York: Teachers College Press.

———. 2002. *Action Strategies for Deepening Comprehension: Role Plays, Text Structure Tableaux, Talking Statues, and Other Enrichment Techniques That Engage Students with Text.* New York: Scholastic Professional Books.

Wilhelm, Jeffrey D., and Michael Smith. 2002. *Reading Don't Fix No Chevys: Literacy in the Lives of Young Men.* Portsmouth, NH: Heinemann.

Wilson, Maja. 2006. *Rethinking Rubrics in Writing Assessment.* Portsmouth, NH: Heinemann.

Wolfe, Patricia. 2001a. "Applying Brain Research to Classroom Practice." *Educational Leadership-Education Update.* (28 Dec.) www.ascd.org.

———. 2001b. *Brain Matters: Translating Research into Classroom Practice.* Alexandria, VA: Association for Supervision & Curriculum Development.

Wysession, Michael, David Frank, and Sophia Yancopoulos. 2004. *Physical Science: Concepts in Action, with Earth and Space Science.* Needham, MA: Prentice Hall.

Yankovic, Weird Al. 2003. *The Ultimate Video Collection.* DVD. Volcano.

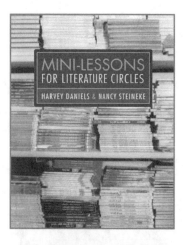

125042